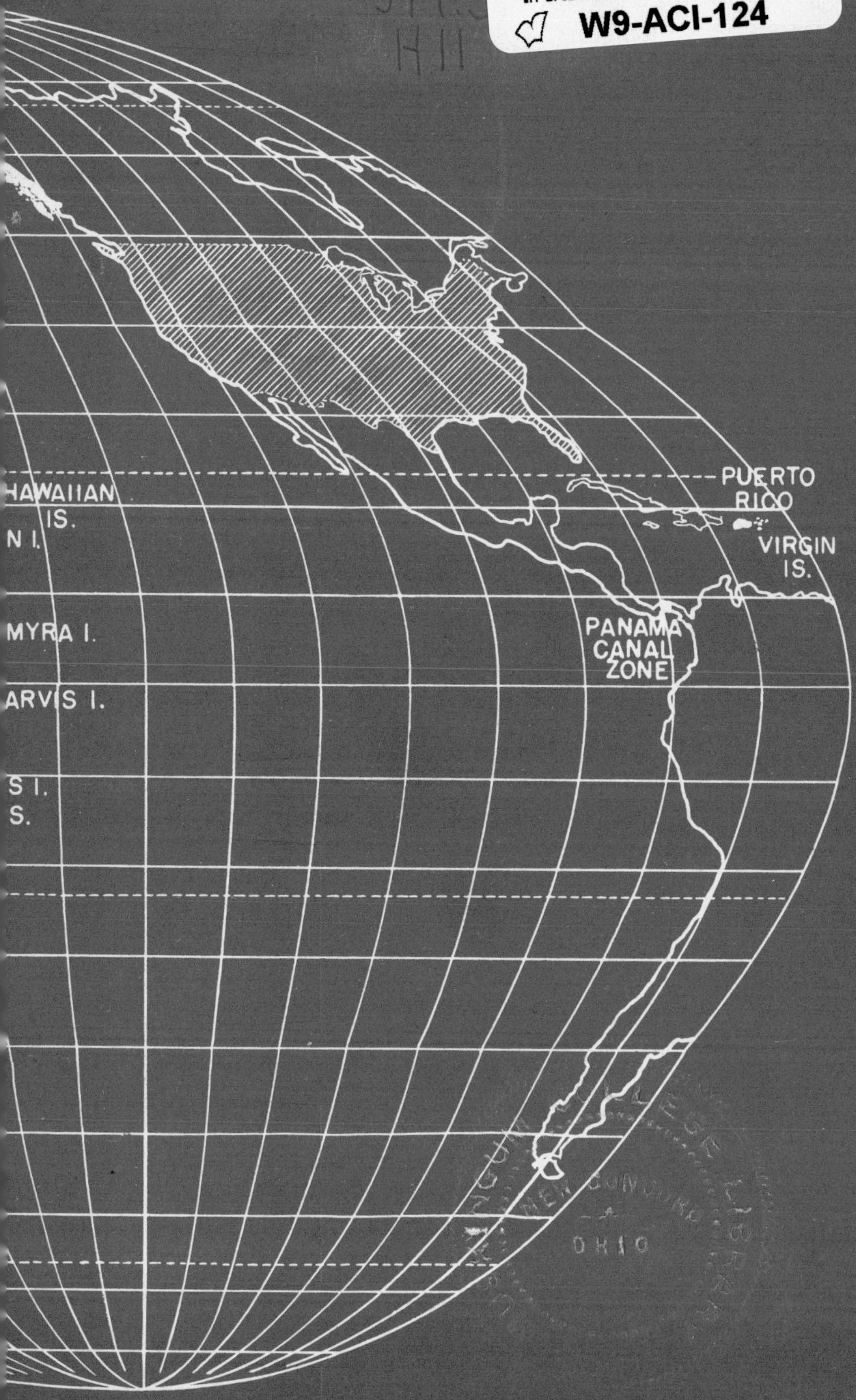

HAWAIIAN
IS.
N I.

MYRA I.

ARVIS I.

S I.
S.

PUERTO
RICO

VIRGIN
IS.

PANAMA
CANAL
ZONE

THE AMERICAN EMPIRE

THE UNIVERSITY OF CHICAGO PRESS · CHICAGO
THE BAKER & TAYLOR COMPANY, NEW YORK; THE CAMBRIDGE UNIVERSITY PRESS, LONDON; THE MARUZEN-KABUSHIKI-KAISHA, TOKYO, OSAKA, KYOTO, FUKUOKA, SENDAI; THE COMMERCIAL PRESS, LIMITED, SHANGHAI

THE AMERICAN EMPIRE ☼ *A Study of the Outlying Territories of the United States*

WILLIAM H. HAAS · *Editor*

CONTRIBUTORS: *W. O. BLANCHARD, University of Illinois, Urbana, Illinois · LUIS J. BORJA, Formerly of the U.S. Bureau of Agricultural Economics, Manila, Philippine Islands · JOHN WESLEY COULTER, University of Hawaii, Honolulu, Territory of Hawaii · ISAAC J. COX, Northwestern University, Evanston, Illinois · CORNELIO C. CRUZ, Mapua Institute of Technology, Manila, Philippine Islands · OTIS W. FREEMAN, Eastern Washington College of Education, Cheney, Washington · WILLIAM H. HAAS, Northwestern University, Evanston, Illinois · RAFAEL PICÓ, Universidad de Puerto Rico, Rio Piedras, Puerto Rico · EARL B. SHAW, State Teachers College, Worcester, Massachusetts*

THE UNIVERSITY OF CHICAGO PRESS
CHICAGO · ILLINOIS

 PUBLISHED SEPTEMBER 1940. SECOND IMPRESSION FEBRUARY 1941. COMPOSED AND PRINTED BY THE UNIVERSITY OF CHICAGO PRESS, CHICAGO, ILLINOIS, U.S.A.

FOREWORD

THE EXTRAORDINARY GROWTH OF A SMALL group of New World colonies into one of the great nations of the world is without historic parallel. None of the nation's founders could possibly have foreseen the superstructure for which they were laying the foundation; nor do the recorded utterances of any of these historic figures delineate, even in a broad way, the present outlines of the United States of America. And yet, during a brief century and a half there has arisen out of a most humble beginning this great commonwealth of states with a productive and a consumptive capacity greater than that of any other country or of any other similar number of people. When such statements are translated into statistics, they loom up larger still and may even take on the appearance of a somewhat characteristically American "bigger-and-better" type of boasting.

During the present period of world-history, however, when among the major nations of the world riches seem much more to be desired than the traditional national honor, these facts, far from being boastful, take on a significance of deep concern. Should the present Old World attitude of aggression become established as justified by need, the American people cannot, by legislative enactments, fence off their own domain or be assured of a peaceful control over their own resources. Already some of the more powerful nations are acting under the principle that natural resources belong to those who are strong enough to defend them, the philosophy seemingly being that, inasmuch as the vital resources are most unevenly, not to say unfairly, distributed, the ultimate title to needed resources must rest upon force.

In the possession of natural resources the American people have been most richly blessed and, unquestionably, have far more than an impartial tribunal would, at the present time, allot them. With a little less than 7 per cent of the land area and a little more than 7 per cent of the people of the earth, the relationship between the two seemingly is well balanced. On this basis 7 per cent becomes a good measuring-stick, a standard of comparison. It is evident, however, even to the most casual thinker, that a nation's riches do not lie necessarily in large areal extent but rather in land rich in a wide variety of resources. In this the United States has no equal, especially in productive mineral resources favorably placed, the foundation of industrial development. It is scarcely ever appreciated that the American people normally produce 80 per cent of the world's sulphur, the mineral foundation of the chemical industry; 33 per cent of the coal and 60 per cent of the petroleum, the leading energy-producers; 43 per cent of the pig iron and 47 per cent of the steel, the harnessers of this energy; and 48 per cent of the copper, the chief distributor of energy into factories, workshops, and homes.

This great productive capacity of only 7 per cent of the world's population is due, very probably, less to native aggressiveness than to the presence of unusually rich resources favorably placed. These resources have made possible a standard of well-being that demands the importation of other commodities from abroad on a scale sufficiently large to round out the economic life of the nation. To do this, it has become necessary to buy, roughly, 50 per cent of the world's rubber, 50 per cent of the coffee, and 75 per cent of the raw silk. With this capacity for production and consumption it is not surprising that the nation has approximately 32 per cent of the world's railway mileage, 50 per cent of the telephones, 70 per cent of the automobiles, and is listed as having 45 per cent of the wealth of the world.

American initiative, however, is not to be ignored entirely. The readiness to run risks and to attack all sorts of problems has led capital into far countries in order to supplement home resources. It is this economic penetration of efficiency under the direction of American capital that is a major cause for apprehension among nations. This peace-time aggression, the result of a highly developed technique learned while exploiting domestic resources, is almost impossible to combat. Resources lie fallow in distant places, and soon Yankee ingenuity controls 20 per cent of the manganese mined, with only an insignificant home production; has commercial control of 76 per cent of the vanadium mines, of which only 17 per cent is within American boundaries; controls 60 per cent of the silver mined, although the country produces only 23 per cent; mines 43 per cent of the aluminum ores, with only 23 per cent coming from within the nation's domain. The adventurous spirit of the early frontiersman is still present but on another kind of frontier.

American industry is not only advancing at a tremendous pace, but it is also increasing its lead over the rest of the world, taken as a whole. As industry basically is so dependent on minerals, the rate of their consumption serves as a fairly safe index of such growth. On this basis, the maximum rate of growth for the United States has come within the present century. In fact, the growth of the first thirty years of this century is more than equal to that of the entire preceding century. The per capita consumption of iron rose from 387 pounds in 1899 to 715 pounds in 1929; copper for the same period rose from 5 to 16 pounds per capita; zinc, from 3 to 8 pounds; and aluminum, from $\frac{1}{10}$ pound to 2 pounds. To round out statistics of this period of internal growth, it should be added that the population increased 62 per cent, agricultural production 48 per cent, the total mineral production 286 per cent, and the installed horsepower—the slave working without reward—536 per cent. No other nation has such a record of growth, and in comparison with the rest of the world the United States is still increasing its lead in most peace-time activities. Foreign nations must view such statistics with concern. Fortunately for the good of the world at large, this 7 per cent of the world's population is not war minded.

Although the data given may be only approximations to the truth, they are, however, sufficiently impressive even if reduced 10 or 20 per cent, to raise the question: "What of the morrow?" This rate of growth cannot continue, nor can one nation hope to use peaceably such a disproportionate share of the world's resources for its own. No longer are large land masses rich in resources to be had for the asking, and many of Europe's resources are being destroyed by wars—destroyed to the vanishing-point. The scramble for the control of strategic places and resources may be expected to become more intense. The United States already is so rich and powerful that, according to the point of view of the Latin-American countries, it oppresses by its potentialities, and the attitudes of those countries are almost always colored by such fears.

Not only has there been a commercial penetration to the

far corners of the world, but the nation has found ocean waters no barrier in its territorial expansion. In the control of its overseas acquisitions, the United States has not been particularly successful. Because their interests and cultural outlooks are markedly different, some of these areas have already become restive under the American flag, and others are held chiefly by economic ties, the bonds of which they dare not break. Already one unit has been granted independence, and in another a strong nationalistic party is demanding similar treatment. Has the limit of territorial expansion been reached? Perhaps there has already been an overexpansion, and the nation cannot, in its traditional attitude of fairness, hold what it already has. In these outlying territories the American commonwealth of states may meet its major tests.

It is a truism that a democracy can survive only with a well-informed citizenry. The people must be in possession of basic facts from which unbiased opinions may be drawn. Material of this type on the outlying parts of America is meager, and that which is in print is not always usable. Most of it is in special publications to be had only in the larger libraries. As a result, the reading public, generally speaking, is pathetically ignorant of the geographic background upon which the superstructure of the country is built. Especially is there lacking an understanding of the problems confronting the outlying territories under the American flag. Strange as it may seem, little effort has been made to make this information available to the general reader anxious to widen his outlook. Even textbooks are silent or woefully inadequate on these areas in which people under the American flag are looking for the full rights and privileges granted in American declarations.

It is to meet this need that this book is presented. The subject matter in the text is, for the most part, based on original data gathered in actual field work by expertly trained university men who either have lived in the area under discussion or have visited it for special investigation and study. The material is presented from the standpoint of the science of geography, and the conclusions drawn are based on scientific data. Each author has made a painstaking study of the region under discussion and takes responsibility for the statements made. To enhance the unity of the work, so difficult to obtain where authors work independently in widely separated regions, the editor has taken the liberty of deleting parts of the original manuscripts and expanding others. In each case, however, authors have had the opportunity to recheck all statements made. By and large, therefore, the editor is to be held accountable for the general point of view and for the arrangement and presentation of material.

In bringing together this material, the editor believes he has rendered a service, especially to the noncontiguous parts of the United States—Puerto Rico, the Virgin Islands, the Canal Zone, Alaska, the Territory of Hawaii, and the Philippines. If, in a small way, this book serves to bring about a better understanding of conditions in these areas and an appreciation of the problems of our fellow-men under the American flag, then the hopes of the authors will be realized.

For the many courtesies and ready help received, each writer is duly grateful and would like to make personal acknowledgment were the list not so long. The editor, however, wishes to acknowledge the earnest and painstaking care of his most efficient subeditor, Elizabeth Erb Ward.

William H. Haas, *Editor*

Northwestern University
Evanston, Illinois
May 1940

TABLE OF CONTENTS

THE ERA OF OVERSEAS EXPANSION

By ISAAC J. COX

AMERICA, WE HAVE BEEN TOLD, WAS AN accident. The statement is true only with respect to its discovery. The conquest and settlement that followed from the Iberian Peninsula were no accidents; nor were the later colonizing swarms that left northern Europe to occupy the upper reaches of the Atlantic Coast mere chance migrations. Both conquerors and colonizers brought to their portion of the New World an expansive spirit that sought to duplicate on virgin continents the life of the homeland without the handicaps—political, social, and economic—that had helped to drive them across the Atlantic.

This spirit of adventurous expansion has seemed especially to mark the British occupation of the North American mainland. Mingled with it was a steady determination to possess and exploit the illimitable wilderness that beckoned to the westward. Spurred on by these expansive and possessive impulses, and aided at times by Europe's needs, as well as by America's opportunities, the tide of Anglo-American settlement gradually pushed into and over the Mississippi Valley and through the Cordilleras beyond, until by the middle of the nineteenth century it rested on the Pacific. It is this spirit, furthered occasionally by seeming accident, that explains the United States and the successive additions thereto of Louisiana and the Floridas, of Texas, New Mexico, and California, and of Oregon.

Less than a hundred years measured this marvelous expansion from the Appalachians to the Pacific. It is small wonder, then, that those who witnessed the acquisitions of the mid-century felt that it was the "Manifest Destiny" of the United States to possess all of North America and its outlying islands. The Oregon Treaty of 1846, however, gave Great Britain a foothold on the Pacific and halted our territorial advance above the forty-ninth parallel, and the war between the states checked acquisitive views to the southward. But, in the midst of the reconstruction turmoil that followed civil strife occurred the purchase of Alaska, late expression of "Manifest Destiny," first hesitant step in a trans-Pacific expansion.

Alaska may be regarded as both a continental and an insular possession. It forms part of the North American continent, but it is connected with the United States by sea and air-borne traffic only. Thus it shares, although belatedly, in the earlier popular urge to dominate North America while showing some of the defensive and imperialistic tendencies that motivated our more recent extensions beyond the continent. Its acquisition was unexpected, even unwanted; but in the brief interval between civil warfare and reconstruction came the opportunity that brought it under American control. In this instance, fortunately, opportunity knocked at the door of the archexpansionist of the period, William H. Seward.

Alaska was not the only region to attract Seward's attention. Like most contemporary disciples of "Greater America," he desired to extend the institutions and the control of the United States to the southward, where Cuba and the other Antilles, Central America and the warring republics beyond, suggested another field. To the northward his ambition sought to bring the Canadas and the other British possessions into the American Union. Hence he welcomed the proffer of Alaska as a means to that end and even looked upon it as a step toward Hawaii and other coveted islands of the Pacific. Certainly its purchase would serve immediately to counteract what he and many others regarded as the unfortunate Treaty of 1846 with Great Britain. Moreover, it would strengthen the traditional but somewhat incongruous friendship between Russia and the United States.

These and similar motives influenced Seward to accept at once the unexpected offer of Baron de Stoeckl, the Russian minister, to sell Russia's possessions in North America. There was no haggling over the price and little delay in completing the necessary details of the purchase. One night's work sufficed to draw up the treaty. It was signed March 30, 1867, and ratified by the Senate within ten days, and Alaska was delivered to the United States before Congress had voted the purchase money. The country at large scarcely realized what was being done. There was some criticism of "Seward's Folly," as the opposition press termed the unwanted possession, and ugly rumors connected the names of a few hesitant congressmen with charges of open bribery. But the majority in favor of the appropriation was too large, 113 to 43, to render a resort to such means necessary.

Both Seward and De Stoeckl exerted themselves in behalf of ratification and appropriation, but their influence was not the decisive factor. It was rather to be found in popular belief that Russia had been truly friendly during the Civil War and that therefore we should reciprocate by relieving her of an unwelcome possession. Strategically, the region was a source of danger to its possessor; and economically, since the failure of the Russian-American Company, it was a definite liability.

Hence the czar's government was ready to sell, Seward was eager to buy, and the American public, however indifferent or unwilling to add to Andrew Johnson's prestige, grudgingly consented to pay something for Russia's supposed friendship. Some features of the transaction, indeed, suggest comparisons with the acquisition of Louisiana, although it was far from offering the immediate advantages of the earlier purchase.

The acquisition of Alaska occurred between the earlier and later phases of American expansion and, as we have noted, partook of the character of each. Economically it has proved a great asset to the United States; strategically it has become an increasing liability. Canada separates it from the main part of the Union and thus gives it an insular position. Its extension toward the coast of Asia, greatly prolonged by the Aleutian Islands, makes it an important element in our strategic policy. With its possession, other acquisitions in the Pacific seemed next in order. Hence arose, during the latter half of the nineteenth century, the various proposals to acquire the Sandwich, or Hawaiian, Islands and the attempts to acquire other insular holdings.

The Sandwich Islands were discovered and named by Captain James Cook in 1778. From that date they have played an important part in the strategy of the Pacific. During the nineteenth century, commercial and missionary enterprises combined to give the islands an importance in American eyes that was intensified during the mid-century by our Isthmian connections. Even then, when domestic problems so thoroughly filled public attention, our interests in the Pacific were not wholly neglected. Our government, it is true, failed to annex Hawaii when the time seemed ripe in the mid-fifties; nor would it join with other nations in giving those islands common protection or even in renouncing an ambition to possess them. Succeeding administrations agreed to defend duly established dynasties. Under that dubious assurance, independent rule in Hawaii continued for another half-century.

Meanwhile the descendants of pioneer American merchants and missionaries became Hawaiian citizens and gradually assumed control of affairs. By the last decade of the nineteenth century the hour had apparently come to convert these religious and commercial ties with the United States into political ones. The resident American minister in the islands heartily supported this idea. "The Hawaiian pear is now fully ripe," he wrote, "and this is the golden hour for the United States to pluck it." Therefore, when the pro-American oligarchy started the revolt, early in 1893, he promptly cooperated by having marines landed from an American war vessel in the harbor "to preserve order." But there was a change in administration at Washington. President Cleveland, unimpressed by the "irresistible circumstances" that seemed to make annexation inevitable, withdrew the hastily drawn treaty from the American Senate and sought to restore the deposed Hawaiian queen. The white planters who had directed the revolt refused to accept the former monarch and for the next five years maintained a quasi-republic, awaiting a more favorable opportunity to achieve their purpose and thus secure access to American markets. As a group, they gained their goal in 1898, during our war with Spain.

This struggle, brief as it was, shows the far-reaching effects of war. Hostilities supposedly affecting only Cuba bore first-fruits in the Pacific. The destruction of the Spanish fleet in the harbor of Manila and the seeming necessity of continuing military occupation there made Hawaii an important post on the route to the Far East. "Sea power," as interpreted by Captain Mahan, came to the aid of "Manifest Destiny" and political necessity. Renewed agitation was already under way to bring about annexation. President McKinley pointed to the Texas precedent of a joint resolution, and in that form the act for annexing Hawaii passed Congress in July, 1898. By that step the United States "plunged into the sea." In 1900 Hawaii was formally organized as a territory. This was the first instance in our history of the incorporation of noncontiguous territory already possessing a government of its own with the United States. In this particular Hawaii differs from the precedent set by Texas.

The annexation of Hawaii was hastened by the situation that was developing in Cuba. This island was early marked out as a prize of American expansion, but our concern in the early days of the nineteenth century for the peaceful acquisition of Florida then kept us from obtaining it. In the filibustering era of the fifties and later during the ten years' revolt in the island, prominent factions in the United States sought to force its annexation. In 1895 began the second Cuban struggle for independence, which speedily degenerated into a guerrilla warfare marked by widespread devastation and inhuman repression. These were conditions inseparable from the reconcentration policy adopted by the Spaniards, but they aroused intense popular resentment in the United States. This feeling of hostility was fanned to a war pitch by an explosion that destroyed the cruiser "Maine" while on a "friendly" visit to Havana in February, 1898. Public opinion at once demanded that Spain withdraw from the island. The Spanish government was then directed by the queen regent, mother of Alfonso XIII. Unwilling to jeopardize her son's throne by immediate compliance, the queen sought to temporize with the American demand. Spurred on by a yellow press, the American public called for immediate warfare; and on April 11, 1898, President McKinley reluctantly acquiesced by asking Congress for power to terminate hostilities between the Spanish government and the people of Cuba. After a week's discussion, Congress, by joint resolution of April 19, empowered the president to force Spain to retire from Cuba and to use the army and navy of the United States to enforce this demand. At the same time, through the Teller amendment to the original war resolution, Congress disclaimed any intention of assuming sovereignty over Cuba "except for the pacification thereof." Thus that island technically escapes inclusion in the present work.

This resolution, signed by McKinley on the next day, was followed on April 25 by a formal declaration of war against Spain. Campaigns followed in the distant Philippines as well as in Cuba. These operations represented both the humanitarian impulse that precipitated the strife and the growing spirit of imperialism that was already influencing American policy. Spain, yielding to the inevitable, recognized the independence of Cuba. That island, released from Spanish domination, was shortly confronted with the Platt Amendment, under which, for the next three and a half decades, it was to keep itself safe, solvent, and sanitary at the behest of the United States.

The war also led to the occupation of Puerto Rico, the chief prize of the conflict. Its acquisition brought the United States face to face with the task of ruling alien peoples. The same problem had presented itself, in slight measure, with the occupation a half-century before of New Mexico and

California. Our Indian wards represented another and not very flattering aspect of the same problem. Puerto Rico brought it still more forcibly to our attention and in a form that called for immediate and thoughtful action.

Few persons in the United States had carefully considered any phase of the problem. This statement would also apply to our attitude toward immigration in general. Yet the circumstances that brought Puerto Rico under American control called for a policy in sharp contrast to the Spanish rule for three centuries. Those years had been marked by continued neglect of the island's economic and social needs. Its inhabitants, numbering nearly a million and living in a restricted area, now made unexpected demands upon our sympathy, our tact, and our generosity. They forced us to face many of the problems that we had neglected in Alaska. Their mere numbers, not to mention the strategic and commercial importance of the island and our reputation in the Spanish-speaking world, called for a serious attempt to meet the varied issues in a spirit of mutual good will and adequate knowledge.

As an experimental ground in American altruism, as well as in cultural effort, the island has given rise to divergent views and often has led to conflicting policies. It presented no unoccupied land for exploitation. Before Spain surrendered it, the people had already increased beyond its greatest producing capacity and were facing a lowered standard of living. They were ready to welcome American control, fancying that it would mean greater opportunities for development. On the other hand, many elements in the United States looked upon the island as affording an opportunity for economic exploitation of which they hastened to avail themselves. Military rule, followed by the Foraker Act, continued the islanders in a state of tutelage without defining precisely the limits and character of their subjection. Thus a decade and a half passed without meeting the political expectations of its population or adequately ministering to their social and economic needs. Territorial status was bestowed upon the island in 1917 without distinctly incorporating it with the American Union. The Puerto Ricans were inducted *en masse* into partial American citizenship, unless they expressly disclaimed it, and in that status they find themselves today. They may become full-fledged citizens by emigrating to the United States. A considerable faction among them demand immediate statehood, while a vociferous minority ask for complete independence. Meanwhile, a rapidly growing population makes increasing demands upon the limited resources of the island.

Lying near Puerto Rico are the Virgin Islands. Discovered, as were the other Antilles, by the Spaniards, they were little utilized until Spain's enemies proceeded to make use of them. After being fought over by various nations for two centuries, they were definitely claimed by France and Denmark in the seventeenth century. St. Croix, the largest of the three principal islands of the Danish group, was held by France until 1733, when it was sold to Denmark, which already possessed the other two, St. Thomas and St. John, and numerous smaller islets. Denmark continued to control them until during the World War, when they were sold to the United States. Twice before the United States had tried to buy them. They were among the acquisitions that Seward hoped to get in the sixties, but at that time the Senate of the United States failed to approve the necessary treaty. Shortly after occupying Puerto Rico, the United States again attempted to purchase them, but this time Denmark refused to sell. The island of St. Thomas, with its magnificent harbor, gave significance to the islands. Charlotte Amalie was a port-of-call for vessels of all nations and an important coaling station for craft in the vicinity. St. Thomas also produced a large proportion of the bay rum of commerce. Its harbor facilities would have greatly aided the United States to maintain its blockade of southern ports during the Civil War. This was the consideration that led Seward to make the first attempt to purchase the island group. Fear that their possession by a potential enemy would prove detrimental to our interests in the Caribbean led to the second attempt, in 1902, which was likewise unsuccessful. But when a new demand for their purchase arose during the first World War, we finally obtained them from Denmark at the greatly enhanced price of $25,000,000.

As in the case of Alaska, conspicuous neglect has characterized the American possession of the islands. To the extent that they have come under American law, they have lost much of their opportunity in other markets. The change in fuel for steam vessels from coal to oil has diminished the importance of Charlotte Amalie as a port-of-call. No other sources of adequate income have been developed, so that the islands form, as President Hoover crudely expressed it, "an effective poorhouse." Recently efforts have been put forth to improve the social and economic conditions of the islanders. They might have been annexed to Puerto Rico, but such a step, if contemplated, should have been taken years ago. Now annexation would help matters but little. Some attempt has been made to stimulate a market for the rum of the islands in the United States. The need for a harbor in that vicinity largely passed with the acquisition of Puerto Rico. Thus the islands remain as they have been for so long in their history, Caribbean waifs, coveted by others through jealousy rather than economic or strategic need. In a small way they test the ability of the United States as a colonizing power.

By virtue of its position, wealth, and importance the United States since 1898 has become the dominating force in the Caribbean. The real center of its control rests on the Isthmus of Panama, the narrowest part of the American continent. Nature has marked out the spot for an interoceanic highway, and within our generation man has furthered its destiny by cutting the Panama Canal. Hard upon the discovery of America, far-seeing pioneers began to devise plans for such a roadway. Early discussions of the project were cut short by a decree of Philip II of Spain, but the idea persisted even against his royal edict. The scientist von Humboldt renewed the discussion, and the early years of the nineteenth century were marked by more than one fantastic plan to realize the undertaking. Then followed a period of intense rivalry between the two highways most favored. Stagecoach and mule train at Panama were matched by stagecoach and river steamer at Nicaragua. A railroad at Panama, completed by an American company in the fifties, seemed for a time to answer the needs of interoceanic transport. This enterprise was carried out under the Treaty of 1846 between the United States and Nueva Granada (now Colombia). Great Britain countered by making pacts with the states of Central America which gave it a negative advantage over prospective canal sites in that quarter. The outcome of this rivalry was the Clayton-Bulwer Treaty of 1850, which sought to encourage the digging of a canal through private enterprise. The passing decades were to demonstrate how weak the individual measures were.

The failure in the late eighties of the French Panama Canal Company indisputably proved their inadequacy.

The activities of this French corporation had aroused keen apprehension among advocates of an American interoceanic canal. Many of these looked forward to closer relations with the republics of the Western Hemisphere. "An American canal under American auspices" became their watchword, and the outstanding representative of this new Pan-Americanism, Secretary of State James G. Blaine, even proposed to abrogate the Clayton-Bulwer Treaty in order to give the United States a free hand in the isthmian region. For the time being, however, less jingoistic views prevailed, and both government and people settled down to watch the Frenchmen waste their money on what still seemed a quixotic enterprise. A few, indeed, sought to rival the French project by constructing a canal across Nicaragua. Both undertakings, after the crash of the French plan, degenerated into competitive lobbying in Washington, where the French stockholders and American promoters each worked against the other's enterprise and in turn faced competition from those who represented transcontinental railroad interests.

From this scene of legislative bickering the Spanish-American War, in 1898, aroused both the American government and the American people. The record-breaking voyage of the "Oregon" around South America demonstrated the necessity for a strategic isthmian canal. National defense thus supplemented commercial demands in urging the immediate realization of better communication between the Atlantic and the Pacific. Backed by this combined economic and strategic urge, the McKinley administration took up the isthmian canal as a promising phase of the "white man's burden." Much preliminary diplomacy was necessary before dirt could fly at Panama. The undertaking must be a national one, with the interests of the United States predominating. Nevertheless, the rights and privileges of Great Britain must be taken into account. Furthermore, the details of construction must be worked out in co-operation with Colombia and Central America. Nicaragua, indeed, was obviously the only alternative route to Panama, but all the isthmian governments felt that the proposed waterway would affect their interests. Such likewise was the attitude of the west-coast republics of South America. All looked upon the prospective canal as a matter of concern to themselves as well as to Great Britain and the United States. None of them singly, nor all of them together, could muster the capital to construct it; but its building would further their individual and collective interests, and their good will would contribute to its easy operation.

The first problem of importance was the selection of a canal site. Two commissions made a careful survey of the whole Central American terrain—its physical advantages and difficulties, its strategic and commercial possibilities—and also examined the resources and liabilities of the French Canal Company and those of its American rival at Nicaragua. Their first report favored the route at Nicaragua; but the vigorous and skilful lobbying of the French representatives, coupled with a considerable reduction in the estimated value of the concession at Panama, led to the selection of the Panama route. In this choice the preference of President Theodore Roosevelt played no little part.

Concurrently with the selection of the route ran diplomatic negotiations with Great Britain. The United States needed to free itself from the hampering provisions of the Clayton-

Bulwer Treaty. John Hay, as Secretary of State, took up the negotiation with Lord Pauncefote, the British ambassador. The first treaty, which continued the idea of a neutral canal, unfortified by the United States, was rejected in the Senate. The spirit of the times was too imperialistic to vision such an enterprise without its military features. A second treaty, which omitted all reference to fortifications but by implication gave the United States power to take such measures for its defense as seemed necessary, was immediately ratified by both governments. This ratification betokened a new *rapprochement* between the former isthmian rivals. It likewise marked an important change in the policy of Great Britain. That power now began to concentrate her naval power in the North Sea and, by withdrawing her war vessels from the Caribbean, left the West Indies under the suzerainty of the United States. This treaty also deprived the mid-American countries of such protection as was afforded by previous rivalry between the United States and Great Britain.

Having determined upon the Panama route and removed the chief diplomatic obstacle, the government of the United States proceeded to take up diplomatic negotiations with Colombia and with the Central American republics. The latter had in some measure to be placated for the loss of advantage that might have been derived from a Nicaraguan canal. More important were the prospective negotiations with Columbia. It would be necessary to treat with that country so as to satisfy her legitimate monetary desires and at the same time protect her honor and prestige. This proved no easy task. One minister from Colombia, convinced that he could reach no agreement in keeping with national honor, withdrew from the negotiation in disgust. A second went well beyond the letter of his instructions in order to sign the pact known as the Hay-Herran Treaty of 1903. This provided for the leasing of a six-mile strip of land through which the canal might be constructed, for the payment of a lump sum of $10,000,000 to Colombia, to be followed after some years by an annual payment of $250,000, and for the exercise of joint sovereignty by the two nations over the canal strip. This, it seems, was the only agreement that either party would accept.

The treaty, although not wholly satisfactory, was promptly ratified by the United States Senate. Far different was the action in Colombia. The congress of that country, called together to consider the pact, proceeded instead to make a bitter attack upon its provisions. Many of the members thought that Colombia should receive a larger indemnity for what it conceded in sovereignty and in material resources. They contended, and with apparent legality, that whatever assets remained to the French Canal Company would in the course of a few years revert to Colombia, and hence their country should receive a part of the $40,000,000 that the United States had agreed to pay the bankrupt company. Despite the covert threats of the American minister, their arguments prevailed, and the Colombian congress, after some weeks of deliberation, adjourned without ratifying the treaty.

During the discussion, the Panama representatives predicted that a failure to ratify would provoke a rebellion on the Isthmus. By the terms of the Spooner Act, which authorized the United States to undertake the canal, the president of the United States was empowered, in case the treaty were not accepted, to address himself to Nicaragua. Thus the residents of Panama might lose the prospective advantages of the canal. Hence its representatives predicted a secession from Colombia, and the predictions were given greater weight by the coercive attitude of the American minister at Bogota. Under such affront, the Colombian congress became still more stubborn and adjourned, as we have noted, without action. Such a proceeding was interpreted as direct defiance of the American government.

Meanwhile, the agents of the French Canal Company were not idle. Upon the ratification of the treaty hung their hopes of salvaging $40,000,000 from their failure at Panama. Philipe Bunau-Varilla, a former engineer at Panama, began to intrigue with the leading families there to bring about the creation of an independent republic. His confrere in New York, William Nelson Cromwell, counsel of the reorganized company, also bestirred himself in behalf of the movement. Through their combined efforts the Roosevelt administration was led to acquiesce in the prospective revolt and to recognize the insurgent group in Panama. In addition, orders transmitted through the Navy Department brought about virtual co-operation of American war vessels at Colon and at Panama to assure the success of the revolt. Furthermore, the management of the Panama Railroad, American in personnel although a subsidiary of the French company, lent its indirect assistance by refusing to transport Colombian troops across the Isthmus and, it is rumored, by using money to buy off the Colombian commander and his troops. Through their complicity and possibly through other bribes to Colombian officials at Panama, separation was achieved on the night of November 3, 1903. On the sixth of that month diplomatic relations were established with the insurgents through the American consul at Panama, and within less than three weeks a treaty was made with Bunau-Varilla, hastily appointed representative of the embryo government. This pact gave more favorable terms to the prospective canal-builders. Panama was to receive the ten millions that had been promised to Colombia. The canal strip was widened to ten miles, and over it the United States was to exercise complete sovereignty. Within this strip, it is true, Colon and Panama were under the jurisdiction of the new republic, but even in those cities the United States might act when political security or sanitary protection seemed to warrant it.

Thus was brought into being Panama, the latest political entity of Latin America. In effect the new republic was only a holding corporation through which the United States might complete the projected canal. It was thus a virtual protectorate of the northern republic, and such it has remained to the present time. Under the circumstances, a minimum of friction has marked this relationship, but it has been characterized on the part of Panama by a growing desire for greater freedom of action. This desire was incorporated in the Treaty of 1936, which recently was ratified by the United States Senate.

The actual construction of the canal also involved difficulties, both in the task itself and in the personnel to direct it. At the outset the work was undertaken by commissions whose members exercised special functions of control and performance. Within a few years, however, such a system proved unworkable, and President Theodore Roosevelt wisely determined to set up a benevolent dictatorship in the zone with an army engineer, Colonel George W. Goethals, in charge. Under his energetic and inspiring leadership the canal was completed in 1913, a full year before the time promised. Thus, this engineering feat, one of the reputed wonders of the world, was brought to fruition through the combined efforts of technical experts, astute diplomats, and determined, if not overscrupulous, executives.

Dewey's guns in Manila Bay aroused imperialistic reverberations in the United States. For some years the American Republic had unconsciously moved toward expansion overseas. The annexation of Hawaii had been preceded by taking possession of Midway Island and by controversies with Great Britain and Germany over Samoa. The American claims in that island group were established in 1878. For a time, in 1889, these claims promised serious contention with Germany. Trouble was then postponed by the device of tripartite control, but the events of 1898 made that method no longer possible, and in the following year the island group was definitely divided among the three contending powers. The United States received as its share the Island of Tutuila, with its harbor Pago Pago. Thus, through these acquisitions, the United States now had strategic outposts in both the northern and southern Pacific.

The spirit of the times seemed to beckon to wider expansion. Dewey was in Manila Bay, far from any possible American base. He was, it is true, reasonably secure from any Spanish attack but not from German intermeddling or general Asiatic complications. Even before 1898 the United States was taking an active interest in Far Eastern affairs. Our statesmen were especially concerned with the possible breaking-up of China. We could not pretend, as did interested European powers, to any territorial claims or commercial concessions there, but Dewey's unexpected foray had given us a possible foothold off the China coast from which we could watch more effectively the machinations of China's despoilers and advance our own commercial interests. We had already taken up the task of the "open door," really a British heritage. Secretary Hay made himself its champion, a function that the British gladly allowed him to assume. Dewey's victory led certain commercial interests to insist upon taking over the Philippines, thus assuming the white man's burden in the Far East and making sure of our share in its resources.

This demand gained unexpected allies. In a moral sense the nation viewed the acquisition of the distant islands as a promising missionary enterprise and promptly moved to undertake the task of organizing a stable government. The first and most pressing need of the hour was to strengthen Dewey's precarious hold on Manila Bay. Hawaii, already in the process of annexation, admirably served to further this purpose. With its help military forces from the United States reached Manila in time to bring about the surrender of that city on August 13, 1898. Thus the Philippines, as well as Puerto Rico, came within the purview of diplomats who were shortly gathering at Paris to settle the issues of the war.

Our imperialistic and missionary zeal was thus in train to encircle the globe. Nor did we lack envious competitors. During the weeks when Dewey in Manila Bay was anxiously waiting for re-enforcements, he narrowly avoided serious clash with an officious German naval commander who sought to gain some advantage for his fatherland in this tumultuous archipelago. Later investigation, indeed, has disclosed that Spain was about to make Germany a dubious gift of the islands. In addition, Philippine insurgents under Aguinaldo were breaking away from Spanish control elsewhere and demanding possession of Manila itself as the capital of their embryo "republic." It was high time to settle the status of the islands.

President McKinley wrestled mightily with the problem in prayer and in timely appeals to public sentiment. Under this double guidance his vision expanded from the city and harbor of Manila to the Island of Luzon, to the whole archipelago, and even to the near-by coasts of Asia. Our diplomats at Paris reflected his expanding vision. Hapless Spain was helpless to resist. In consideration of $20,000,000 it agreed to transfer the sovereignty of the islands to the United States, together with a way station at Guam in the Carolines. The other islands of the latter group went to avid Germany.

In the course of a few months the United States had moved to incorporate alien peoples in the body politic. Such expansion in the Caribbean and in mid-Pacific had aroused apprehension in many quarters. It meant not only the acquisition of noncontinguous territory and the assumption of more extended means of defense but an attempt to bestow political privilege upon those ill prepared to use it and not likely to acquire the necessary skill and experience to profit by possessing it. This departure from practice in former acquisitions was still further heightened by the proposal to acquire the distant Philippines. Such an acquisition would, indeed, affect the character of our fundamental institutions. It would seem impossible to admit the Filipinos into the full privileges of American citizenship even if such status should be given to the people of Hawaii or of Puerto Rico. The proposal to acquire the Philippines brought the question of alien control before the American people. Public sentiment divided over the issue. The treaty annexing the islands passed the Senate through the influence of William J. Bryan, who hoped to make imperialism the leading political issue in 1900. He realized his aim in part, but in the election of that year the anti-imperialists failed to convince the voters that expansion across the Pacific endangered our fundamental political institutions, and McKinley was triumphantly re-elected. Nevertheless, the experiment being carried on across the Pacific continued to excite apprehension among many American observers.

One cause for their disquiet was to be found in the resistance to American rule which broke out even before the ratification of the treaty. The three years' struggle that followed meant the loss of more than four thousand lives and the expenditure of nearly $200,000,000. The struggle was not ended when a commission, headed by William Howard Taft, established civil government there. It was the purpose of Judge Taft to prepare the Filipinos for self-government as rapidly as possible. With that end in view, the islands, on July 1, 1902, were made an "unorganized" territory under the protection of the United States. The commission was expanded to include Filipino members, and the islanders were given a representative assembly. The commission continued to function as an upper house. Successive governors-general sought to develop the material resources of the islands and to increase the facilities for public instruction, but there was no substantial progress toward self-government until the advent of the Wilson administration in 1913.

By that date it became apparent that the commercial advantages anticipated from the Philippines had proved largely illusory. Trade between the islands and the United States had vastly increased since the beginning of the century, but by no means in the same proportion as trade with Hawaii or other recent acquisitions. Nor did our costly possessions off the coast of Asia bring us a correspondingly increased trade with China. Our presence there, it is true, enabled us to participate in the occupation of Pekin during the Boxer Rebellion of 1900. In this episode the United States sought to show moral leadership, and its attitude toward China strengthened the traditional friendship between the two countries. On the other hand, our Chinese policy helped to alienate Japan, and this alienation was further increased by an immigration policy which placed the Japanese at a distinct disadvantage in comparison with most other nations and destroyed much of the friendship of an earlier period.

With the coming into power of the Wilson administration and the appointment of Francis Burton Harrison as governor of the Philippines a new era was introduced into our relations with those islands. Their more advanced residents were given a large measure of self-government under the Jones Act of 1916, with a governor-general and a vice-governor appointed by the president of the United States, in the usual manner, and with the latter executive exercising a final veto on Philippine legislation. In his last annual message in 1920, President Wilson asked for complete independence for the islands, claiming that the Jones Act had given their inhabitants a stable government. Congress failed to heed the suggestion. The Harding administration sent a new commission to investigate conditions, and this body recommended that independence be postponed. The administration of General Leonard Wood, who remained as governor-general, reversed the policy of the Harrison regime and aroused the opposition of nearly all the Filipino leaders. Despite this deadlock between executive and legislative departments, the movement for self-government continued to grow even under Republican administrations at Washington. Later governors-general reestablished more cordial relations with the legislative branch and paved the way for complete independence.

That status has not yet been achieved but is well advanced toward realization under the Tydings-McDuffie Act of March 24, 1934. This act, substituted for an earlier one that was rejected by the Filipino legislature, created the Philippine commonwealth, a temporary form of government to bridge over the ten-year transitional period that is to precede complete independence. During this decade the islanders enjoy complete self-government, although the American flag is still recognized and technical sovereignty remains with the United States. Trade with the latter country in certain products is on a quota basis and will so continue for five years, when export duties, annually increased, will be levied on these products. At the end of ten years, with full independence of the islands, Philippine trade will be subject, like that of any foreign nation, to American tariff laws.

Elsewhere overseas, expansion may also reverse itself. Discontent with American administration exists in Alaska. Though recently given territorial status, its people still feel that their contributions to national wealth lack appreciation. Its population during the last two decades has slightly declined—not a hopeful sign for the future. Nevertheless, its dominant element, closely in touch with the continental portion of the Republic, has no thought of looking elsewhere for relief. Such is largely the case with Hawaii and its polyglot population. Far different is the situation in Puerto Rico, where, despite American efforts, the people still adhere to their Spanish culture and resist efforts to make English even a second language. What the future has in store for them is uncertain. One might vision a possible confederation of the Spanish-speaking islands in the Caribbean, of which they might form a part; but up to the present that appears only as a dream. Beyond Hawaii, the Midway Islands, with Wake

Island, Guam, and the Philippines, afford an airway to Asia. To a certain extent Tutuila, in the southern Pacific, offers a stepping-stone to Australia. These are advantages that were unperceived when we began our imperialistic experiment in the Pacific, but today they constitute the chief advantage of that costly procedure.

The United States will profit, it is to be hoped, from a reserve of good will that may flow from our educational and other tutelary effort in the Philippines and elsewhere. One hesitates, however, to make predictions concerning their political and economic future and hence refrains from any attempt to measure the contribution thereto by the United States. The same statement applies in large measure to the Caribbean, where at the turn of the century our country initiated its other outstanding phase of short-lived imperialism. The present administration has declared its intention to abandon the system of protectorates in Cuba, Haiti, the Dominican Republic, Nicaragua, and Panama. The system has proved a financial liability, productive only of local restrictiveness and widespread criticism. Thus we may liquidate one of the chief by-products of the imperialistic era. The Canal Zone will remain, as it is today, part of the coastline of the United States until mankind arrives at that remote golden age when the nations of the world agree to neutralize all strategic waterways. Puerto Rico, restless and unsatisfied in its political aspirations or economic outlook, and the near-by Virgin Islands still remain and will doubtless long continue as reminders of our expansion overseas. We can only hope that this expansive movement, promising in its inception, exasperating in many of its most cherished features, has profited alien peoples more widely than our own.

PUERTO RICO

By RAFAEL PICÓ and WILLIAM H. HAAS

As DON JUAN PONCE DE LEON IN 1508 ENtered the spacious harbor of San Juan on the north coast of Puerto Rico, legend has it that his surging emotions found expression in "Que rico puerto!" Perhaps this historical phrase, as some historians believe, was the product rather of some fertile imagination of a much later date, Ponce being more intent upon what the hills beyond had in store for him than upon the magnificence of the setting at hand. Yet the intelligent traveler with a feeling for the exquisite in nature and a fair appreciation of the centuries of history and romance represented will not consider "Ah, what a magnificent haven!" at all extravagant. Even the blasé tourist with an eye for only what is evident recognizes in this splendid gateway, dominated by ancient fortifications, a harbor of striking beauty. At the end of the journey, no less interesting to the serious minded is the bustling, modern-old San Juan, with its teeming hinterland rich in history and in problems, where a tremendous change is taking place, a metamorphosis of the old into the new, the medieval into the modern.

The oldest city under the American flag is the focal point of this setting. San Juan, the capital of the island, was a settlement long before St. Augustine, Florida, came into being and a full century before the Pilgrim Fathers set foot on Plymouth Rock. The city, naturally, is rich in historic structures associated with an adventurous and bloody past. El Morro, the old fortress overlooking the town and added to as funds permitted, became the second strongest fortress in Spain's New World empire. Parts of its thick walls still survive—a striking monument to a day of pirates and corsairs long since left behind. Parts of the wall which once inclosed the town still stand, while other parts have disappeared with time, giving way to structures that serve a new need. A similar situation, only to a lesser degree, prevails throughout the island, with its old-fashioned towns taking on a modern aspect and outlook.

Despite its antecedence, San Juan is an active business center where the new mingles with that which is antiquated and ill fitted for current business activity. A building without an elevator, yet with high ceilings, surrounding a flowering patio must serve a progressive business firm the best it may. There is also the inevitable congestion of traffic in the narrow, one-way streets with their single-file sidewalks, congestion increased by the loading and unloading of merchandise, to the discomfiture of those who have business errands to perform. Huge trucks, busses, streetcars, automobiles, taxis, pushcarts, burden-bearers—even pedestrians—express their impatience in noisy clamor. Moreover, the persons so engaged may, when at home, be surrounded by all the modern conveniences of life or live with their utter lack, as did their ancestors a century or more ago.

Throughout the island the sharp contrasts between the old and the new, the medieval and the modern, are much in evidence. A primitive conveyance carrying some product to market, an oxcart, or a native with a razorback at the end of a rope may be passed by ultramodern automotive equipment. In the smaller towns are many houses upon stilts whose architecture is almost a replica of that of earliest Spanish days. In

EL MORRO, THE FORTRESS AT THE ENTRANCE OF SAN JUAN HARBOR

It was added to little by little until it became the second strongest fortress in the New World. Parts are now used as soldier barracks.

ONE OF SAN JUAN'S BEAUTIFUL PLAZAS

Within the city of San Juan are many beautiful plazas. The love of the beautiful, where poverty is not too much of a handicap, is evident throughout the island.

"Old San Juan," as in other towns, there still are the flat, chimneyless roofs, jutting balconies with fancy grilles, tiled floors, shuttered windows that know no glass, flowering patios, and pastel-shaded walls of plaster. These outward evidences of the old and the new are an index also of what is less evident—the change in the outlook of the people passing from one cultural stage into another. A new life is growing out of an older one, which in turn was impinged upon a still older or native culture. Each of these three phases of culture has a part in the present outlook.

Out of this background a new Puerto Rico is rising, coming out of all the past. Puerto Rico at present, therefore, is not American; it is not Spanish; it is not pre-Spanish. It is a mixture, not a compound of all; it is new, yet still unamalgamated. In one section one element of cultural life is dominant; in another part, another element. In time, all is sure to be fused into a unit. Modern Puerto Rico, however, cannot be understood without an appreciation of all the forces that are now a part of life's outlook and activities.

THE PRIMITIVE PERIOD

Like other parts of the New World, Boriquén, as the island was known to the indigene, was inhabited by a race which had the name of "American Indian" thrust upon it. This race represented a cultural development as distinct from that brought in by the Europeans as though it had developed on another planet. In some parts of the New World where the two cultures met, the native blood was fairly quickly and completely wiped out by the white invader; in other parts it has persisted and may even be dominant today. In sections where the phrase, "The good Indian is a dead Indian," was current, as in most parts of the United States, little remains of that older culture. In other sections, where the good Indian was a slave, as he was in the mining regions of the New World, the native culture still prevails. Puerto Rico in this respect occupies a median ground; no Indians are left, but many of their cultural traits still persist. As was inevitable, the coming of an advanced people was sure to bring on strife, no matter how sincere the desire for peace. One group had to give way; better equipment and growing numbers, not ability or bravery, commonly decided the struggle. In Puerto Rico the native disappeared early, but not before he had left his imprint upon the newcomers.

Where exploitation, and not settlement, was the dominant motive, the natives were needed to supply the invaders with labor and food. To insure a certain regularity in supplying these needs, some form of enforced labor became essential; but the native, by nature proud and haughty, was not fitted for slavery. He chafed under the first restraint and, with added burdens, rebelled, but unsuccessfully. This was the story in Boriquén as well as elsewhere under similar conditions.

Although the natives of the New World had never, at their best, been able to get much beyond true Stone Age in spite of an environment so favorable and stimulating to the more advanced immigrant group, nevertheless they had gone much beyond the best that is known of the Stone Age in Europe. Because of their insular environment, it is natural also that the natives of the West Indies should have developed their own island culture, remarkably distinct from that found on the near-by mainland of North America.

The origin of the people and the basic elements of their culture in both the Lesser and the Greater Antilles may be traced with fair assurance to the mainland of South America. This is not strange, for both the flora and the fauna are distinctly South, not North, American. The islands in their wide arch come fairly close to the southern continent, thus forming more or less definite stepping-stones to the north and west. The gap between Cuba and Yucatan, on the other hand, is too great to expect any interchange of peoples, except perhaps through accident. Although Cuba lies fairly close to Florida, the moderately swift-flowing Gulf Stream with its attendant roughness also proved a fairly effective barrier. The Bahamas, which might have acted as stepping-stones between Cuba and the mainland, are, for the most part, low and unfavorable for any development by primitive people.

In its relation to the other West Indies, the position of Boriquén is significant. It lies about midway in the large festoon of islands extending in a wide arch from Venezuela to Florida. It is also the first of the major group large enough and sufficiently differentiated to have many different physical settings. There is a flat coastal region; and in the more mountainous interior are wide, open valleys with rich alluvial soils, readily accessible from the coast. Each of these areas offered new conditions and new possibilities. As time went on, the South American migrants gradually spread through the Lesser Antilles and to the larger islands north and west. However, at the time of discovery the cultural progress westward had been by no means complete, for the early conquistadors found the western end of Cuba less advanced than the eastern, and this part, in turn, more primitive than Boriquén.

Although the indigenes of the New World have all been grouped under the same general head of "American Indian," they had been in the New World long enough to have become

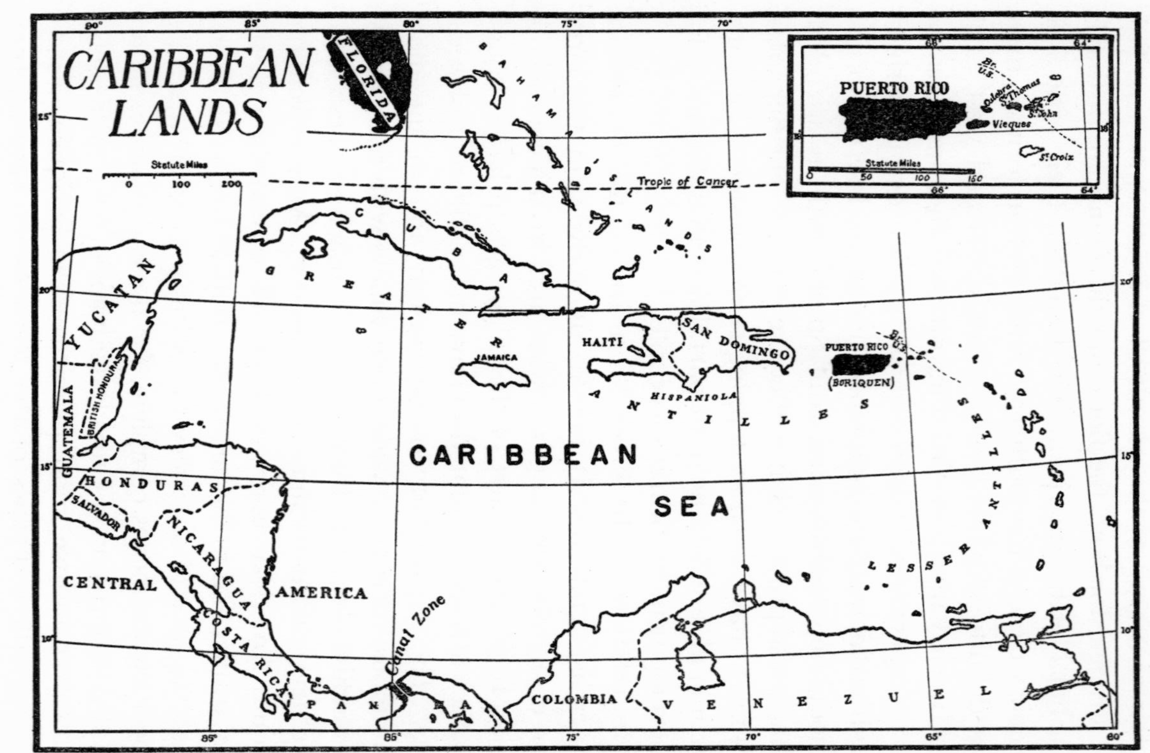

MAP OF CARIBBEAN LANDS

The distribution of the islands made the cultural development distinctly South, not North, American

differentiated into a wide range of languages and cultural stocks. In the West Indies had arisen two markedly different cultural groups, seemingly from the same South American (Tainan) stock, each a product of its new island environment. The larger and evidently older branch, known as the "Arawaks," had migrated or had been pushed north, and at the time of Columbus occupied the Greater Antilles. They had become an agricultural people who, through sedentary habits of life and love of peace, had lost some of their original virility and aggressiveness. They were, however, far from being a decadent people, as the severity of their struggle with the better equipped white invaders bears full testimony.

The other offshoot of the Tainan stock at a later date began also to spread over the islands by way of the Lesser Antilles. The Caribs, as this branch was known—a fierce, warlike, non-agricultural folk—were ever crowding the gentle Arawaks from the rear. At the time of the discovery of Boriquén, the two groups had become implacable enemies. The home-loving Arawaks lived in constant fear of the fierce warriors who came in their great *piraguas* to raid their villages for food and to carry off their young women and small boys. The bravery and fearlessness of the Caribs, as well as their fierceness in time of battle, brought dread even to the better equipped Spaniard. Their warlike characteristics made such an imprint on these adventurers that the sea surrounding the islands became known as *El Mar Caribe* ("the sea of the Caribs"), or, in English, the "Caribbean Sea." The Caribs were reported also as "eating like a dog" (*canis*) some of their prisoners, and thus was born the name *canibales* as a designation for man-eaters.

Puerto Rico, or Boriquén, thus not only was the first major

island to the north of the lesser group but was also at the northern frontier of this savage group and bore the bulk of its raids. The Boriqueños, as the inhabitants of the island were called, were, at the time of the discovery, being forced to give further ground, for the Caribs were already in possession of the two small islands to the east and were also in control of parts of eastern Boriquén. How much farther west the Caribs had at one time or another extended their control is not known, but there seems to be some archeological evidence of their presence in the western part of the island and of their activity in the other islands of the major group. Thus the native stock of Boriquén was dominantly of the quiet, peace-loving Arawak type, with only a slight addition of the fierce, warlike Caribs.

The cultural base[1] of the Boriqueños was a tropical one, and many of its elements have been traced to Venezuela. The migrations, therefore, meant merely different environment and, on the whole, a more favorable one. Tropical vegetable foods on the island were available throughout the year. Although there were definite seasons for the planting and harvesting of certain crops, there was not much need for the storing of foods, as some vegetable food was procurable at all times of the year. The temperature never was low enough to make the heating of homes imperative. Over none of the agricultural areas was the rainfall so heavy that fire could not be used at some season or other in clearing wooded areas for agricultural purposes. Like other natives of the tropics, the

[1] Much of our knowledge of the indigenes comes from writers who knew native life from direct contact: Las Casas, Oviedo, Ramon Pane, and Pedro Martyr. Of all, Las Casas (1474–1566) seems to write with most insight, perhaps with some partiality. He was their friend, living with them and doing all in his power to ameliorate the harsh conditions officially imposed on them.

Boriqueños had learned to kill trees by girdling, felling some and then setting the whole on fire. The ashes counteracted the acidity of the tropical soil and added available potash as a fertilizer. In a relatively few years such areas again were leached, then abandoned, and a new hillside area burned over. It is not at all improbable that the greater part of the island may have been cleared again and again by this "milpa" or "fang" or, as locally known, *conuco* system of agriculture.

Animals, as well as plants, had an important part in the native food supply, although never to the same extent as in parts of North America. Marine foods were to be had and, if shell heaps may be taken as an index, were highly prized. The manatee was a regular inhabitant of the lagoons and lower courses of rivers, where lived also many edible fish, turtles, and various kinds of shellfish. Inland were birds, reptiles, and other animal foods, such as iguanas, rodents, and the larvae of insects. The much greater density of population in the coastal regions may have been due, at least in part, to the greater abundance of food there.

The Boriqueños were primarily agriculturists and only secondarily hunters and fishermen. They were mainly dependent upon starch foods, such as maize, yuca (manioc), yautía, yams, and potatoes of various types. There was also a wide variety of legumes, squash, and squash-like or citron-like foods, as well as tropical fruits. According to the writers of the day, the natives had learned to use both "sweet and bitter herbs" in their quest for sufficient food. Strangely enough, of the two hundred or more food plants that they had domesticated or semidomesticated, none is listed in the island at present as a major commercial crop.

The natives were widely distributed over the entire island

but largely in villages. These villages were never in direct contact with the coast but were placed inland some distance and in the sheltered valleys of the interior, presumably as a protection against the marauding Caribs that came via the sea. Food and water supply seemingly were the dominant factors in the selection of the sites. Many of the Boriquén settlements became Spanish centers as the conquest proceeded and have since continued as centers of activity. Some of the towns, like Coamo and Caguas, may well have had their first inhabitants hundreds of years before the white man came and have been continuously occupied ever since. In many of these antiquated centers away from the major lines of travel much still remains that is Boriquén—a rich field of untouched study.

Unfortunately, the homes these people built were shortlived. There were no mound buildings, no pueblos or cliff dwellings, nor any type that might make possible some sort of permanency. Consequently, an architectural art could not have advanced very far. With a wide variety of plants to select from for their buildings, there was little need in the tropical environment of the more permanent type of material. The fragile frames, tied together with fibers, soon rotted away, especially when once abandoned. The modern *buhío*, or grass hut, seems such an accurate counterpart of the earlier types, as described by the early chroniclers, that there is little difficulty in visualizing how these people were sheltered. The framework was covered with bark, palm leaves, or grasses, and the roofs were thatched with material most easily available. Placed on stilts, perhaps an inheritance from a Venezuelan custom, they were admirably adapted to combat dampness and insect pests. This, or some modified form, is still the common type of architecture in the rural sections.

Clothing and house furnishings were not only simple but scanty. Only married women wore any body covering, and this was only in the form of a small apron. The only furniture possessed was a *duho*, or carved reclining chair, of which several are in archeological collections. The "bedroom suite" consisted of a hammock, in which the native was conceived and in which he breathed his last, in case of natural death. In many homes throughout the island the homemade hammock still persists instead of a bed or cot. Some families also still manufacture most of their kitchen utensils and other paraphernalia as of old from gourds, *ditas* of the *higuera* tree. Crude, unpainted earthenware, adorned in part with grotesque monkey-like heads, must have been widely used if the number of shards found is an index. Some of the relics have real artistic merit. To be noted especially are the beautifully carved mysterious stone collars, the three-cornered stones, idols, stone heads, masks, and necklaces.

The most characteristic element in the culture of the Caribs, on the other hand, was the canoe-like seacraft, *piraguas*, in which they traveled from island to island, far out of sight of land. These pirogues were made of huge logs, several feet in diameter, and were equipped with many oars and even with sails in addition. It is not at all surprising that the simple Arawaks, because of the strangeness of the craft of the Caribs and the unpredictableness of their coming, should have considered these fierce fighters as more than human. In fact, there was little likeness between the two groups. The peaceful Arawaks had nothing in common with the sea-roving Caribs, who in their knowledge of the sea had advanced far beyond any other group in the New World, a striking example of the great differentiation, due to environment, that had taken place. Their strange craft was the objective expression of a maritime life that must have taken centuries to develop. In no other part of the New World was there a culture like it.

The island, with its many limestone caverns, still has its pictographic writings. These are fairly common and, in view of the solubility of the rock and the rapidity of rock disintegration in tropical climates, fairly well preserved. From the number and character of the inscriptions it has been inferred that a pre-Arawak cave-dwelling people occupied the island earlier. Certain archeological evidence seems to support this view; and, if early chroniclers are interpreted rightly, these people were still to be found, at the time of discovery, in the remoter parts of the island. On the other hand, it is also known that the Arawaks hid in the caverns at times of Carib raids and made use of them at other times in carrying out certain religious rituals. The Arawaks may therefore have been responsible for the inscriptions.

The number of natives in Boriquén at the time of conquest will ever remain conjectural, as the early conquistadors were not interested in a study of the natives or in their number. Casual references or haphazard guesses as to population density vary greatly. Estimates as high as 600,000 found their way into the early writings, and one estimate is as low as 5,500. From a study of the possible food supply the one estimate seems much too large, and, from allotments made under the *repartimientos* system, the other seems absurdly small. Recent studies indicate that the number at the time of discovery very probably did not exceed 50,000 and may have been as low as 30,000. Whatever the number of the native peoples at the time of conquest, the rapidity with which it decreased is almost unbelievable. It may be stated with considerable assurance that in a brief half-century after Spanish occupation the indigenous race became a negligible factor in Spanish-Indian relationships.

THE SPANISH PERIOD

On his second expedition to the New World, Columbus learned from some Arawak women, enslaved by Caribs, of a beautiful and rich land to the north by the name of Boriquén. Following this clue, he sighted the island on November 16, 1493, and a few days later entered a small bay on the west coast, probably Aguada, where, to the rear, he found a neat Indian village of twelve houses grouped about a much larger structure, all facing a spacious plaza. From this plaza a broad, cleared roadway, separating well-kept gardens, led to the bay. The beauty of the place impressed the sailors greatly, and the gardens especially reminded them of those in their old home in Valencia, Spain. A thorough search made it evident that the inhabitants of this beauty spot had fled precipitately, perhaps mistaking the caravels of Columbus for some new invention of the dreaded Caribs.

In this setting, Columbus, with elaborate ceremony, took possession of the land in the name of his sovereign and named it *San Juan Bautista* ("St. John the Baptist"). With this declaration, the old, euphonious Indian name of "Boriquén" gave way to a cumbersome Christian one, and a new chapter in the history of the island was begun which, fates decreed, was to extend through more than four centuries of time. Of course the villagers had no appreciation of the importance of this visit and continued in their normal routine of life without interference for another fifteen years. The christening similarly meant little to Spain, for *San Juan Bautista del Boriquén* was only another name in the records. Lands were being added to the colonial empire much too rapidly for Spain to know what to do with them. Only Santo Domingo on the neighboring island of Hispaniola was maintained as a continuous settlement from the time of Columbus' first voyage. The city (now Trujillo), therefore, is the oldest permanent white settlement in the New World.

A new era for *San Juan Bautista* began when Ponce de León, who had been present at the naming, set out from Hispaniola on the military pretext of conquering the island for the protection of Santo Domingo. In 1508 he entered a bay on the north coast where, as already stated, he was overwhelmed by the beauty of the setting. To establish a base for his operations, he took his group inland about two miles to a place, near the present town of Cataño, where higher ground was bounded by a small plain, the whole inclosed by low hills. Here he built a fortified house and a chapel and had his men clear two separate areas for the growing of food crops. The one located on the *Rio Toa*, named *Los Reyes Católicos*, later became the chief testing- or proving-ground for various crop introductions. The settlement, named *Caparra*, separated from the harbor by a swamp and also proving unhealthful, was later moved across the bay to the site of present San Juan.

During the early part of his stay Ponce and his men were most hospitably treated by the natives. They were always greeted as superior beings, feted, and well supplied with food. Every now and again ceremonial dances (*areitos*) and games were held in their honor. Indeed, the natives felt most highly honored in the continued presence of these bearded, white immortals, god-men. During one of the ceremonials, Ponce much admired the yellow disks that hung from the chief's neck and expressed the desire to know the source of these beautiful objects. The chief readily explained that they represented the work of scores of men who painstakingly had collected the material, bit by bit, from the river sands in the hills. As a gift of friendship, he even gave Ponce some of them for his own enjoyment. Moreover, he ordered a tour of inspection in order better to explain how the natives separated the yellow flakes from the sands. All the processes were shown in detail, the chief, of course, having no premonition of the calamities and tragedies that the desire to possess this metal was to bring not only to him and his people but also to the people in other regions. At his earliest opportunity Ponce dispatched the disks to the homeland to be assayed. In due time came the report that they were pure gold and with it the request that he be most diligent in his search for more. With these disks had come, for the first time, the full awakening in the homeland that here was a possibility in the New World that had thus far received too little attention.

The aid of the natives was at once solicited to help supply the great white father across the sea with the desire of his heart. Naturally, at first they worked freely and willingly; but when pressure was brought to bear on them in order to increase the amount extracted and they were forced to work even beyond their strength, they lost their enthusiasm, then protested, and finally precipitated an open revolt in 1511, only three short years after having declared their friendship so ceremoniously. The revolt came, so the story runs, only after an experiment to test the white man's divinity had been made upon a young man by the name of Salcedo. After a ceremonial visit, the chief, giving instructions on the side, ordered several natives to carry the young hidalgo across some swollen streams. When in the center of one, they stumbled and then sat upon the poor Salcedo. At sundown they laid him upon the bank and, as fear seized them, pleaded divine forgiveness for three long days. Only after decomposition set in did they decide that the white man was mortal also.

The striking reversal of the native point of view is significant. They no longer looked upon the whites as gods but enemies that were to be exterminated at all costs. In their first organized assault they were highly successful, burning the town of Sotomayor and killing many of the settlers, among them the founder of the settlement. In open combat, however, the natives were no match for the better equipped whites, who, the experiment to the contrary, seemed nevertheless possessed of some supernatural power. With reinforcements from Santo Domingo, three expeditions which were sent out routed them completely within a three months' period. Those who would not submit had to go into hiding or exile. Quiet prevailed for a short time only; they had been defeated but not conquered. A guerrilla warfare was started with the aid of the Caribs as allies, but the cause was lost. Where formerly the kindly Arawaks had to fear only the fierce attacks of the Caribs from the outside, now they had an enemy in their midst against whom their blows seemed strangely unavailing. After this futile revolt, the island definitely lost its native status and became a dependency of Spain, being spoken of in the records as *San Juan Bautista de Puerto Rico*, or, in short, "Puerto Rico."

What, in large part, had been the cause for revolt was the establishment of a system of allotting or apportioning the natives to some white overseer or overlord. This system, widely in force throughout Spanish America with a slight modification from one region to another, was known as *repartimientos* (distribution), or, in a slightly different form, as *encomiendas* (by villages). It was developed ostensibly for the good of the native in order better to regulate pagan life. Someone had to be his sponsor to see that he became a Christian and was made subject to civil regulations. The system, seemingly so well intended, soon led to terrific abuses under the ruthlessness of some to whom the allotments had been made. Unmasked, it was an effective system for enslaving a whole population by decree, especially since public opinion of the day was not averse to slavery in any form.

The system was suggested by Columbus, who could not have foreseen the debasing effects. With its introduction into the island by Ponce, it became easy to tax the natives and, in their helplessness, to levy a tribute on them so heavy that it was in many cases absolutely impossible for them to meet requirements. The first tribute on record was imposed by Columbus in 1495 on the natives of *La Española* (Hispaniola) to the extent of gold the size of a sledge bell (*cascabel*) and an arroba (25 pounds) of cotton every three months for every native above sixteen years of age. It has been customary to blame the mother-country for everything that happened in America, but it should be kept in mind that this system did not originate in Spain and that reports of conditions in the New World took a long time in reaching home. Leaders were wont also to curry favor by giving reports that put themselves in the most favorable light. The fact of great vital importance is that with the coming of the white man a drastic change was forced upon the food and life habits of the natives of the island, to which they were unable to adjust themselves. As a result, some migrated to the Virgin Islands, there to become allies of their former enemies, while others who did not succumb to hardship lost their identity in miscegenation.

How many natives succumbed to harsh treatment and diseases to which they were not immune, how many died in war, and how many emigrated can never be known. Whatever the number, the native population decreased so rapidly that by the middle of the century the number remaining was negligible. Velasquez, who made the second allotment under the *repartimientos* system, wrote the king of Spain under date of April 15, 1557, stating: "Excepting your highness' Indians and those of the crown officers, there are not 4,000 left." In another letter a short time later, he wrote: "The smelting brought little gold. Many Indians have died from disease caused by the hurricane as well as from want of food."

The 4,000 Indians spoken of by Velasquez may not all have been of Arawak stock. As a result of the scarcity of labor, a considerable Indian traffic developed within the Antilles from the more to the less populated sections. There is record also that some natives were brought to the island even from far-off Mexico. In his desire to help the natives, Las Casas at this period advised the introduction of Negroes as workers—advice which, it may justly be said of him, he profoundly regretted later. Thus, as early as 1513, King Ferdinand authorized the introduction of Negroes as slaves into the West Indies.

The Negroes, however, had already been brought to *La Española* in five caravels, "free of duty," as early as 1502, only ten years after the discovery of the New World by Columbus. The first record for Puerto Rico is of a certain Geron, who, under oath that they were for personal services only, received permission in 1502 to bring his two slaves. The traffic in slaves for the island, however, was never very large. The gold workings had never been on a scale to warrant large numbers; and other needs, such as personal servants, plantation workers, and beasts of burden, were also very limited. As the white population never was very prosperous, the Negro was always more or less of an expensive luxury. So true was this that some owners were brought to court for their inability to pay for their slaves, and as early as 1533 the authorities petitioned the queen of Spain not to permit the importation of any more slaves, as it was impossible for the people to pay the prices asked. The general poverty of the people during this early period accounts, in large part, for the relatively small percentage of Negro blood in the island today.

The lack of prosperity, moreover, was due, in the main, to the small amounts of gold to be had. Even as early as 1536 the island was looked upon as having little or no gold, and all mining activity was officially abandoned about the middle of the century. There were, moreover, many other factors to keep the people poor. In 1519 an epidemic of smallpox broke out, with a fatality that reduced the number by at least a third. The fierce Caribs also found the island more defenseless than ever and the booty greater and much more to their liking.

The great scourge of the island, however, the fear of which people never outgrew, was the tropical hurricane. These storms were relatively numerous even if the records of only the most disastrous ones are considered. The first record is for July, 1515. In 1526 another was described by Vadilla: "There was a great deal of wind and rain which lasted twenty-four hours . . . . the damage caused by the flooding of the plantations is greater than one can estimate. Many rich men have grown poor." In July and August of 1530 there were three such storms. After the third the people had little heart to rebuild. Half the houses in San Juan were down, and the other half were without roofs. In the direct path of the hurricane not a house was left standing. "Everybody is impoverished and thinking of going away." "The city prays that all debts will be postponed for three years." Seven years later several hurricanes in close succession again devastated the island. "The floods have carried away the plantations along the borders of the rivers, many slaves and cattle having been drowned. Want and poverty are universal." Such laments, as the centuries come and go, are not at all uncommon.

As the first century of trials and sorrows came to a close, the natural beauty of the island was still there, the vegetation as luxuriant as ever, but the Indian villages in the more accessible regions had disappeared and with them the many gardens which Columbus' men had so much admired. There still were depleted tribes in the hill country with their superabundance of women where they had gone to escape slavery, and where an occasional runaway Negro slave found asylum. Some white men, to escape the rigorous discipline of the *presidio* (military garrison), also succumbed readily to the generous and kindly native. Many sailors of various nationalities, tired of the discipline and hardships of the open sea, readily entered the simpler life of the native under tropical skies. Even men of title who, because of the law of primogeniture, had been forced to seek their fortunes in the New World, disillusioned and ashamed to go home, found an asylum among the simple hill folk. Out of such beginnings came the present people of the interior—the country peasant, or *jíbaro*. As more immigrants came, the cultural landscape took on more and more of a white-man aspect. At no time was there a white frontier.

This first century of Spanish domination had many changes but little cultural progress to record. In this respect Puerto Rico was not unlike the mainland, the nations of Europe being more interested in exploiting the New World than in building up colonial empires. The sparsity of the island's white population at the time is an index of this attitude. The estimates given are all exceedingly small, altogether probably not more than a tenth of the number of people Columbus originally found there. The whites numbered about 2,000, the total population being somewhere between 4,000 and 6,000 people. It is very possible that at the end of the sixteenth century there were fewer people on the island than there had been at any time since the Arawaks became established, this in spite of the fact that Puerto Rico, because of its strategical location, was the favored daughter of Spain.

This century of Puerto Rican history can be interpreted only in the light of Spain's activities. The island had no identity of its own, the people had no feeling of unity as Puerto Ricans, and the homeland's interest was only as a means to an end. These facts are very evident in the records of the period. Reference is rarely made to the island as a whole, but the harbor was the all-important element. During the century the island served roughly three purposes for Spain: (1) it was looked upon as a frontier in the protextion of the major islands from Carib raids; (2) it was a base for outfitting expeditions, the best known being that of Ponce de León in his search for *la Fuente de la juventud* ("the Fountain of Youth"); and (3) it was a base in the conquest of the tropics, a proving- or testing-ground for both plants and animals. Strangely enough, in spite of Ponce's proving-ground on the Toa and the excellent work done later in plant introduction, America nevertheless proved to be for the conquistadors ever *un continente hambreado* ("a continent of hunger").

During the century not only had many of the old activities

been uprooted and replaced, but also to a very large degree the food crops of the island had been changed. Under the native culture the people had developed an economy that represented a balance of nature—a balance between numbers and their ability to wrest a living from the environment. With the advent of the whites this balance of nature was disturbed, the old order was upset, and the new did not furnish enough to maintain the former numbers. In their long search for food the natives of Puerto Rico had domesticated, partly domesticated, or introduced more than two hundred different kinds of plants. Strange as it may seem, some of these plants may still be found growing in the garden patch of some *jíbaro* in the hilly interior.

To replace these native domestications, plants from all parts of the world were tried out by the conquerors. The major introduction was the cane from the Orient, the product of which was so highly prized in Europe at the time. Columbus brought it to Hispaniola on his second voyage in 1493, and from there it reached Puerto Rico in 1514. The first mill on the island was built in 1523. Ten years later a little more than a ton of sugar was sent to the king as tribute, and, in 1540, a government loan of 6,000 pesos was granted to aid in the erection of ten mills. Such items of record show the slow growth of the industry in Puerto Rico, where it never reached major proportions, although the West Indies and Brazil became Europe's chief sources of sugar during the seventeenth and eighteenth centuries. To Hispaniola also came the banana from the Azores, in 1516; its importance as a food to the islanders can scarcely be overestimated. The general usefulness of the coconut tree and the value of its fruit as a food are enthusiastically spoken of by 1549.

The astounding feature of this century, however, is the tremendous energy displayed by Spain in exploring and in annexing the New World. The division of the world into two parts by papal decree was the real beginning, and the end of conquest came with the loss of the *Armada invencible* in 1588, perhaps more specifically with the death of Philip II in 1598. In the earlier years the Antilles received the major attention as a possible source for tropical products; but soon the discovery of Mexico and Peru, with their accumulated wealth, absorbed all attention. Puerto Rico, however, considered as the *Llave del Mar Caribe*, or "Key to the Caribbean," had to be held at all costs and made secure; even *situados*, annual assessments on Mexico for its support, were established and continued to the time of the Mexican revolution in 1810. All hope for holding the new empire was placed in building an impregnable fortress on the Bay of San Juan de Puerto Rico.

If the sixteenth century was one of expansion, the seventeenth was one of trying to hold on to what had been acquired. If the mother-country had been neglecting the island for more profitable regions elsewhere, it was not forgotten, however, by sea-roving pirates and freebooters such as Drake, Hawkins, Abercrombie, Bowdoin, and especially Lord Cumberland, who actually had possession for 157 days. This second century of Spanish domination under the recurring raids by the French, English, and Dutch was probably the most trying period for Puerto Rico. Aside from the strain of constant attacks, the people of the island were also so harassed and handicapped by restraints and regulations from the home offices that progress was well-nigh impossible.

During most of the eighteenth century, Spain was little more than a satellite of France. Fortunately, Puerto Rico was left alone and enjoyed an uninterrupted peace for more than ninety years. This gave the people of the island an opportunity for developing their own resources, gradually at first, then more rapidly. Enormous strides were made during the latter part of the century largely by the founding, in 1756, of the first commercial organization. In 1759 there was also a re-examination of land titles with a view to a more equitable land distribution. Many adjustments were made, and the feudal character of some of the landholdings was to a large degree eliminated.

The long-continued peace, moreover, brought its increase in immigration as favorable reports of the wealth and beauty of the island spread. In 1776, 70,000 people were listed; in 1786, 96,000; in 1796, 133,000; and in 1800, 155,426. The population was added to by immigrants from many walks of life as well as from widely separated regions. According to the records of the day, the new arrivals were soldiers, many of whom married *mulatas* and "other girls of the country"; *confinados*, prisoners; and *desterrados*, exiles; escaped slaves from neighboring islands; a group of families from the Canary Islands; deserters and ship passengers who prolonged their stay indefinitely; sugar experts; French refugees at the time of the Haitian Revolution; people from Santo Domingo who left when France took over the island; and, of course, the adventurous spirits from the mother-country. With such an influx the interior did not remain long a virgin forest, for people soon occupied all the more favorable, though distant, parts of the island. By the end of the century there had developed not only a genuine *criollo* ("creole") population but also a well-organized, civil government, which for the first time considered itself Puerto Rican.

For the nineteenth century there is again a different story. The people had become conscious of their condition and in the early part began to make demands on Spain. A governor reported that on the whole island there were only two schools and that literacy was a rarity. The country people were pictured as ambitionless, taking supreme satisfaction in rocking themselves to sleep in a hammock. But it was said also that their numbers were so small relatively and the soil so fruitful that much exertion by them in order to make a living was not necessary. There seemed generally to be an abundance of bananas, maize, beans, and fish, and some of the people even had a cow or two. They had little or no household furniture or kitchen equipment.

Not only in Puerto Rico but throughout the Spanish colonial empire was there a growing sense of personal values and individual rights, which, unfortunately, the mother-country did not understand and whose seriousness she did not appreciate. Starting out with demands for simple reforms, an emancipation movement spread rapidly through the colonies from Mexico to Argentina, and all the mainland colonies of Spain in the Americas ultimately declared their independence (1810–24). In the Antilles, however, the Spanish flag continued to wave for many years, although Cuba was and continued to be restive under the restrictions imposed. To Puerto Rico, during this early part of the century, came one of the most amazing announcements of the entire century. Perhaps it came as the result of the stirring events of war-torn Europe; perhaps the reverberations of the French and American revolutions were at the bottom. Or perhaps Spain was just beginning to realize what was happening to her colonies on the mainland.

Whatever the reasons, in August, 1815, came the royal

decree, *Cédula de gracias,* or "Regulations for Promoting Population, Commerce, and Agriculture of Puerto Rico." This decree of thirty-three articles was like a proclamation freeing a people from bondage. It was a most amazing document of liberality in view of past policy. It gave the people on the island the same status as that of the inhabitants of Spain. Land was allotted, free of all expense, in amount according to the ability to cultivate, as measured by the number of slaves owned. Property rights were to be protected, and Catholic foreigners with capital were encouraged to come and invest. Among the many benefits established were freedom of trade with foreign countries, the free importation of agricultural machinery, and a host of other most liberal provisions.

As the good news spread to the other colonies, especially where political unrest prevailed so generally, many of their best and wealthiest families migrated from these countries to the new haven, bringing with them not only wealth but industry, zeal, and skill. In a single month in 1821 there is record of nine shiploads from Venezuela alone; even seventy-five "gentlemen" are reported arriving from Louisiana. This influx seemingly was all that was needed to bring new life and vigor to a discouraged infant colony. The arrival of this, a dominantly cultured class with its wealth, helped to emphasize the distinction of the two classes of people on the island—one a cultured, landowning class, the other the country peasant, or *jíbaro.* Many of the upper class today with pride trace their ancestry back to one or another of these immigrants.

The change, however, was too radical to be without its setbacks, for it meant an adjustment of thinking among conservative officials that was beyond the spirit of the time. Yet, in spite of all ups and downs, the hard times from 1820 to 1823, and the unusual prosperity from 1823 to 1833, the general trend was upward. So evident was this that Flintner (1834) could report to Her Majesty the Queen:

> A country that a few years ago was covered with impervious woods and unhealthy swamps, we now find intersected with roads. Unfordable rivers that in the rainy season cut off all communication between one part of the island and another are now rendered passable by bridges. Flourishing towns and smiling villages have risen as if by magic, where the gigantic trees of the tropical forest, a few years ago, stood in tropical grandeur. The swamps where stagnant waters lay infesting the surrounding air with their effluvia, are now covered with cane fields and luxurious pastures. This scene is enlivened by the comfortable cabins of the islanders. Surrounded by groves of plantain and fields of Indian corn, the numerous seaports resorted to by ships of all nations exhibit everywhere manifestations of the active and extensive commerce carried on by both the mother-country and by foreign nations.

Flintner may have been overenthusiastic about the changes wrought; yet the contrast in the point of view of the people and in their general welfare must have been very great.

The general trend for the better continued, although with many interruptions. More progress was made during the last century under Spain than during the entire three preceding ones. The progress, however, may not have been due alone to any particular act, like the *Cédula de gracias*, for the period in question was one during which the whole civilized world underwent great economic changes and advancement. The progress in the island is indicated also in a measure by the increase in population from 155,426 in 1800 to 953,243, in 1899. This was a sixfold increase within the century and meant the very high density, for an island of only 3,400 square miles, of 280 per square mile. The century was momentous for the mother-country also, only in a different way. Before the first quarter of the century was over, all the mainland colonies in the Americas had revolted; and by the end of the century Spain could look back and see how, step by step, the largest and richest colonial empire the world had ever known had dwindled away into a relatively insignificant part.

The loyalty of Puerto Rico to the mother-country, however, is one of the facts in history of which Spain well could feel proud. The people of the island have always acted with great forbearance, and the country has never been beset with rebellious movements, as have many of the Latin-American countries. The situation in the neighboring island of Cuba was quite in contrast. The only genuine revolutionary movement (*Grito de Lares*) in the history of the island broke out on September 20, 1868, in the interior with the proclamation of the new republic of Boriquén. Premature pronouncements, moderate leadership, and the lack of support from neighboring municipalities combined to make the attempt a fiasco. The movement was the result of trying economic conditions and great suffering, and not of political ambitions. It was a period of unusual severity: the treasury was empty, poverty everywhere was being intensified, and even people with money were losing what they had. Real estate values were dropping to ridiculously low prices, and many who had not lost all were migrating to other lands. The break for the better, however, did come and with it more outspokenness in demanding greater local freedom in regulating local affairs. The early nineties again were a period of great suffering and poverty; but, although unrest was growing, there were no revolutionary outbreaks, as in Cuba.

In the general unrest prevailing on the island during the last third of the century, two major questions agitated the popular mind: one was the complete abolition of slavery; the other was greater autonomy in handling purely local problems. The full emancipation of slaves was granted by Madrid in 1873 and was received with great local rejoicing; but the question of autonomy, not so easily disposed of, then became the all-absorbing political topic.

The local situation during the period in question was complicated by the ever increasing unrest in Cuba, climaxed by one open revolt after another. Puerto Rico could not remain wholly immune to Cuba's plight, especially as there was a growing group who would make Cuba's cause its own. Two points of view developed in this fight for greater freedom in handling local affairs: the *autonomista* and the *separatista*. The one, loyal to the mother-country, believed that in a spirit of conciliation and co-operation all the pressing local problems could best be solved; the other group, having lost all faith in the political leaders at Madrid and all hope of ever winning real concessions, held that secession was the only course left open.

Whatever the reason for Madrid's liberality, a far-reaching autonomy was granted in *La Carta autonómica* and put into effect February 9, 1898. Although the charter still left the governor-general the supreme head of the colony, the commercial concessions, such as the right to levy taxes and tariffs, were sufficiently far-reaching for the whole to be considered a great victory, and in that spirit the charter was received. The right to settle local affairs locally was considered a fitting climax to years of tireless effort. But the fruits of these efforts were not to be enjoyed long without interruption.

Other events, over which Puerto Rico had no control, were

rapidly spinning their web of destiny for her. Only six days after the principles of the *Carta* had gone into effect, the American battleship "Maine" was sunk in Havana Harbor. On April 25 Congress declared war on Spain; on May 12 Sampson bombarded San Juan; on July 25 the first troops were landed at Guánico, Puerto Rico. Hostilities on the island were suspended on August 13, and the political transfer took place October 18, 1898. A new power now had assumed control over the island, and the principles of *La Carta autonómica* were in the discard. The time during which this partial autonomy was in force was all too short to test its significance. The fact remains, however, that under the American rule the principles of the *Carta* have not been reinstated. A feeling at present, therefore, is widespread that the work of four hundred years was blown away with the breeze that unfurled the American flag.

The full political transformation, however, did not come until May 1, 1900, with the inauguration of an American civil government. This seems an unusually long delay under the peaceful conditions prevailing. The transfer of status with its many changes and petty restrictions in an attempt to give the island an American form of government is a matter of history readily available and does not show the highest degree of statesmanship. Dissatisfaction was inevitable, but much of the irritation could have been, and still could be, eliminated without economic harm to the United States by the granting of another *carta autonómica*. When the United States took over the island as a booty of war from Spain, not in a war with Puerto Rico, it became responsible for far more than political stability. The chief end of any people is economic betterment, to which may then be added other good things. If, therefore, the island is not at its best under the American continental form of government, then it were better to develop some modified form under which it can reach its highest destiny. No Anglo-Saxon nation can remake a people steeped in Spanish traditions, a fact not appreciated in the American relationships. Where possible, local conditions should be determiners of the destiny of the island, and therefore it is vital that all continental Americans appreciate to the full the background, the resources, the problems, the inherited attitudes, and the points of view of these their fellow-Americans, who feel hard pressed and unfairly treated.

THE MODERN PERIOD

That a nation's economic life rests on a physical background is axiomatic. Equally so is the fact that no nation, by changing its form of government or by fiat, can add basically to its original endowment. The change of sovereignty, therefore, has not added any new wealth to Puerto Rico, and the island's problem of developing its natural resources more effectively still continues. During the centuries of man's exploitation of the island, it is only natural that some of these resources have become more or less depleted and that some have disappeared entirely. All the readily available gold has long since been worked out, and the magnificent forests which once covered the island live only in the early accounts. Some of the land, through long, unscientific cropping, has become seriously impoverished, yielding very limited returns. Indeed, Puerto Rico must be thought of as a very old country exploited to the full during the centuries of occupation. In this respect it is quite unlike some other Caribbean areas, where the land is still largely in a virginal state.

Although there is no way for a nation to add to its original stature, it may, nevertheless, make its resources more valuable by putting them into greater service. Were there coal deposits on the island, of which there are none worthy the name, they would have meant little to the Boriqueños and little more to those who followed. Yet an exploitable bed of coal would mean more to the people of today than all the gold ever taken from the island's stream gravels. It is barely possible, though not at all probable, that unused resources may still be lying fallow, some day to add to the wealth of the island. It is safe to conclude, however, that if there is to be an improved well-being for the people, it must come in making the exploitation of present known resources more profitable to them. The future progress of the island, we may feel assured, also will come most permanently through a more intensive use of the land in producing raw materials that may be turned into useful articles, and also through the application of technical skill in exploiting the lesser resources more effectively. Fundamental to any plan is the raising of the standard of well-being and efficiency of the peasant class.

In looking forward to any long-range policy for improving the outlook of the people on the island, a thorough understanding not only of the past but of the present is necessary. A survey of active and potential resources and the problems of their exploitation, the nature of the population that is to develop these, and the interrelationships with the outside world on which Puerto Rico must depend are some of the questions about which there must be clarity of thought. Puerto Rico unquestionably is much too small for the number of people within its shores, its resources too limited to make it a self-sustaining country. Outside relationships are its only salvation. Since it is a tropical country, competition with whatever it produces will continue necessarily to be very keen. Lying at the edge of the most extensive and undeveloped tropical areas of the world, it may expect an increasingly competitive development from these more or less virginal lands. Wages, although low on the island in comparison with those paid on the United States mainland, are nevertheless high in comparison with those of other tropical lands and will necessarily continue so, thereby offsetting other advantages.

THE PEOPLE

The character and energy of a people is always one of the major elements in the development of a tropical region. The Puerto Rican people are dominantly of Spanish descent with some admixture of Negro and Indian blood among the lower classes. The upper class is much like the same class in other Latin-American countries, although it is well to remember that in no two are the stocks exactly the same. Politically, the Puerto Rican is much more stable than his Latin-American brothers. The general outlook of the people is Spanish, not Anglo-Saxon; and the basic elements of culture, history, and law are drawn from Spain and not from England. A change of sovereignty has made them Americans only in name. They are still Latin, with a different point of view, different ideals, different manners and customs, and with a different temperament from that of continental Americans. To judge them by mainland ideals is as unfair as to be judged by them according to the standards on the island. The attitude of superiority taken by some continental Americans accounts in a very large measure for much of the ill feeling prevalent.

Class distinctions on the island are very marked. Members

of the upper class do not take readily to even the simplest physical tasks. Their superior social background, education, and standard of living are ever present reminders of differences and give to them a sense of superiority over those who, through generations of need, have become servile. In this group are the rich or even moderately well-to-do, who, through competence or family inheritance or both, are the equals of cultured people anywhere. Fortunately for the island, there is developing also a virile middle class, which, largely by sheer effort and native ability under great handicaps, is rapidly forging ahead. As opportunities come, this group is sure to take a major part in the evolution of the island. The bulk of the population, however, belongs to the lower class, whose major distinction is poverty, of which there are many kinds and degrees. Some of the poor are still poorer than others, until hunger, nakedness, wretchedness, and hopelessness of outlike are the lot of many.

The wretchedness of the poorer classes beggars description. It is impossible to escape the ever present piteous spectacle of poverty in going about the island. The inland districts "seethe with misery." Housing facilities, no matter how makeshift, are wholly inadequate. Many are the cases where a family with its numerous brood occupies a small, one-room cabin. Such a makeshift home may be on the edges of a swamp or within a tidal marsh. Some of these people surely are misfits, incompetents; but, in the main, they are poor merely for the want of opportunity. Theirs is largely an animal-like existence outside the pale of the economic life of the country. Their childish intensity while they try to serve well may be hunger driven, but it also disproves any wantlessness so commonly attributed to tropical peoples. They are peace-

ONE OF THE POORER HOMES

The poorer homes are built, for want of land, along the roadside. Nearly every such home has a *cocina*, or kitchen lean-to. There is no chimney; and when poverty forces the use of twigs and leaves instead of charcoal, as in this case, the food prepared tastes of dead smoke.

ONE OF THE BETTER JIBARO HOMES ACCOMMODATING SEVERAL FAMILIES

The valuable breadfruit tree is just beyond the house. The seemingly bare hillslopes in the distance are under cultivation. The wooden house is patterned after the grass *buhio*.

able and kindly, ready to share their meager store with the stranger and, for the most part, are not resentful of those who so mercilessly exploit them. All countries have their poor; but where nearly three-fourths of the population belongs to this class, the burden is too heavy for the nation to carry permanently and prosper.

The difference between the various groups has been and is largely a matter of opportunity. The ultra-poor peasants, almost without exception, are absolutely without opportunity of betterment in their present situation. The island is and has been overpopulated, and in a land where this is true those least favorably situated are the ones to suffer most. It is difficult to see how, under present conditions, the younger generation, even in the more favored groups, can become established in the economic life of the island and be an asset as citizens. The sad part is that the future of the young will depend much more upon opportunities available than upon native ability.

The present overpopulation with its pathetic aspects is not a new situation. Even during the last quarter-century of the Spanish period there were too many people for the possible returns from the island's resources. At the time of transfer there were 280 people for every square mile[2] of territory, which was seven times the density of Cuba with its much better agricultural lands, and eleven times the density of the United States mainland, with its high degree of industrialization. The criticalness of the situation is emphasized by the fact that the development on the island has been little other than agricul-

[2] The War Department took the first census on October 16, 1899, and recorded 953,253 people. Recent measurements gave the area as 3,339.5 square miles; including the islands of Vieques and Culebros, the area is 3,400.6 square miles.

tural. This means that little wealth is being added to raw materials by the addition of labor.

The dominance of the land in the economic life of the people is emphasized by the fact that at the time of the 1899 census, when there were nearly a million people on the island, only two cities had a population of more than 25,000 each.[3] At that time only 21.4 per cent of the people lived in towns of 1,000 or more; in contrast, in Cuba with the smaller density, the proportion was 41.7 per cent. Such a concentration of people dependent wholly on the land for a livelihood can mean only that the per capita income must be ridiculously small, with a consequent extremely low standard of living for the landless class. Of the "gainful workers" listed in the 1930 census, grouped in some thirty industries in the three leading cities, the larger number by far for females is in "domestic and personal services" and, for males, in "wholesale and retail trade, excluding automobiles." Manufacturing, therefore, as the term is understood in continental United States, scarcely exists on the island.

The census of 1899 disclosed also that there were an unusually large number of children under ten years of age (30 per cent) and a corresponding scarcity of people over forty-five (11.8 per cent). Again in comparison, under similar climatic conditions Cuban percentages during the same period were 14 and 22.7, respectively. Cuba proportionately had less than half the number of children and more than twice the number of people of middle age and older. For Puerto Rico it is a case of many being called into the world but relatively few chosen to remain there long. The high birth rate may be explained, in a measure, by the low standard of living in a

[3] San Juan had 82,048, and Ponce had 27,952. By 1940 this number was changed to three, with San Juan having 169,255; Ponce, 105,110; and Mayagüez, 76,482.

large rural population, where an extra child is not much of a financial strain and may even be an asset. The peasant group is also highly religious, almost to the verge of superstition, and fervidly Catholic, which precludes much hope from birth control.

In view of the extremely high birth rate there is an unusual situation of the marital state. In reporting the status of persons of marriageable age, fifteen years and older, the census lists 43.2 per cent of the males and 38.8 per cent of the females as unmarried; the legally married persons, on the other hand, are 39.1 and 39.4 per cent, respectively. That an unusually large number of men and women are living together consensually is evident; yet, bad as this may appear, it does not mean, necessarily, great promiscuity. In the great majority of such unions there is no feeling of wrongdoing or idea of immoral living. Nor does their status carry any stigma among their fellows. It has been suggested that this is a hold-over custom from the time when the colonizers came alone and took Indian or Negro women as their marital companions. This in part is borne out by the fact that almost invariably this type of living is found in the more isolated sections of the island, where the more modern social outlook has not yet penetrated.

Before the 1900 census it was believed that the Negro population was much larger than it actually is. For a tropical and a former slave country, the percentage of 38.2 is surprisingly low, lower than in many of our southern states. From a very early date, probably as early as 1531, when the Negroes represented 87.9 per cent of the total, the percentage trend with each census has been more or less regularly downward. This proportional reduction is due to the early stoppage of Negro importation, with a continued white immigration, and to the dilution of blood through miscegenation, Negro characteristics becoming too faint to be recognized positively. Among the lower classes the color line is only faintly drawn, and the Negro blood is rapidly being diluted more and more. This amalgamation is going on chiefly along the coast, for there is little Negro blood in the interior. The color line among the upper classes is sharply drawn, the antecedence of the prospective bride and groom being most carefully investigated by the families concerned.

The first census showed also a remarkably low degree of literacy—only 22.6 per cent for the entire island. A small percentage of illiteracy is never very serious, but when three people out of four cannot read even a word, much less interpret a printed page, it is almost impossible to reach the individual in any attempt at social betterment. It should be stated however, that most of those making up the other fourth are well educated, highly cultured, and of the highest social order. The unusual efficiency of the present school system is, in spite of many handicaps, rapidly making the island more literate. By 1930 for persons ten years and older the literacy had been raised in the urban areas to 72.6 per cent and in the rural areas to 52.8 per cent. The appreciation of the need of some schooling, commonly up to the fifth grade in the rural districts, is reflected in the increase in the number of pupils in the schools from 28,000 in 1900 to more than 250,000 in 1930. The present high illiteracy statistics are somewhat misleading, since little has been done in adult education. As might be expected, the literacy of people sixty-five years old or older is still only 22.4 per cent. Yet, in the light of the encouraging statistics of 1930, it is well to remember that there are still people without any school facilities whatsoever and that a large percentage of those that drop out after the fourth grade do so because of poverty.

The problem which in a measure overshadows all others is the extraordinary increase in numbers. From a population of 953,243 in 1899, the number rose to 1,118,012 in 1910; 1,299,809 in 1920; 1,543,913 in 1930; and 1,869,245 for the census year 1940. These figures show that there was an annual increase equivalent to 1.69 per cent from 1920 to 1930, and this rate rose to 2.11 per cent for the ten-year period of 1930–40. The density per square mile has grown from 280.3 in 1899 to 329.8 in 1910, to 382.2 in 1920, to 454.0 in 1930, and to 580 in 1940. As there are practically no immigrants, the growth is due almost wholly to an excess of births over deaths. With a birth rate that has no relation to possibilities in making even the barest living, the problem of finding gainful employment on the island for the ever increasing numbers and of providing any decent standard of living is a task which seems beyond the power of any government. In an area with two people where only one should be and with the number increasing so rapidly, making two blades of grass grow where only one grew before, even if this were possible, cannot give a permanent solution of the problem.

At present there seems to be no feasible way for reducing and keeping the number of people on a basis where the resources of the island will assure a reasonable standard of well-being. An increase in sanitation and improved health conditions has a tendency to intensify the situation. A wholesale migration of half or even a third of the people is not practicable and would not solve the problem permanently even were it feasible. With the present rate of increase it would be a mere palliative and not a cure. Already in New York City there is an unamalgamated colony equal in size to the largest city on the island. An annual migration sufficient and more to counterbalance a birth rate of approximately two times the death rate is also not to be taken seriously. The gradual reduction of the birth rate through education until it is equal to, or less than, the death rate is the ideal to be hoped for ultimately. The pathetic aspect of the question is that only in a reduced and a stationary population can the people of the island look forward with assurance to maintaining a decent standard of living.

THE NATURAL LANDSCAPE

The island as a whole may be designated as mountainous. Thirty-two per cent lies below 250 feet. The rougher parts, with elevations of about 2,500 feet and a maximum of 4,398 feet, trend from east to west and separate the island roughly into a narrow southern and a wider northern part. There is, however, no continuous ridge producing a sharp barrier. Roads crisscross the island freely, and no part is far from some sort of highway. The major route from north to south is the "Old Military Road" from San Juan to Ponce, built by Spain. Over its ups and downs, winds and turns, many times each day various types of private and commercial vehicles pass in four, five, or six hours. The island, it is to be remembered, is small, having the form of a parallelogram roughly one hundred miles from east to west and only about half as wide from north to south.

The physical features, however, are fairly effective in dominating the life-activities of the people on the island. The more level lands are by far the more important. Along the north coast even the area close to the sea is patched with low hills which break up level stretches. The greatest extent of almost flat coastal land is in the south. There are also some excellent alluvial valleys of considerable extent, especially in the north,

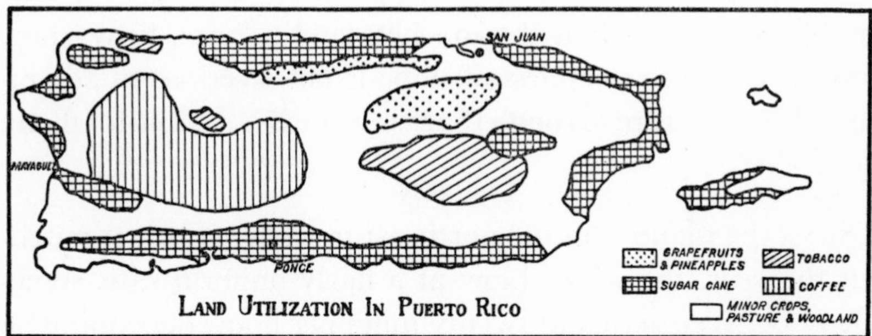

RELATIONSHIP OF CROPS TO PHYSICAL FEATURES

The distribution of the crops is distinctly related to the physical features: cane lands are profitable only in flat or moderately flat lands, while the coffee tree is a product of the steeper hillslopes.

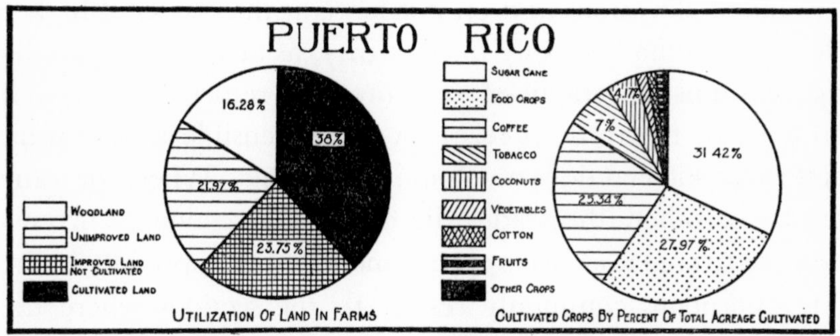

PERCENTAGE OF LAND UNDER CULTIVATION

The small percentage of land of the island under cultivation in view of the high density of population indicates the character of the terrain. Of this small area of cultivated land, the small percentage in foodcrops is anomalous.

such as those of the La Plata, Arecibo, and Loíza rivers. In the interior valleys, such as those of the Cayey, Caguas, Utuado, and Jayuya rivers, there are moderately flat to rolling areas that contrast sharply in their fertility with the bare, steep hillsides surrounding them. The lack of flatness in the interior is not so much of a handicap as it might be, for the simple, primitive agricultural practices know few, if any, implements other than the machete and a large, heavy hoe, and for their use steepness of slope is not a serious disadvantage. Few areas are so rough that some use is not found for them.

CLIMATE

Since the island is in the northeast trade-wind belt throughout the year, the winds blow at a fairly uniform rate, somewhere between zero and twenty miles per hour, depending on location and other factors. The trades by nature are drying winds and evaporate ground moisture quickly except when forced to rise, as in the Luquillo Mountains in the northeast, where an extremely heavy precipitation is the result. On the lee side of elevations and on flat lands within areas of higher elevation rainfall is likely to be scanty, as at Ponce, where irrigation must be practiced to secure crop returns. Where not obstructed, the trade breezes lower the sensible temperature and make such sections much more desirable. When, for some reason or other, the trades die down, convectional currents become stronger, clouds appear, and showers, especially in the late afternoon, commonly result. In the sections where the trades are active, the heat is never intense, shaded areas being surprisingly comfortable and pleasant.

Puerto Rico, together with other West Indian islands, has a moderately warm but equable and comfortable climate. The small area, moderate elevation, and little variation in wind velocity or direction give it a uniformity of temperature characteristic of most tropical island areas. There is a much more marked contrast between shade and sunshine than in higher latitudes, and, for that reason, personal impressions by those accustomed to mid-latitude conditions may vary greatly. Moreover, as meteorological observations are always made in shade, temperature data for low, mid-, and high latitudes are not always exactly comparable. The mean annual temperature for all stations on the island is 76.3° F., a very comfortable and healthful temperature. The stations along the coast have a slightly higher record, about 78° or 79° F., than the interior with its higher altitudes.

To one accustomed to the marked seasonal changes of middle latitudes, the contrast between summer and winter in Puerto Rico seems small and insignificant. The contrast is nevertheless marked, especially for people living within the tropics, who become very sensitive to slight temperature changes. January is the coldest month, with an average temperature of about 73° F.; August, on the whole, is the warmest, averaging about 79° F. A fairly constant difference of from 6° to 8° is maintained in the records of coast and interior stations, the latter, because of their higher altitudes, having the lower temperatures. A visit of a native from one of the coastal towns, therefore, to a higher part in the interior of the island seemingly is as effective for him as the much more marked seasonal change is for a person living in the higher latitudes.

Although the temperature does not vary much from day to day or from month to month, there is a real difference between the temperatures of day and night and even between those of very early morning and afternoon. In the coastal areas this diurnal range is much smaller, 10° or 11° only, than in the interior, where ranges from 20° to 30° are common. No frost has ever been recorded, even at the highest stations.

The diurnal range especially is of tremendous importance in maintaining a stimulation similar to that produced by the seasonal changes in the middle latitudes. The feeling of comfort induced by the cool of the evening, a night temperature that assures a refreshing sleep, and a cool early morning account unquestionably, in large part, for the vigor and energy displayed by the lower classes in spite of their handicap of poor food and an unbalanced diet. Unquestionably, also, the outdoor life throughout the year, in a land with such a high percentage of sunshine, explains the straight limbs and erect bodies of the young of the undernourished poor. The large part of the body exposed to the sun from one year-end to the next leaves less need for vitamins from an artificial source.

In continental United States, where 20 inches of rainfall is regarded as necessary for agriculture, the rainfall of the island, varying from 26 inches at Enseñada on the south coast to 145 inches in the Luquillo Mountains, seems unusually heavy. However, such statistics are largely meaningless when compared with those of the mid-western states, as many other factors, such as cloudiness, rate of evaporation, time and kind of rainfall, and the like, must be considered in estimating the amount of moisture available to plants. As already stated, the trade is a drying wind, and a rainfall of half or even an inch disappears rapidly under its influence and that of a hot sun which commonly does not wait for the end of the shower. Rain comes very easily, and it is literally true that rain falls out of a clear sky. In spite of the great amount and frequency of the rain, the evaporation is so rapid that a period of two weeks without any precipitation becomes a drought period and is so spoken of. Under normal soil conditions without irrigation at least 60 inches, well distributed, are considered necessary for agriculture.

Rainfall on the island varies greatly both in distribution and in amount. For the island as a whole, the general mean of 76 inches is divided as follows: winter, 11; spring, 16; summer, 23; and autumn, 26 inches. Although there are no definitely wet and dry seasons, the winter, December–March, is notably drier and thus becomes the more specific harvesting season. The rainfall on the north side of the island differs from that on the south not only in its greater quantity but also in the certainty of its more uniform distribution. On the south side periods of four or five weeks with little or no rain are common, and periods of two or three months with less than an inch are not exceptional. Here in places a true xerophytic vegetation is dominant, and it becomes necessary to irrigate.

Parts of the island are under irrigation, and others would be were irrigating waters more readily available. The sugar lands at Ponce are irrigated, as is also the mixed farming district of Isabella, in the northwest. The cost of irrigation, which may amount to as much as from $25 to $50 per acre annually, is the real limiting factor. But as the income from good cane lands is high, irrigation is practiced with a rainfall of 60 inches or less. At present more than 80,000 acres are under water, chiefly in the sugar district about Ponce.

A serious climatic handicap is the tropical hurricane, with wind velocities up to 200 miles or more per hour. As already noted, the early history of the island is replete with their devastating effects, and even the Indians named them after their evil god, *Juracán*. At present Puerto Rico, interestingly enough, names them after the saints' days on which they occur. The most recent of the severe hurricanes, the San

Ciprián (1932) and the San Felipe (1928), in spite of the very specific warnings by the weather bureau, caused deaths of at least 225 and 300, respectively, with property losses estimated at $30,000,000 for the San Ciprián and $50,000,000 for the San Felipe. The hurricane season lasts from July to October and is, therefore, a period of great apprehension for all. The oncoming of the storm in its slow progress is announced, step by step, by the weather bureau, and man's helplessness intensifies his fears. In its wake buildings are leveled to the ground or damaged, palm trees are stripped of leaves, cane fields are flattened, coffee trees are stripped of their berries and even crushed by falling shade trees—in fact, there is almost a total destruction of everything in its path. Since so many people live on the very margin of elemental needs, the resultant hardships can scarcely be overemphasized. With good crops gone and no credit, life-conditions for many after such a storm become deplorable in the extreme.

RESOURCES

Puerto Rico is very definitely a land of limited resources. Originally it must have been densely wooded, for even to the earliest explorers the magnificent trees were a never ending wonder. But during the centuries of agricultural occupation the Boriqueños had cleared much land by girdling the trees and then burning over the land as a part of the *conuco* system of agriculture. Then, during the four centuries of white exploitation, the forest areas were being culled more or less continuously, especially to furnish timber for ship construction. The only primeval forest remaining is now being preserved in all its beauty and luxuriousness with its orchids and lianas in the Luquillo Mountains as the Caribbean National Forest.

However, occasionally on some landed estate magnificent but lone specimens of mahogany or other native woods have been preserved.

Today practically all the lumber is imported from "the States." The price is sufficiently low so that many homes and other minor buildings are constructed of wood, displacing the much more picturesque but also much more expensive brick and plaster or cement. The major use of the local woods is for the manufacture of charcoal, made in pits of the most primitive type by a *carbonero* who has access to wood. The charcoal is then carried into towns and cities, on hand carts commonly; and the early-morning call from the seller of *carbon* is one of the strong impressions of every visitor to the island. Practically all the *peon* homes have a small *cocina*, a kitchen lean-to without chimney, within which the cooking is done over a small charcoal glow. The scanty smoke thereof commonly reaches the outside through cracks in the sides or roof of the building. However, the kitchen becomes a veritable "smokehouse" when poverty forces the use of leaves and small fagots in place of charcoal. Because it is much cheaper and perhaps because its use is a habit, charcoal is commonly burned when a sustained heat becomes necessary, even by the upper classes, in whose homes gas and electricity are available.

Fortunately, tree growth in Puerto Rico is rapid and readily replaces the cut necessary to supply the household charcoal needs. The rapid growth of vegetation also becomes an important factor in the prevention of gullying. The countryside has, therefore, in no sense a desolately barren, denuded aspect, such as is found in some tropical regions with a specific dry season; and the problem of erosion is by no means a serious one, in spite of the heavy rainfall, even where slopes are cultivated up to a 45° angle. The wash is dominantly in the form of sheet erosion and somewhat counteracts leaching by carrying some of the worn-out surface material down to lower slopes. It also carries away other debris and waste. As there are few human-free catchment basins and as a large percentage of the hill people have not even a semblance of a latrine, the water in streams very readily becomes polluted through such wash. In spite of a naturally developed immunity among the natives, typhoid is still all too common and might become most serious were it not for the vigilance and prompt action of the health authorities. The hope to combat the disease lies in the education of the people to dig wells and use latrines, since the chlorination of all stream waters is not practicable.

The necessarily high gradient of the rivers, owing to the nearness of the mountain areas to the sea, their year-round flow, and in places the narrowness of valleys act favorably for the building of dams and the development of waterpower on small-scale units. It has been estimated that at least 60,000 or 100,000 housepower could be generated, twice or more than twice the amount now produced. The La Plata, the Island's largest stream, now leads in electrical development, with two plants. The island is so small that electric power may readily be furnished to all parts from a single plant, and in time many small manufacturing industries may become widely distributed in the various small towns of the interior. In electricity lies a possibility of making outlying communities more attractive by offering opportunities of wage-earning through manufacturing.

Even a slightly industralized Puerto Rico would seem to offer considerable possibilities to this highly overcrowded island. The greatest possibilities would arise from small industrial plants in which manual operations would be more dominant than is the case in the highly mechanized industries. The latter are far less likely to succeed and in time would necessarily be large exploitative enterprises rather than the builders of domestic capital so urgently needed. Such handwork factories might, with reason, be expected to supply most of the cheaper clothing and many of the items of demand sold in stores handling goods of low value. There is a market for such goods not only on the island itself but also in the neighboring islands, as well as in the tropical sections of the mainland of both North and South America.

In the possession of basic materials to be used in manufacturing, Puerto Rico is extremely limited. This is especially true of minerals; but it is to be remembered that little information has been gathered, largely because of the density of the vegetation and the great depth of rock-weathering over the major part of the island. With such handicaps, the possibilities of reward are too few to warrant exploratory work. The known deposits of ores are neither rich nor extensive enough to be worked on a very profitable basis. A little placer gold is taken from gravels near Corozal. Manganese ore, with an annual export of about 2,500 tons, is taken from the hilly region north of Juana Diaz. Although this mineral is widely distributed, capital is needed to make its possibilities evident. The quantity, however, is too limited to make its mining important so long as there is a readily available supply elsewhere. There are deposits of lateritic iron ore but not enough to fit into modern large-scale mining methods.

Practically the entire economy centers in the soil. Studies now being made show almost an infinite soil variation.

There are all gradations and types, and no broad generalizations can be made except to say that in general the soils are acidic and deficient in plant food and that they are fairly well adapted to certain types of plants and very poorly adapted to others. Through much abuse some of the soils have become extremely heavy and cloddy; others, as in some of the cane districts, have had their humic content enormously increased by a regular system of plowing under leaves and tops of cane. Even the best lands held by well-to-do owners or by the large corporations are very heavily fertilized, for the higher yield warrants the extra expenditure. The unfortunate fact is that the poorer the lands, the poorer the tenants in the main, and fertilization is beyond their means. With the exception of the alluvial deposits, the soil ranges from medium to poor, but under intelligent control it may be counted on to give fair yields.

For various reasons only a small part of the acreage of the island is under cultivation. In the United States 2.5 acres per capita has been taken as the amount necessary for maintaining the American standard of living; and were this standard applied to the island, the Puerto Rican people would need more than 4,000,000 acres, or about twice their total area (2,176,384 acres). The census for 1930, however, lists only 756,642 acres in crops, or 0.49 acre per capita. This acreage, of course, includes the sugar, tobacco, and coffee lands whose products are largely exported. On the food crops listed, there is only about 0.16 acre for each person.

In addition to the foregoing, there is also the "unimproved land," mostly in pasture and brush, 434,743 acres, and "woodland," 322,447 acres, all of which in some form or other enters into the national economy. At whatever angle the situation is viewed, the crop land available is woefully inadequate. Even Italy, with its industrial development, has a larger acreage of arable land per capita.

Agriculture is so basic in the life of the island that almost all other activities may be said to be subservient to it. This is evident in the comments by businessmen and in the editorials of daily newspapers. With conditions favorable or unfavorable for the production and sale of cash crops and their products, such as sugar, tobacco, coffee, and fruits, the business outlook rises or falls. Since these exports find their only free market in the United States, the economic relationships are even closer to the average man than the political ones. As a result, only too often are political relationships blamed for conditions purely economic; and, as a corollary, the conclusion arises that either statehood or complete independence will solve forthwith all problems. Local unrest, therefore, is largely an agricultural problem, as the only basic source of money is some crop product. Even foods grown for home consumption may be sold or bartered, only to be bought back a little later. The *jíbaro*, no matter how meager his supply, may sell his beans, bananas, yams, yautias, lone pig, or whatever he may have, at the local market and be at once in need. Part of the suffering for want of food is this seeming mania, or perhaps necessity, for selling.

Sugar is the leading commercial crop, occupying 238,000 acres in 1930. Practically all the good level land in the coastal regions and some in the interior is now in sugar cane, crowding out other crops wherever the growing of cane is feasible. Its increase since 1900 has been truly phenomenal. In 1897 the total production for the island was 63,500 tons of sugar; in 1934, before restrictive measures were put in effect, it reached its peak of 1,103,822 tons. Machinery, fertilizers, irrigation, higher yielding varieties, strains of cane more immune to disease, and laboratory experimentation—all resources capable of being mustered by capital have been used to stimulate production. This concentration on sugar has been at its strongest during the last decade, during which production has practically trebled as a result. The crop has even spread into what are truly marginal lands for cane, over and beyond steep foothills, growing on slopes of 30° or more. Other crops have been crowded out even from land where the cane yields are low, since profits from sugar are more certain.

In spite of the profitableness of cane-growing and the efficiency shown in its production, the industry is looked upon with disfavor by those not directly connected with it. The antisocial evils of sugar-cane production are stressed. Sugar cane tends to concentrate lands into large corporate holdings, some of them reaching 15,000–20,000 or more acres. A goodly part of the sugar return leaves the island in the form of dividends and high-priced personnel coming from "the States." Those in control are grouped on company lands, with beautiful homes and surroundings, de luxe clubhouses, tennis courts, and imported foods and furnishings—a truly foreign colony taking little or no interest in local conditions. This luxury and the general aloofness of the personnel even to the upper class of Puerto Ricans, in contrast to the landless native laborer with about 90 cents per day for ten or twelve hours of work, and that work seasonal, arouse resentment and even hostility. Under the circumstances, the worker on the plantation, undernourished, probably suffering from both malaria and hookworm, cannot be a very efficient or progressive citizen.

Not all the sugar lands are in the hands of great American corporations; some are partly or wholly controlled by local capital. A small part of the cane land is still owned by the *colono*, the rich landowner and independent operator who pays a relatively high charge for having his cane processed by the large corporation. The antisocial attitude of this local sugar man in no wise differs from that of the "heartless" corporations with their main offices in New York. The display of wealth by the local multimillionaire sugar man is perhaps even more flagrant.

The question of the wisdom of taking so much of the best land for the production of sugar for export when there is such dense population and so little land for food is one that must be answered in the very near future. It is particularly pressing now that so many persons are on relief; and, unless there is a drastic change in the land policy, the situation is almost sure to have its serious consequences. Recently the insular government decided to enforce the intent of the clause in the Organic Act, which limits tenancy by corporations to 500 acres. The subterfuges to prevent the enforcement of the intent of this act have been many and the test case has been carried beyond the Supreme Court of Puerto Rico.

During recent years fruits have ranked in value next to sugar as an export crop. The citrus fruits—grapefruit and oranges—have been the leaders. The industry is the product of the opening of the American market that took place with the transfer of the island. Shortly after the transfer a number of continental Americans bought lands and began to set out grapefruit trees. By 1908 the export already exceeded the million-dollar mark. The peak was reached in 1928, with an export value of $7,500,000. In sharp contrast to the situation on the sugar lands, most of these owners live on the land with their families, buy local supplies, and are a distinct asset to the cultural evolution of the island. The orchards are, in general, concentrated along the north coastal region between Barceloneta and Carolina, and the relative nearness of the region to San Juan aids materially in lowering the cost of shipment to New York. However, in recent years little could be marketed abroad profitably because of prohibitive ocean shipping rates, so it is claimed, and as a result the surplus fruit has been left to rot.

The pineapple is thoroughly at home on the island and thrives particularly well on some of the more highly acidic soils. The same general problems in growing and marketing hold for the pineapple as for the grapefruit. The fruit is grown, however, chiefly in the municipalities of Bayamón and Corozál. The quality is high grade, and the yield fairly good —as much as 350 cases per acre when the plant is properly cared for. It is believed that the production can be made more profitable still and that the industry should expand greatly. As in the case of grapefruit, the early crop of pineapples commands fair prices; but the later crop, in keen competition with Cuba, gives small returns. The acreage devoted to the crop is not known, but the normal production is only slightly less than half a million cases annually. With the abundance of sugar it may be that the major outlet ultimately will be in the canned form.

Other fruits, although in general fairly abundant, are of little importance in export. In the main, oranges and bananas are grown as temporary shade for young coffee trees, and the fruits are sold widely in the town market places and by peddlers at low prices. Rarely does either fruit reach the New

York markets, as competition is too keen. Coconuts are widely distributed, more specifically along the west coast near Aquadilla and in the north near Loiza. Partly ripe coconuts are sold in off seasons by street vendors for the water they contain. Small quantities of the ripe fruit may reach the New York markets when prices are favorable, but the industry is wholly unorganized. Other tropical fruits, especially the mango, are grown in a semi-wild state and are a great blessing to the poorer classes, with their limited diets. The tropical hurricane is one of the real limiting factors in the growing of the various tree crops. To find a grove that has just come into bearing, after five or six years of cultivation without any returns, hopelessly ruined in a few hours is not conducive to further planting. The San Felipe and especially the San Ciprián took a very heavy toll, and many of the growers, even if they had the courage, did not have the capital to replant.

Coffee occupies the largest acreage (192,000 acres in 1929), next to sugar cane. The groves are in the high interior, mainly in the west-central part of the island, on a type of terrain that precludes most crops. The tree is grown for individual home use in practically all parts of the island, but commercial production is centered in the mountainous sections of the municipalities of Las Marias, Maricao, Lares, San Sebastian, Yauco, and Mayaguez. The groves are kept moderately clean of weeds, except for shade trees, grass, vines, and other underbrush, but receive little or no actual cultivation. Some of the slopes are so steep that the workmen need to hold on with one hand while working with the other. From a distance these groves look like any other forested slope except that the leaf cover appears darker. Some coffee groves are very heavily fertilized.

More than either sugar cane or fruits, coffee is specifically an island product. During the entire Spanish period it was the leading crop, much sought after in European markets. The decline has been more or less constant since. The coffee groves are in the hands of native farmers, who own and manage their own farms of from 15 to 1,500 acres and who make up more or less of a landed gentry. Workers live on the same property with an allotment of a small plot of ground for the growing of food crops, a few chickens, and perhaps even pasture for a cow. The wages paid are small, as measured in the large; but the amount received may, almost in its entirety, be expended for things other than food. Furthermore, the work on a coffee plantation is never strenuous, and the laborer not uncommonly takes a pride in the estate as though he were joint owner. The *jíbaro* on the coffee plantation, therefore, is probably as well off as are unskilled workmen anywhere on the island. Living on the same farm establishes a personal relationship between employer and employee that is most wholesome and that is rarely or never found on the large corporate holdings.

The coffee-grower's plight is perhaps more serious than that of any other of the landowning classes. A large percentage of the growers find it necessary to work on borrowed capital, supplied mostly by merchants who charge from 8 to 12 per cent interest and secured by the current crop. Conditions have been so bad that in many cases the owners have lost confidence and have turned their plantations over to mortgage-holders, or, where the land is fitted, have shifted to tobacco, food crops, or even sugar cane. This reduced acreage, however, has not brought relief. In the economic life of the island, coffee is considered so vital that newspapers have devoted long editorials and full-page advertisements appealing to the loyalty of the people to buy home-grown coffee, in an attempt to develop a greater home market. The grower, however, can scarcely hope to prosper without a larger outlet for his product since the normal commercial production of some 50,000,000 pounds is more than the island can absorb.

The plight of the coffee-grower has been cumulative. The crop prior to the World War found a ready market in Europe, principally Spain, where a decided taste had developed for the rich Puerto Rican aroma and flavor. Other European countries also favored it for demi-tasse servings and were willing to pay a higher price for it. During the war, when regular shipments to Europe were no longer possible, Puerto Rican growers had to content themselves with shipments to the United States, in large part for re-export. After the war Cuba was the best market until 1925–26, but her imports now are negligible. There is no market in Spain. Other countries, like Germany and Italy, are limiting their buying mainly to reciprocal arrangements. At present there is no direct foreign market outside that of the United States, and American firms are adding to the distress by offering vacuum-packaged coffee in competition to the local product. Also, during the hurricane of San Felipe in 1928 plantations were so damaged that the normal production of some 50,000,000 pounds dropped to 7,000,000 in 1929. As the grower must depend now upon the American market, where no preference is shown his crop, the competition with other mild coffees, such as those from Colombia, Costa Rica, and other Caribbean countries, will necessarily be keen. Whether Puerto Rico can meet this competition only time can tell.

Tobacco-growing has undergone a great transformation in recent years. No longer are the cheesecloth slopes to be seen, appearing from a distance like snow-covered areas, as they were in the days of the cigar and a brisk demand for a high-grade wrapper tobacco. With the shift in taste from the cigar to the cigarette, this demand fell off and with it disappeared the cloth-covered fields. The tobacco now grown must meet the competition of the "filler leaf" produced elsewhere. As the United States leads the world as an exporter of such tobacco, competition is necessarily keen; and the Puerto Rican growers, as a result, have found themselves hard pressed and, by voluntary agreement, as a protest against the low prices offered in contract, reduced their output from 30,000,000 pounds in 1931 to 6,000,000 pounds in 1932. This, if anything, intensified their distress, with the natural result that the normal commercial area of some 50,000 acres is again being planted.

Aside from the commercial or money crops, there are also the subsistence, or food, crops, so vital to the masses. In a country of such dense population, with so little cultivable land available and practically all the good land in commercial crops, food at prices the poor can afford to pay is a serious matter. Even the poor must eat, and the type and quantity of food they can afford is determined, in the main, by what can be grown locally. Only a small minority of the rural working-class families have gardens of their own or raise foods on share-cropping. They must buy, or, as is commonly the case, they must go without. In a survey made by Professor José C. Rosario, of the Universidad de Puerto Rico, for the Brookings Institution and covering two thousand families, the standard menus were tabulated, by classes, as follows:

Breakfast.—Class I, black coffee; Class II, coffee with milk; Class III, coffee with milk and bread.

Midday meal.—Class I, corn meal and bananas; Class II, rice and beans; Class III, corn meal and codfish; Class IV, corn meal; Class V, corn meal and rice; Class VI, rice.

Evening meal.—Class I, rice and beans; Class II, rice; Class III, rice and beans and corn meal; Class IV, corn meal and rice; Class V, soup.

Even selecting the three most desirable meals listed, the food consumed by the workman is pitifully inadequate.

It is almost inconceivable that with such a meager diet, even with the addition perhaps of a little wild fruit, the members of the *jíbaro* family have any energy for work. The worker who has only a cup or two of black coffee for breakfast may find it necessary to walk from his hillside home several miles to his work, when there is any to be had, and be active from dawn to dusk at less than a dollar per day. At noon he eats his lunch in the field; and at night, after working ten or twelve hours under a hot tropical sun, he trudges home for his evening meal, rarely with meat, there not to enjoy the luxury of a rocking chair, which he hopes to have some day, but to sleep in a hammock or upon the floor, without undressing, only to wake up for a repetition of the previous day's experience. His case is not an isolated one; it represents the common lot of the *jíbaro*. The monotony and inadequacy of the diet must have a more vital effect on the energy of the people, especially when other life-conditions are on a par.

The people, for the most part, respond to help offered, and an improvement on conditions is possible. The Red Cross, after the disastrous San Felipe hurricane, gave an immense stimulus to home gardens by a free distribution of seeds. A practical education that can be carried into the home is the crying need. At present several agencies are doing splendid work through the university, but activities have been severely handicapped by a scarcity of funds.

To a large extent the foods found in the public markets come from sharecropping. Where this system is found, the specific arrangements made depend much upon the character of the landowner, upon the crop that predominates, and upon the land available. Upon some of the American owned and managed pineapple plantations there is an insistence that the resident laborers raise some garden crops for themselves, and land is provided for the purpose. Upon other plantations any effort at home gardening is discouraged and in some cases even definitely forbidden. This is especially true in the sugar regions, where land is said to be too valuable to be put into food crops in the hands of an ineffective group. In the tobacco areas the land lies dormant during a part of the year, and much of it is double cropped in tobacco and food crops. On most of the coffee plantations, where a more intimate relation exists between the worker and the owner, the problem of getting enough land to grow food is not a serious one. The family may even be the proud possessor of a cow.

Unfortunately, a census of all food-crop acreages is not available, as nearly all the food crops are grown by *jíbaros* who are much more interested in the yield than in the possible acreage of an irregular plot. Many of these have a system of intercropping or growing two crops, such as corn and beans, on the same land at the same time. Then there is also the system of double cropping, growing two successive crops on the same land during the growing season of twelve months. Thus, food acreages may total up considerably more than the land in crops would seem to indicate. As such land is generally poor and as the price of fertilizers is prohibitive, the yields are necessarily small. The estimated acreages for the leading food crops are strikingly small: corn, 70,000 acres; sweet potatoes and yams, 48,000; beans, 41,000. Out of the total of 2,176,000 acres in the island, certainly not more than 1 acre in 10 is given over to food crops. This means seven to ten persons for each food-crop acre. As this acreage is wholly inadequate to supply food needs, the rest must be imported at prices out of reach generally of the poorer classes.

An island people with a scarcity of agricultural land might well be expected to look to the sea for part of its food. Yet, just the opposite is the case in Puerto Rico. The people have never become sea-minded, even along the coast, in spite of the fact that fish, not meat, forms the leading nonvegetable diet for the masses. The consumption of about 20 pounds of fish per capita is small, even when compared to 32 pounds for the Virgin Islands. The abnormal aspect of it is that, of this, only 1½ pounds are of local origin, the rest being imported as salted, pickled, and smoked fish, mainly cod, from Canada and Newfoundland primarily. Many people of the interior have never tasted fresh fish. The chief reason seems to be that the sea offers relatively little because of the great offshore depths near the more densely populated centers. Only to the east is there a shallow submarine bank, extending to, and including, the Virgin Islands; but the area has never been thoroughly tested as a fishing ground. The poor roads that in former days were a hindrance to transportation are no longer an excuse, but habits of life continue long after conditions that brought them into being have changed.

An answer to the question "What of the future?" is not an easy one to outline. It will depend much on the point of view held. Has American control been a grand success, as some would have it and as trade statistics seem to indicate; or has it been a miserable failure, as others insist and the wretchedness of the masses seems to prove? President Coolidge in his statement, "The United States has made no promises to the people of Puerto Rico that have not been more than fulfilled," represents one attitude. Professor Diffee, in his book *Puerto Rico, a Broken Pledge*, represents another. President Hoover, upon visiting the island, expressed himself as highly pleased and said: "All is good." Luis Muñoz Marín, Liberal party leader, is equally convinced that

> the development of large absentee-owned estates, the rapid curtailment in the planting of coffee—the natural crop of the independent farmer—and the concentration of cigar manufacturing into the hands of the American Trust have combined to make Puerto Rico a land of beggars and of millionaires, of flattering statistics and distressing realities. More and more it becomes a factory worked by peons, fought over by lawyers, bossed by absentee industrialists, and clerked by politicians. It is now Uncle Sam's second largest sweatshop.

Whichever point of view be taken, the facts remain that the investments in the island of millions of dollars of American capital have been very profitable because of a much greater efficiency and a much higher mechanization than had ever been known on the island. But for this capital there could have been little progress, and Puerto Rico today would very probably be much the same as it was at the beginning of the century. It is also true, on the other hand, that American occupation has done comparatively little for the social and economic betterment of the poorer classes. The facts still are as Governor Theodore Roosevelt pointed out in 1929:

> Riding through the hills, I have stopped at farm after farm where lean, underfed women and sickly men repeated again and again the same story—little food and no opportunity to get more. . . . . I have looked into kitchens where a handful of beans and a few plantains were the fare of the entire family. . . . . Housing facilities, of course, are woefully inadequate.

Six or seven people sometimes live in one small room. In some of the poorer quarters I have seen as many as ten housed in a makeshift board room not more than twelve feet square.

Such pictures are not overdrawn. They are in certain sections the common lot of the masses.

Few countries of the Western world have had more ups and downs than Puerto Rico, and in few has there been more periodic distress. At the beginning of the century American capital, fortified by technical skill, found the island in a backward state and ready for exploitation, an opportunity not to be neglected. Millions upon millions of dollars were poured into the island, the like of which had been undreamed of by Puerto Ricans. The men who invested or controlled these sums were primarily interested, naturally, in the profits to be made. Absentee ownership, as it always does, demanded "results" from those in charge and rewarded their efforts according to the efficiency shown, whether it was in the interest of the people of the island or not. The owners were not wilfully indifferent to local problems, but "business is business." Huge corporations are not organized because of their humane interests. In time resentment naturally has arisen, as locally there has been no way of bringing about a regulation of activities in the interests of the people. The system is one of exploitation, since it practically prohibits the development of local capital so sorely needed on the island. Furthermore, American entry, like Spanish entry of old, has brought for crop land a new economy to which the people seem to be unable to adjust themselves.

Statistically, the progress made is most phenomenal. The case of sugar is most outstanding and in a measure typical of other lines of development. Occupying only 15 per cent of the cultivated area in 1900, by 1930 it had more than 31 per cent. What is more striking still is that productivity increased four times faster than the acreage. The total export trade grew from $5,000,000 in 1898 to more than $100,000,000 in 1920, 1921, 1927, and 1928. During this same period the exports per capita rose from about $10 to nearly $70. The wealth of the island, not of its people, increased from $100,000,000 to more than $600,000,000. Available revenues for local improvements have increased even in greater proportion. The increase in amounts expended for roads, sanitation, and education reads like a fairy story.

Why, then, should there be so much agitation for a change and a growing restiveness with the present economy? There are those whom nothing short of a complete independence will satisfy. They believe that what is grudgingly granted when one political party is in power at Washington is taken away when the next one has its say and that local problems can be decided justly only by those most vitally concerned. On the other hand, there are those who look forward with a certain dread to the time when independence may be granted. To them economic conditions are unsatisfactory now, but with independence the situation might be much more serious unless special trade advantages are granted the island by the United States. Then there are those who look to more or less complete autonomy under the American flag in order to have the advantages and not the disadvantages of the American tariff system. Aside from all political aspects, there is the universal feeling that for the good of Puerto Rico some economy, radically different from that of the present, should be put into force at once to bring regulations more in line with Puerto Rican interests.

A UNIVERSITY BUILDING AT RIO PIEDRAS

Instruction is given in either English or Spanish at the discretion of the instructor, and the earnestness of the students is not exceeded anywhere.

THE ADVANCE GUARD OF A DEMONSTRATION PARADE OF SEVERAL THOUSAND PEOPLE ASKING LEGISLATORS TO ENFORCE THE ORGANIC LAW, LIMITING THE SIZE OF LANDED ESTATES SO THAT MORE FOOD MAY BE MADE AVAILABLE FOR THE POOR

As already pointed out, there is a growing dissatisfaction on the island with the political and economic outlook. In these days of intense nationalism there is naturally a resentment in being a people subject to the dictates of another with so little voice in adjusting matters of the most vital local interest. To most Americans the island at present is only a possession which is to be fitted into the larger unit at any cost with the dominant thought that in no way must its products become competitive with those of any part of continental United States. The treatment accorded the island at present in this respect is analogous, the Puerto Ricans believe, to that received by the American colonies and against which they rebelled. They cannot understand the present attitude of the continental American who is not willing to grant the Puerto Rican, as an American citizen, the same rights that he himself prizes so highly.

One of the typical illustrations given is the tariff system. The island must buy within this protected market at high prices, benefiting by the protection only in products it has to sell. As a result and because of high ocean freight rates, many of the prime necessities of life cost much more on the island than they do in New York. As sugar is the leading export by far, the producers of this commodity benefit by the high tariff; but sugar in the main, it is pointed out, is an American, rather than a Puerto Rican, industry.

The application of the coastwise shipping laws to Puerto Rico is manifestly unfair, for they are not being applied to the Virgin Islands. As a result of these laws, all goods between American ports and Puerto Rico must be carried in American bottoms at higher-than-standard rates, an important factor in both import and export trade. This is readily understandable, since two shipping companies have a monopoly on the trade, against whose charges there is no recourse by the shippers.

Puerto Ricans resent also the concentration of so much power in the hands of a governor who, as a political appointee, cannot have, they feel, the interests of the island uppermost. Although such appointees intrinsically may be men of the highest caliber, it is true that rarely have they an appreciation of the Latin-American outlook, rarely have they the ability to read the local publications and thus also are not able to read between lines, and still more rarely are they able to converse with the people in the language of the island. Consequently, it is scarcely possible to have an intimate knowledge of intricate and troublesome problems. Wisely or unwisely, the governor is forced commonly to cast his lot with one or the other of the political factions, and then, naturally, he is criticized for the things he does by those who are not part of the inner circle. The appointment of a native Puerto Rican for governor, who has the confidence of the people on the island and who knows their language and points of view as well as the local conditions, should be nearer the ideal. More ideal still would be the election of the governor by the people.

That autonomy or even complete independence would solve all Puerto Rican problems is far from true. The plight of the *jíbaro* must be alleviated before the island can be said to be on a sound footing. His number is far too large to be disregarded; no nation can advance with such a handicap. These people must be educated to reduce the birth rate so that it will be in line with economic standards of well-being, even if birth control is forbidden by the church. There must also be an adjustment in the agrarian situation, for no nation can prosper when its best lands are being used by a foreign group, no matter how efficiently.

In view of the dependence of the island upon the land, one of the most perplexing problems is a new distribution of farm income without a decrease in efficiency of production. To this end the Puerto Rican Reconstruction Administration as early as 1935 began to buy land; the first parcel was of 10,000 acres, for subdivision into units less than 500 acres to be worked as co-operatives. Its members work as common laborers as before purchase and receive current wages under steady employment, and in addition are entitled to a share of the net profits. This experiment of far-reaching social and economic significance may bring about drastic changes in the island's economy and reorient the entire outlook.

There are other encouraging features in the various attempts to answer some of the more perplexing questions. Especially so are the various plans to solve some of the complex agrarian problems. Whatever plans are to be made for the *rehabilitación de Puerto Rico*, a more sympathetic understanding of local points of view and less thought of continental interests must be brought to bear on the many open problems. The American people as a whole condemn wholeheartedly any so-called *imperialismo industrial norteamericano* when its object is purposefully to exploit the island and to make Puerto Ricans subservient.

THE VIRGIN ISLANDS OF THE UNITED STATES

By EARL B. SHAW

In the minds of many, the Virgin Islands of the United States suggest little more than Spanish treasure ships, pirate sea-rovers, and quantities of hidden gold. In the past, books and magazine articles have emphasized this phase in the evolution of the islands more than any other. Such stories have a general interest, but they add little to a solution of present-day economic problems. To the geographer, on the other hand, an interpretation of the factors that have led up to the present economic conditions is by far the more important. Only through studies directed toward such an interpretation can a solid foundation be laid upon which to build an economic structure that will serve for an improved well-being of the people.

LOCATION AND PHYSICAL SETTING

The Virgin Islands of the United States form a northeastern outpost of the Caribbean Sea and comprise our farthest east possession in the Atlantic. The group lies at the outer bend of the Antillean arc, approximately 1,200 miles southeast of New York, 1,000 miles east of Panama, and 40 miles east of Puerto Rico. Included within its boundaries are about fifty islands, but only three—St. Croix, St. Thomas, and St. John—are large enough to be of significance. These three make up a combined area of about 132.5 square miles and contain a population of 24,890, most of whom are colored.

Geologically the islands may be considered as a group of extinct volcanic peaks whose base is a submarine plateau. Erosion has modified the original outlines until at present the Virgins are characterized by rugged relief in a postmature stage of dissection. They have undergone many periods of differential uplift and subsidence with marked effects on the coastal sections. St. Thomas has probably been influenced most by subsidence, through which it has gained a well-known harbor.

The islands have a trade-wind climate without any marked extremes in temperature. At Christiansted, a typical station for the islands, the mean is 79°.3 F. Blowing equatorward and becoming warmer, the winds, in general, are moisture absorbing and consequently very drying except when cooled in rising over topographic barriers. At the same city there is a mean annual rainfall of 46.3 inches, from which, however, there is great variation from place to place. The contrast throughout the islands between the precipitation and vegetation of windward and leeward slopes is most marked. The latter are characterized by low rainfall and may be clothed with cacti and other drought-resistant plants, whereas the former, with heavy orographic precipitation, may support a vegetation that borders on the tropical rain-forest type. Although tropical hurricanes add a dangerous and undesirable element, the climate, from the standpoint of living conditions, may be considered generally healthful and, for the most part, delightful.

HISTORICAL AND GEOGRAPHICAL BACKGROUND

Columbus discovered the Virgin Islands of the United States, together with the British Virgins, which lie to the east, on his second voyage to America in 1493. In this part of the

Caribbean, hundreds of engulfed mountains dot the water surface; and the famous Genoese sailor, realizing the almost insuperable task of applying an individual name to each, decided to settle the problem by calling them the Virgin Islands, after the eleven thousand virgins of St. Ursula. According to tradition, St. Ursula and her company left Britain in the fifth century on a crusade to the Holy Land and suffered martyrdom at the hands of the Huns.

Whether the Caribs inhabited all the Virgin Islands when Columbus discovered them is not known, but there was a settlement on St. Croix when he dropped anchor near there in November, 1493. The village was built near Salt River, which flows into Sugar Bay; this stream provided fresh water except in times of extreme drought (there are no perennial streams in St. Croix). The ceiba trees of the northwest upland furnished the wood for the Carib boats; other vegetation yielded fruits and nuts for food. The limestone and marl soils locally favored the growing of root crops to supplement a diet contributed largely by sea and forest. Furthermore, the coastal location gave opportunity to enjoy the refreshing, health-giving sea breezes of the tropics. The Caribs were not primarily agriculturists, like the more civilized Arawaks, dominant in the Greater Antilles, but gave much attention to fishing. Evidently shell fish were plentiful, for heaps of shells may still be seen around the sites of old villages. The seaside location gave excellent opportunity to practice this industry. An examination of the shell heaps discloses the fact that at least two dozen varieties, including numerous conch, found place on the Carib bill-of-fare. Green turtles and land crabs were not ignored, and these were eaten just as they are by the Negro inhabitants of today.

The forest supplied the framework for the Carib houses, and the heavy leaves and branches of palm trees provided roofs to keep out rain and the piercing rays of the high sun. However, the palm-covered dwellings were not as staunchly constructed as the stone cottages of many Negro workers on the sugar plantations of today, and consequently few Carib villages survived the onslaughts of the tropical hurricanes which ravage the Caribbean region. After such storms the Caribs were compelled to build new villages or to go on a marauding expedition and usurp the settlement of a more fortunate group. Destructive storms and droughts surely contributed to the lack of permanence of many Carib settlements and gave impetus to the interisland movements so characteristic of these early Americans.

Although never densely populated, within a century after their discovery the islands were without people. When the Spaniards discovered gold in the stream gravels of Hispaniola, natives of that island, as well as those from many of the Lesser Antilles, were enslaved to work in the placer mines. Several of the small islands were completely depopulated by the slave hunts; and the aborigines, unaccustomed to hard labor in the hot humid environment of the gold fields and especially susceptible to the white man's diseases, died by the hundreds after short periods of service. Whether the Virgin Island Caribs were enslaved, killed in attempted capture, or driven out by the Spaniards is a matter of conjecture, but it is probable that one or more of these methods accounted for the early depopulation of the islands. When the Earl of Cumberland passed the Virgins in 1596 he described them as wholly uninhabited. Nevertheless, the islands did not cease to be of service to Spain. Their location at the northeast corner of the

Caribbean and the numerous harbors which indent their shorelines made them valuable as an assembling-point for Spanish treasure ships. Many of these craft carrying the Aztec and Inca gold to Europe met at the Virgins on their way homeward and sailed the longest portion of the trip in group formation, so as to provide better protection from pirates infesting the sea. Both pirate and treasure ships used coastal indentations through choice or necessity, in order to play hide-and-seek with pursued or pursuer.

Permanent settlement by Europeans did not take place until the latter part of the seventeenth and the early part of the eighteenth centuries. Prior to this time ownership changed so frequently that nation after nation claimed the islands as its possessions. St. Croix belonged to four different countries in a period of 26 years. Finally Denmark established definite claim to St. Thomas in 1672, St. John in 1717, and St. Croix in 1734; and they remained her colonies until the United States purchased them in 1917.

The lateness of permanent settlement and the many changes in sovereignty are reflections of conditions and times. No gold was present. No large native pastures similar to those in Cuba were available for cattle-raising, which was one of the first industries tried by Europeans in the Caribbean. No significant area of smooth topography like that which early attracted Portuguese and British to Barbados for sugar production was to be found. Finally, no large islands were included in the group, a fact which limited their economic value in the early days just as it does at present.

Unlike the Caribs, whose culture was based largely on fishing, the Danish settlers lived primarily by agriculture. The Indians changed the landscape but little; a few palm-thatched huts along the coast, a few big piles of shells, remnants of the shellfish diet, several large, seaworthy canoes along the shores —these were major items in the cultural pattern of the aborigines. The Danes, on the other hand, built substantial houses of stone and wood instead of thatched huts, lived off the harvests of the land more than from the harvests of the sea, and used better boats than the Indian canoes. Moreover, their activities were not confined to the coast. They planted fields of cotton, tobacco, and sugar on level land where they could find it and on hilly land where level fields were not available. Sugar soon became the dominant crop, and a monoculture sugar economy existed for decades on all the islands. On St. Thomas and St. John, isles characterized by rugged topography, hill lands were terraced and hoed from top to bottom. St. Croix, where arable land was more plentiful, soon became the leading sugar-producer.

In the earliest years of settlement the Danes tried out white indentured labor in the fields, a practice which proved unsuccessful. When this failed, Danish planters, like those in other West Indian islands, imported African Negroes, and a constantly increasing number of Negro quarters dotted the Danish cultural landscape. Between 1691 and 1715 the Negro population of St. Thomas alone increased from 555 to 3,042. The descendants of these and other slaves make up the bulk of the present Virgin Islands' population.

At the close of the eighteenth century more than 30,000 acres were planted to sugar cane, more than a third of the total area. However, when European sugar markets fell in response to the increase of beet sugar and the severe competition of East Indian areas, only regions topographically suited to machine cultivation could continue to produce cane profitably. Because of their rugged terrane, St. Thomas and St. John were forced by these world-changes to discontinue cane production. The latter island turned to a subsistence economy, while the former focused attention more strongly on shipping. Only in St. Croix, where an arable coastal plain made plow-farming feasible, did sugar continue its agricultural dominance. But even there physical conditions were not ideal; and when the United States purchased the islands in 1917, only 12,000 acres were devoted to cane.

The cultural landscape of the islands changed but little after the transfer to American ownership. Shipping continued important in St. Thomas, subsistence farming remained dominant in St. John, and sugar plantations were still conspicuous on the level acres of St. Croix. In St. Croix, however, sugar production declined to a new low in 1938, when only 4,362 tons were produced.

ST. CROIX

The story of the principal causes for the decline in sugar production illustrates one of the major economic problems of the Virgin Islands. A description of the marginal character of production in St. Croix, as well as a glance at the prospects for other agricultural industries in the island, very readily make evident the fact that St. Croix, under the present system of land use, is an economic liability to the United States.

St. Croix ("Isle of the Holy Cross") lies 40 miles south of St. Thomas and St. John and rests on a submarine platform separated from that of the northern islands by profound block-faulting. The island, with its 84.25 square miles, includes two-thirds of the area of the American Virgins, and its 12,902 people make up more than half the population of the group. As previously indicated, it possesses the only arable land of im-

RUINS OF AN OLD CANE MILL

Old smokestacks on St. Croix are mute evidence of a former prosperity in sugar. In the foreground is an abandoned cane field. The home of the plantation manager, right center, is now occupied by Negro families.

portance in a rich limestone plain, one of the major physical regions of the island. The upraised sea bottom extends in a general northeast-southwest direction between the rugged volcanics of the northwestern highlands and the arid hill-lands of the east.

The coastal plain has been the economic heart of St. Croix. Here are the Negro villages; here are the two major urban

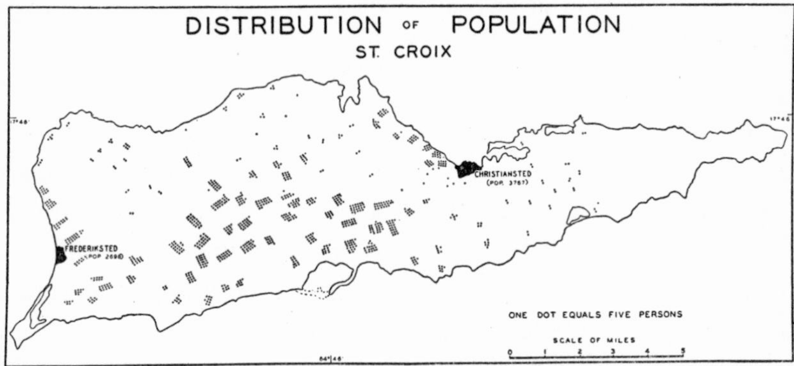

DISTRIBUTION OF POPULATION, ST. CROIX

The distribution of the population is very closely related to the relief. Parts, such as the east and the northwest section, are rough and have little agricultural land available. The regular arrangement of the dots in each group agrees fairly closely with the stone or frame houses of Negro workers in the sugar areas.

centers, Frederiksted and Christiansted; and here, for centuries, sugar has been king. Nevertheless, this dictatorship has long been weakening—weakening because the island's physical background does not provide a basis for competing on equal terms with the world's low-cost sugar-producers.

The great limiting factor which at present prevents the success of sugar in St. Croix is rainfall. Because of the drying effect of the trade winds, there must be at least 45 inches of rain well distributed through the year to give even a fair yield of cane. In only half of the eighty years of weather records has the total been as great as this, and in 1873 less than 30 inches fell. In 1938 drought conditions were so severe that the governor's report contained the following statement:

> Sugar production fell from 8,211 tons in 1937 to 4,362 tons in 1938. Hundreds of acres of drouth-stunted cane were uncut and plowed under. Plowing and planting costs that should have been spread over three or four years of sugar-cane production were totally lost. Sugar factories with heavy investments in sugar cane grown on so-called administration land were even more seriously affected than were small farmers whose chief investment is their own and their family's labor.

Not only is the annual total of rainfall uncertain, but distribution as well. In some years, as a result of tropical hurricanes, one-fourth to one-third of the entire precipitation may fall in a single month, and the remainder may be insufficient for a good cane crop even though the amount for the year is high. In general, sugar production rises and falls with the annual rainfall, in contrast to production in Cuba, where rain during the growing season is much more dependable.

The causes for the unsatisfactory rainfall regime are to be found in a combination of circumstances. The convectional rain that reaches a maximum at the time of the high sun is variable in occurrence and, because of the small size of the island, is seldom heavy. The hurricane control, an important influence in the rainiest period, is likewise erratic. The northwest upland is insufficiently elevated to present an effective barrier to the northeast trades, and the resulting slight increase in rainfall gives little advantage to the sugar region because it lies in the lee of the hills.

The use of deep wells or reservoirs to obtain water for irrigation of the cane does not seem feasible in St. Croix. The smallness of drainage basins and the flatness of river valleys which might be flooded make reservoirs impracticable. The inflowing water to be stored would not always be adequate, and the evaporating surface would be so large in proportion to depth that the supply would be further diminished. Geologists report adversely upon the possibilities of deep wells, and even the most optimistic consider that water obtained thus could increase the moisture available for sugar cane by only 10 per cent of the total precipitation.

Whereas climate affects adversely the possibilities for cane-growing in the entire island, relief restricts cultivation by machinery to the coastal plain, a very small section, which is too limited to provide the amount of cane necessary for cheapest production. On the whole, soils are not unfavorable; and if all the physical background were as advantageous as the marl and limestone earth of the plain, the dominant industry of the Virgin Islands would not have sunk so deeply into the doldrums.

Goods and passengers enter and leave St. Croix by lighters from ocean vessels which lie at anchor some distance beyond the coastwise shallows. The necessity for lighters constitutes a marked disadvantage to the sugar industry by adding to the cost of transport; it is more expensive, of course, to lighter sugar to the ship than to load it at the dock. It is also more costly to operate small sugar centrals than to run large ones. In Cuba and Puerto Rico huge mills grind as much in a single week or even half a week as those of St. Croix do in a season. There is thus a high overhead charge in manufacture, which forms a further drawback to the industry.

The boon of tariff-free entrance to continental United States, the world's greatest sugar market, only partly compensates for the long list of handicaps to sugar production in St. Croix. Although the industry has survived by means of this prop, it is literally losing ground in the struggle, for in the last twenty years field after field has been abandoned to grass and pasture. The sugar area in 1909 was 14,007 acres, whereas pasture comprised 31,255 acres; in a recent year cane occupied less than 5,000 acres, whereas grazing land has increased to 41,500 acres.

Throughout the Virgin Islands it is possible to maintain natural and improved grasses suitable for pasturage. Although rainfall is too scant for good forest, and relief, with the exception of St. Croix's coastal plain, too rugged for cultivated crops, both factors, in general, permit a vegetation upon which cattle may thrive. Shallow wells furnish water except in times of extreme drought; the animals need no shelter against cold; and until recent quarantine measures were enacted, Puerto Rico, with its crowded population has provided a good market for beef. With these advantages the cattle industry ranks second to that of sugar in St. Croix and forms the dominant agricultural activity in St. Thomas. There are, however, distinct handicaps to cattle-raising which preclude the possibility of its forming the basis of prosperity. During the dry season the parched grasses are not nutritious, and scenes in years of extreme drought show lean and half-starved cattle wandering about over parched pastures in search of food. Ticks and fever form an ever present menace. And, finally, the present Puerto Rican quarantine shows the extreme danger of a dependence on one market. Even without the environmental handicaps, the industry could never benefit St. Croix and the other islands significantly because it employs such a small number of people. Although at present cattle-raising occupies approximately 80 per cent of the land, it gives employment to only about 3 per cent of the labor.

Cotton, which would undoubtedly be a great boon to St. Croix, has been suggested as a substitute for the declining sugar. This crop, which thrives under the rainfall regime of the island, could not only be grown by renters on small plots of land unsuited for cane but would fit into a rotation system with sugar cane itself. The fiber would provide an outlet for much idle labor and would increase the revenue of the people as a whole. Yet the plant cannot be grown successfully because of the pink bollworm, successful control over which is not likely.

Vegetables are also considered a possibility. Again, many physical features seem favorable, for machines may be used on the flat, rich earth of St. Croix; averages show that sufficient rain falls during the growing period from September to January; labor is plentiful; and the crops ripen at a time when the manufacturing centers of northeastern United States are demanding a fresh product which cannot, at that season, be raised near the market. Although no frost occurs and the major growth of vegetables comes after the hurricane period, one serious climatic handicap stifles the industry. The uncertainty of the rains frequently results in late planting, which consequently delays the harvest until the northern market is flooded by producers in continental United States. In addition, insect pests and plant diseases are rife. A paragraph from the governor's report for 1935 indicates the difficulties encountered:

> The third year of tomato growing for the northern winter market proved a failure. Variable weather throughout the planting and growing season, together with certain pests, increased costs and decreased yields to the end that losses were suffered. The first year showed a profit on small acreage,

the second year showed an even break on larger plantings. . . . . Few men can or will take the risks particularly attendant upon the more perishable products subject not only to weather but to the uncertainties of the New York commission market.

Neither vegetables nor cotton offer a money crop more favorable than the marginal sugar cane. Cattle-raising will not provide labor for a population density based upon cultivation agriculture. What the island needs is a major cash crop suited to its limited physical advantages and minor diversified crops for subsistence agriculture. The problem is easily seen, but a solution is yet to be found. The island thus far remains a distinct economic liability to its purchasers.

ST. THOMAS

Like St. Croix, St. Thomas also is an economic liability for the United States. As in St. Croix, prosperity waxed high during the early years of European settlement and declined during the nineteenth and twentieth centuries. But in contrast, the ups and downs of St. Thomas were based upon shipping rather than upon sugar. A glance at the physiography and geologic history of the two islands discloses the reasons for the difference.

St. Thomas is a maturely dissected upland consisting of irregular angular ridges which extend across the island in a general west-east direction. Only to the east is there any land even approaching arability, and this is suitable only for the planting of improved grasses. In St. Thomas no level sea bottom arose to afford diversity to the folded, tilted, and faulted volcanic sections, like the former subsea limestone strata which emerged to unite the two previously isolated volcanic regions of St. Croix.

Again, although both islands had major periods of submergence, that of St. Thomas was greater. The downward movement in the northern island caused the drowning of a system of river valleys which joined at the base of the main ridge in the vicinity of the present town of Charlotte Amalie and gave the island one of the best harbors in the Caribbean. St. Croix, with lesser subsidence and with no well-defined valleys so necessary in the production of an embayed shoreline when there is any significant coastal sinking, possesses not even one good harbor. In consequence of these differences, the development of the one island has always been closely connected with shipping, while the economy of the other has been associated with agriculture.

During the period of discovery, colonization, and commercial development the harbor of St. Thomas was a natural port-of-call for ships of all nations. Here shipping lanes crossed. Here late in the nineteenth century ships found cable connections with all parts of the world, and long before this time they stopped at the port for food, fuel, and water. For many years Charlotte Amalie was an entrepôt where cargoes were unloaded for transshipment and other goods obtained in exchange. Moreover, during most of its history it has been a free port, a fact which has added to its popularity. As a result of all this, the merchants of Charlotte Amalie made profits rivaling those of the St. Croix sugar-planters during their golden age. But, like the heyday of St. Croix, the prosperous period of St. Thomas came to an end not because of any decline in the physical background of the harbor but because of changes in world-conditions. The time factor, so little stressed in geography, was a major influence.

Several factors contributed to the decline of shipping at

Charlotte Amalie. Steamships burning coal and oil replaced sailing boats; ships traveled longer distances without refueling, and frequent stops at fueling-points like Charlotte Amalie were less necessary; refrigeration eliminated much of the food problem of ships, and sea-water condensers eliminated stops for water; wireless and radio gave vessels constant contact

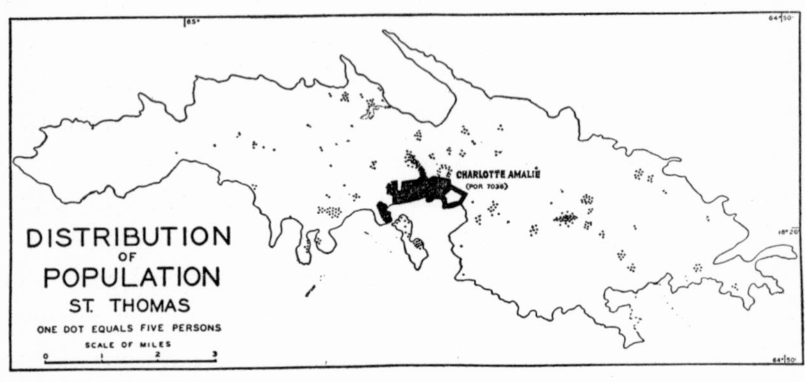

LAND UTILIZATION AND POPULATION OF ST. THOMAS

With scarcely 500 acres of arable land out of a total 18,000, it is not difficult to see why the Island of St. Thomas does not support a dense rural population. Because of harbor activities, about three-fourths of the entire population is in the town of Charlotte Amalie.

with the outside world, and docking at strategic islands for orders was discontinued; other islands in the Antilles became commercially important and ordered full shiploads, as did St. Thomas; and foreign countries developed ports in their own colonies, by the aid of patronage and subsidies, to afford stronger competition for Charlotte Amalie. All these and other changes brought about by scientific advance and commercial competition have lessened the early advantages of the port. About the only shipping of importance is associated with the fueling of ships. This is done by the oil pipe line, the elec-

A VIEW OF THE TOWN OF CHARLOTTE AMALIE AND THE HARBOR OF ST. THOMAS ON THE ISLAND OF ST. THOMAS

The beauty of the harbor beggars description, and very active attempts are being made by the government to develop a tourist traffic. The strategic value of the harbor is being superseded by San Juan Bay, Puerto Rico.

tric cranes, and the picturesque Negro coal-carriers, both men and women.

The island of St. Thomas, like St. Croix, is looking for a system of land use which will bring back the shipping profits of early colonial times. The grazing industry which occupies much of the land will help little because it has the same handicaps as those enumerated for St. Croix. Market gardening affords no hope, for less than a thousand acres can be considered arable, and uncertain rainfall discourages investment. Forestry and tree crops have been suggested; but frequent droughts, hurricanes, and other climatic variables offer slight encouragement. The bay-rum industry brought temporary prosperity to some, for production rose from less than 10,000 gallons in 1910 to 140,000 gallons in the early 1930's. Recently strong competition from other West Indian producers has caused a drop to less than 55,000 gallons.

Other industries have been attempted or suggested to take the place of the declining shipping trade, but the ones already cited are sufficient to indicate the economic dilemma of St. Thomas and the American government, which is attempting to improve conditions. The strongly subsidized tourist industry may afford improvement; but most of the ships which stop are cruise ships, and their passengers contribute little to island economy. The fact that cruise boats provide hotel accommodations to passengers while stopping in port is a situation worrying the managements of the new and recently remodeled hostelries of Charlotte Amalie, as well as those of hotels on tourist islands like Bermuda and the Bahamas. Moreover, St. Thomas is off the main travel routes, and passenger service is none too regular. There seems little chance to balance the island's economic budget.

ST. JOHN

In contrast to St. Thomas and St. Croix, the island of St. John causes but slight drain upon the treasury of the United States. The present island economy, based largely on subsistence agriculture, provides the sparse population—709 Negroes and 13 whites—a comparatively low standard of living with but little outside aid. A picture of the physical background and the adjustments in land use are of interest.

Although generally similar to St. Thomas in its ruggedness, St. John lacks the well-marked east-west mountain ridge so characteristic of the former island. There is little arable land, but the upland consists of a somewhat dissected erosional surface which is so consistent and characteristic that wherever it appears, whether in St. John or in the rest of the Virgin Islands and Puerto Rico, it has been given the name of the "St. John peneplane." It marks the oldest erosional surface appearing in these islands.

Like that of St. Thomas, the coastline of St. John is characterized by marked irregularity. Both islands were subjected to two stages of submergence in Quaternary time, which produced excellent harbors. Coral Harbor on St. John is said to approach the ideal as closely as does the famous indentation on St. Thomas. Yet the latter far surpasses the former in port development. It is possible that the earlier settlement of St. Thomas, its location near the Virgin Passage, its nearness to Puerto Rico, and the ample capacity of the harbor for all shipping which came to it may have influenced greater development. Moreover, the position of Coral Bay with reference to the mountains of Tortola, the British island to the east, where guns of heavy caliber could be mounted and thus jeopardize the safety of a fleet, may have limited the chance for port development.

Climatically St. John also resembles its close neighbor, St. Thomas, but contrasts exist in both vegetation and soils. The soils of St. John are slightly deeper, because the removal of natural vegetation has been less, and the more consistent forest cover has reduced soil erosion.

Although the two islands, St. John and St. Thomas, which lie within 3 miles of each other, are similar in physical background, there are definite reasons for their dissimilarity in economic structure. During the early days under Danish rule St. John was fairly prosperous in the production of sugar. However, with an expansion of the sugar-beet industry in temperate latitudes, the emancipation of slaves, and the presence of other competing factors of the period, new adjustments became necessary, and cane production disappeared. St. John had no well-developed shipping industry, like that already under way in St. Thomas, or any arable coastal plain for machine agriculture, like that in St. Croix. Consequently, the decline to a subsistence agriculture status caused a rapid reduction in population. In 1841 St. John had 2,555 people; today they number 722, a decline of 72 per cent. Most of this drop came before the turn of the century, for during the last fifty years the population density has remained relatively stable. In short, St. John has made the necessary adjustments from an economy based on sugar to one which depends on more diversified, although more primitive, pursuits. These include the grazing of cattle, a small production of forest products, a widespread practice of subsistence farming, and a minor interest in fishing.

Cattle-raising is a major industry on the island. Whereas

the growing of sugar in colonial days demanded large numbers of laborers, the cattle business requires few workers. There is no cultivation, no careful planting, no hoeing, no harvesting, and no process of manufacture in the raising of beef cattle in St. John. Little labor is needed to plant the fields with improved grasses once in several years, to clean out the brush growth once or twice annually, if it is done at all, and to look after other limited requirements of this extensive type of occupation. Moreover, there is no need for the skilled labor so necessary in some highly developed lands. Hence, the sparse and unskilled population affords an adequate labor supply. Environmental conditions offer the same advantages and handicaps for the cattle industry as those in St. Croix.

The forest industry of St. John is slightly different from that found in St. Croix or St. Thomas. The tree crop for which the island is most widely known is bay leaves. Through some unknown cause the indigenous *Pimenta acris* has developed naturally without intermixture with other but closely related species, which yield an inferior and almost worthless bay oil; and it is largely because the bay leaves are obtained from this desirable species that the oil of St. John has long had an enviable reputation in the world's trade in perfumes and cosmetics.

The industry is not a plantation occupation. Hence, like cattle-grazing, the gathering of bay leaves requires but few laborers from the island's small number of people. No attempt is made to plant the trees, but birds eat the bay berries and, with the wind, are scattering agents for the seeds. Plants spring up, and, if the landowner wishes to encourage a favorable growth of trees, other vegetation is cleared from the new seedlings. The few native families who perform this work, pick the leaves, and assist in other tasks incident to the industry are permitted by the landowner to occupy little plots of ground where they built rude huts and supplement the small bay-leaf income by raising fruits and vegetables for their own subsistence.

The gathering of bay leaves and their manufacture is not the large development that may be supposed. Sales in a recent year amounted to approximately $5,000. Although there are four stills, only one, slightly more modern than the other primitive types, is operating, and that intermittently. There are hundreds of acres of bay trees growing up in brush, but new markets and better methods of production are needed to bring about significant expansion. In addition to bay oil, the forests contribute other products. The natives make charcoal, cut fence posts, weave basketry, and gather fruits and nuts. However, forest industries show no immediate prospect of expansion, and sparsely settled St. John is well adjusted to such pioneer activities.

Subsistence farming is practiced by almost every family in St. John. Several vegetables grow well, and plots of tanias, okra, casave, yams, pigeon peas, sweet potatoes, and beans are planted, along with Cavendish bananas, papayas, and a few drought-resisting tropical fruits. Further variety is added to the food supply by fish, which may be obtained in the shallow waters above the submarine banks surrounding the island.

The government is attempting to attract tourists to this isolated primeval land. Were it closer to densely populated regions and nearer to much-traveled trade routes, there would be a better chance for success. Many world-travelers would be intrigued by its primitive culture, lack of roads, rugged trails, forest cover, white sand beaches, and beautiful views. But an

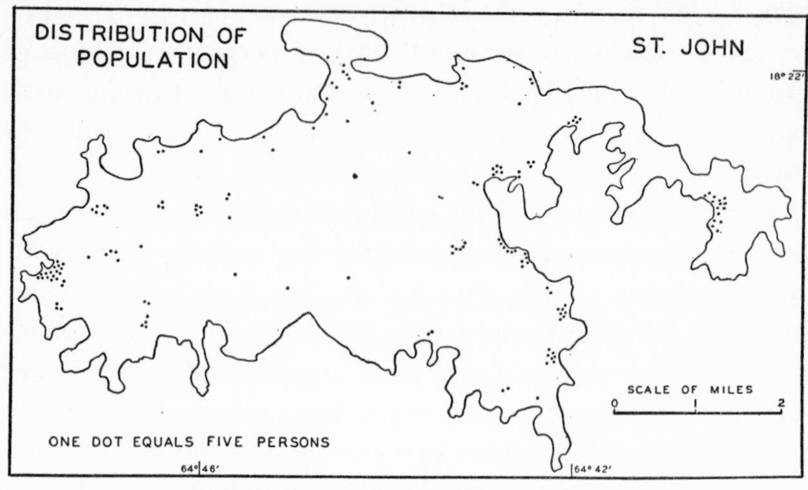

POPULATION IN ST. JOHN

St. John is a highly dissected upland with little level land. The maximum elevation, approximately, for St. John is 1,250 feet; for St. Thomas, 1,550 feet; and for St. Croix, 1,100 feet. Most of the people live at or near the coast.

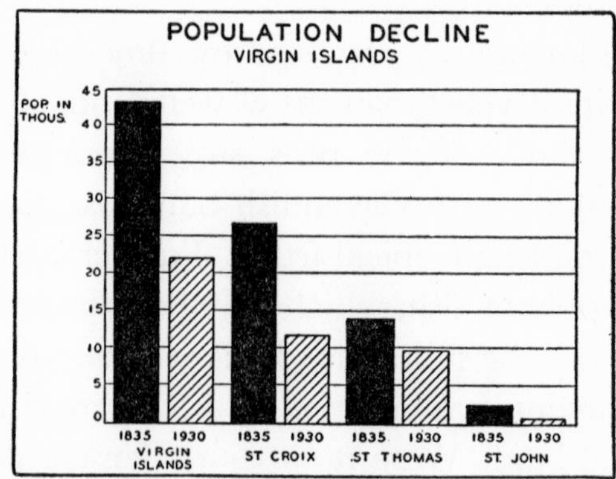

POPULATION DECLINE IN THE VIRGIN ISLANDS

The present population is only about one-half (51 per cent) that of a hundred years ago. There has been a similar or even greater decline in the sugar industry. In the early part of the nineteenth century Europe looked to the West Indies for its sugar, produced with slave labor; now the major supply comes from home-grown beet sugar.

influx of tourists would upset the present balance. There would be a change in the cultural environment, and a development of economic desires among the natives which at present they sense but little and which they would find difficult to satisfy. Hence it is a question whether it would be better to encourage a change or to let conditions remain at the present level—in many ways a situation ideal. At any rate, under the present land-use system, St. John affords few problems to the United States government and cannot be considered an economic liability in the same class with St. Croix and St. Thomas, although the latter have more favorable physical conditions.

CONCLUSIONS AND TRENDS

To some students of the Virgin Islands the balanced economy of St. John affords a suggestion for tackling several of the problems of the whole group. But one must remember that a subsistence economy for 722 people on 20 square miles is one thing, whereas a similar type of land use for 24,167 people on 112 square miles is another. In the latter case the density of population is approximately 215 per square mile, whereas in the former the average is approximately 36. In short, St. Croix and St. Thomas are overpopulated for a subsistence economy like that of St. John; and if such an economy is tried, one of three situations is likely to result: the standard of living will be lowered; emigration for a substantial fraction of the population will be necessary to maintain the present living standard; or grants-of-aid will be necessary from the government.

One may ask: If subsistence agriculture holds no hope for St. Croix and St. Thomas, what then? The ideal goal is a money crop, which can be raised well on the islands' niggardly environment and which will find a ready sale in the world-market. Some geographers believe that an island devoted to profitable monoculture can maintain a higher standard of living than one devoted to subsistence agriculture. This may be true, provided the price level remains high enough to maintain an adequate profit, and therein lies the argument for diversification. Many authorities believe a country signs its economic death warrant the moment it focuses all attention upon one crop.

Profitable diversification is easy to suggest but hard to apply in the tropics. Even one profitable money crop is hard to find for the Virgin Islands. The record of sugar in St. Croix is not encouraging. Improper soil conditions and limited rainfall preclude any significant development of citrus fruits, which have proved profitable in Puerto Rico. Lack of rainfall inhibits successful banana-growing, an industry which has been an economic mainstay for Jamaica during recent years of depression. Coffee, another major crop of the Caribbean, would find an inhospitable environment because the plant requires abundant moisture. In fact, a long list of important agricultural crops are ruled out because of climatic, edaphic, or topographic conditions. Expansion and diversification of the livestock industry would also meet serious drawbacks.

If a limited choice is available in agriculture, even less opportunity is present in other basic industries. Geologic processes have not favored the islands with mineral resources. There are small deposits of clays that might supply a local pottery industry; but, aside from that, mining offers no possibilities. The outlook for manufacture provides no joy to the optimist. No coal or petroleum is present, and water power is impossible because the rainfall is small in amount and faulty in distribution. A lack of basic raw materials, such as iron and good timber, so vital to the development of important manufacturing, further emphasizes the limited resources. A small labor supply exists; but the people are little adapted to manufacture, either because of racial handicaps and climatic influences or on account of years of association with shipping or agriculture. The manufacturing possibilities of the Virgins seem limited to activity on a small scale in such handicraft work as textiles, furniture, toys, and basketry.

With industrial possibilities limited and an agricultural money crop difficult to find, and with subsistence agriculture like that of St. John holding slight hope for the overpopulated islands, one may well wonder what system of land use may be followed successfully. It is difficult to say, but a hybrid scheme of land use involving both subsistence agriculture and monoculture may achieve as great a measure of success as is possible on these marginal isles. Such a plan is being followed by the government at the present time.

Several thousand acres have been purchased, homes have been built, and the subdivisions have been sold to purchasers. Under an easy amortization plan approximately four hundred homesteaders are acquiring possession of these plots of land, averaging 6 acres each, together with comfortable houses. In general the record of meeting amortization rentals has been fairly satisfactory. The government has also purchased two sugar mills, a commercial rum distillery, and several thousand acres of land for planting cane. Besides grinding its own cane for sugar and rum, the government purchases crops from homesteaders and private owners in order to operate its centrals more nearly at capacity.

Critics of this hybrid scheme of land use point to the fact that private capital will not invest in Virgin Island sugar and rum industries because of the unfavorable geographic environment and that the government will lose money on its venture. There is surely some foundation for their prediction; but if any organization can make a success of an agricultural enterprise in a marginal farming land, that organization is likely to be one composed of a large number of individuals like the government, which, much better than the private individual, can stand the losses of drought years and wait for heavy rainfall seasons to recoup failures.

The homestead plan is much more likely to succeed on the arable land of St. Croix than on the rugged hills of St. Thomas. Yet, if the Negroes are as willing to work as the farming Chachas on the windward, rainy slopes of the island, a measure of success may be achieved. The Chachas are a colony of French who came to St. Thomas from St. Barts several decades ago. Many of the immigrants have eked out a hard living by a semiterrace agriculture without government aid. Others are fishermen who prefer the harvests of the sea to those of the land. And they have some reason for their preference. Fishing should be an economic ally to subsistence agriculture. The islands are favored by submarine banks, numerous coastal indentations, and a variety of species of fish. Just as in early Carib days, fish supply an important food element not only for the Chachas but for a large percentage of the population of the whole island group. Both farming and fishing Chachas form one of the few white colonies in the Caribbean who have largely maintained their racial purity for generations.

Government aid in St. Thomas has not stopped with the homestead plan, for thousands of dollars have been expended on hotel facilities; one improvement involved the development of the well-known Blue Beard Castle Hotel on St. Thomas. As previously indicated, tourism has possibilities; the physical environment is generally ideal for attracting lovers of scenic beauty and enjoyable climate. Nevertheless, distance from large population centers and lack of frequent ship service are two handicaps which may not easily be overcome.

No doubt an improvement to the harbor both in the way of dredging and in the addition of facilities for the shipping industry would stimulate economic conditions in St. Thomas. But a significant change is unlikely. An interdepartmental committee, appointed by the Secretary of the Interior, to study and report on the relative advantages of the ports of St. Thomas and of San Juan, Puerto Rico, as sites for a graving dock made a report on November 7, 1937. They found that, if a graving dock were to be constructed in the Caribbean area, it should be in the harbor of San Juan rather than that of St. Thomas. If the dock is established at San Juan, the only commercial industry of St. Thomas will receive a serious blow.

Besides emphasizing homesteading and the manufacture of sugar and rum, the government has invested large sums in all the islands on health and education. Drainage projects have lessened the dangers of malaria and other tropical diseases, and progress in education has been achieved. Illiteracy has declined from 24.9 per cent in 1917 under the Danish regime to 13.4 per cent in 1940. Moreover, greater stress on vocational training in the educational program should provide the native with a better understanding of his problems and a greater ability to meet them. Much is yet to be accomplished. One of the most serious difficulties is the chaotic conditions of the home. Marital relations are so irregular and illegitimacy so common—60 per cent of the children born—that for most of the humbler people little family life exists.

The preceding paragraphs are filled with implications of large expenditures being made by the government for the welfare of the Virgin Islands. One writer has indicated that they have cost the government $15,000,000 since their purchase in 1917. However true this may be, it is certain that the United States Treasury has been drained of several million dollars in its attempts to improve conditions.

Large expenditures and small receipts emphasize the liability quality of these Caribbean white elephants. But there is another way of looking at the Virgin Islands besides gazing at their sorry economic balance sheet. One may consider their potentialities in time of war. The United States did not purchase the islands because they were considered a wise economic investment. The United States did not pay Denmark $25,000,000—a price of $295 an acre, in contrast to 2 cents an acre for Alaska; less than 3 cents an acre for California, Nevada, Colorado, and Utah; approximately 4 cents an acre for the Louisiana Purchase; less than 14 cents an acre for the Philippines; and but $35.80 an acre for the Canal Zone—in order to increase our sugar lands. The United States bought them for war purposes.

War has been the spur which has encouraged all attempts to buy the Virgin Islands, for their strategic importance has always been recognized in time of conflict. A deep, spacious, protected harbor on the south coast of St. Thomas, which itself is located near the outer bend of the Antillean arc, offers possibilities for a naval base highly acclaimed by military experts. Not only does St. Thomas possess one of the few good harbors in the West Indies, but its structure, with its central ridge, is especially fitted for the emplacement of fortifications commanding both shores of the harbor at the same time and making any approach by an enemy difficult. Moreover, although near the other islands, St. Thomas is practically in the open ocean and permits entrance and egress of a fleet with little chance of observation. Hence, with these advantages it is little wonder that Admiral Porter of Civil War fame called St. Thomas "the keystone to the arch of the West Indies," and Major Glassford of the Signal Corps said: "St. Thomas might be converted into a second Gibraltar."

Our first serious attempt to purchase the Virgin Islands came after the close of the Civil War. During that struggle the North needed a naval station in the Caribbean. Both British and French harbors had been hospitable to Confederate cruisers and blockade-runners, but Federal warships found it difficult to obtain coal and shelter from storms. With the harbor of St. Thomas as a base for coaling, supplies, repairs, and shelter it seems likely that the United States could have rounded up privateers, blockade-runners, and contraband traders in half the time and with half the trouble.

The negotiations failed at this time, and certain phenomena which have always been economic handicaps to the islands exerted no small influence on the outcome. On November 18, 1867, while a commission from the United States was visiting the Virgin Islands in the interest of the purchase, there occurred several severe earthquake shocks, which not only caused damage to life and property but also set in motion a tidal wave severe enough to throw the "Monongahela," the American commission ship, high and dry on the shore of St. Croix. This event, coming after the terrible hurricane of October 29, gave active opponents to the purchase a chance to sneer at the attempt to buy a region of earthquakes, hurricanes, and tidal waves. Moreover, several newspapers joined the opposition and influenced public sentiment in the United States against the transaction. In the Virgin Islands antagonism to the sale also appeared, for many ignorant natives believed that the earthquake showed the displeasure of Heaven at the contemplated change of sovereignty.

In 1902, only a few years after the war with Spain, the United States made another determined effort to buy the islands. Just as at the close of the Civil War, a feeling developed that the Danish possessions provided definite military advantages, the lack of which was felt all too keenly during the war with Spain. Authorities argued that, had the harbor of St. Thomas been in the hands of the United States, Cervera might have been barred from the Caribbean, Puerto Rico would have fallen into American control more easily, the expense of hasty harbor defense need not have been incurred, and the loss of life and money very likely could have been reduced considerably. But again the American-Danish negotiations failed—this time, however, through Danish opposition, possibly brought about by German intrigue. However, in 1917, with the fear of the German U-boat uppermost in the minds of the people, the transfer was made.

It is well at this point to keep in mind that the United States did not purchase the islands in 1917 because it needed a naval base in the Caribbean. The Spanish War gave us harbors in Puerto Rico and Guantanamo Bay in Cuba. United States ownership of the Virgins came as a result of fear that Germany might acquire them. Admiral Dewey states the case clearly:

> There is no "military reason for acquiring the Danish West Indies connected with preparations by the United States itself for a campaign in the

Caribbean. The harbors and waters of Puerto Rico and the adjacent islands now under our flag afford as good facilities for an advanced base as do those of any of the Danish West Indies, and they are so near that the acquisition of the Danish Islands for the mere purpose of establishing a base upon which the United States fleet could rest would not be worth while.

"The Danish Islands, however, do afford several harbors and anchorages more or less protected from prevailing winds and seas, and more or less capable of artificial defense, that would be very useful to a foreign nation conducting a campaign in the Caribbean. If that nation were an enemy of the United States the resulting situation would be exceedingly embarrassing in the conduct of a campaign by the United States. Denmark is a small nation with limited sea power, and would not be able to prevent the seizure of the Danish Islands by a strong military power desirous of using them as a base. It might not even be able to withstand an attempt by such a Power to purchase the islands.

"In a military sense, that of forestalling a possible enemy rather than that of endeavoring to gain a favorable position for ourselves, it is advisable that the Danish Islands should come under our flag by peaceful measures before war."[1]

Was the purchase of the Virgin Islands a sound investment? From a military point of view no one can fully evaluate all the factors involved. No one can fully forecast the needs should the United States become involved in a major war on the Atlantic. Nevertheless, there is no doubt that the Virgin Islands could be utilized to an advantage by an enemy power. At present all the remaining islands of the Caribbean are owned by democracies. It is not likely that they will be allied against us in any coming struggle. However, it is not so certain that the fascist nations will be on our side. Had we failed to purchase the Virgins, had they become bases for Germany, the picture might be far different. Moreover, they may con-

[1] C. C. Tansill, *The Purchase of the Danish West Indies* (Baltimore: Johns Hopkins Press, 1932), pp. 481–82.

tribute to the guardianship of the Panama Canal as well as furnish an extra naval base in the Caribbean. Considered from a military standpoint, then, the price paid may be insignificant. Economically, on the other hand, there is little hope that the people on the islands can ever maintain a normal American standard of living with their own efforts and own resources. Unquestionably the islands can never be made to pay dividends on the investment. In the long run, even the costs of administration will always be greater than the revenues available.

THE PANAMA CANAL ZONE

By W. O. BLANCHARD

STRAITS AND ISTHMUSES HAVE ALWAYS been of peculiar interest because of their influences on transportation. Thus, straits, if on important routes, serve to focus water traffic and to facilitate intercourse between oceans or seas. Likewise, isthmuses, the land counterparts of straits, seemingly ought to function as connecting links for the regions joined; but, as a matter of fact, they seldom do. Isthmuses are important commercially not as facilitators of land communication but chiefly as barriers to ocean shipping.

The Isthmus of Panama is an excellent illustration of the general principle cited above. Physiographically it was the tie that bound together the two Americas; commercially its significance lay in the fact that it separated two oceans and hence was an obstacle to ocean trade. In the four hundred years since Balboa first crossed it, it has never functioned as an important link in land routes but always as a barrier to ocean commerce. Only since it was cut and transformed into a strait has it become a great focus of transportation routes.

The Panama Canal Zone, as a political unit, was organized for administering control over the canal, and for all practical purposes it is a territory of the United States. Technically, however, the relation of the Canal Zone to the United States is different from that of other noncontiguous areas. It is not, strictly speaking, a territorial possession of the United States but was formed and is now being controlled by reason of authority granted by the Republic of Panama, an independent country in Central America, in a treaty dated 1903. According to this agreement, three rights were granted to the United States in perpetuity: (1) to use, occupy, and control a Canal Zone, 10 miles wide, and to have sovereignty over it; (2) to take any additional lands and waters outside of the original Canal Zone which may be convenient and necessary for the construction, maintenance, operation, sanitation, and protection of the canal; and (3) to enforce sanitary ordinances and maintain order in the cities of Panama at the west end and Colon at the east end of the canal, in case the government of the republic should not be able to do so. In return for these grants the United States agreed to pay Panama the sum of $10,000,000 and, after nine years, an annual rental of $250,000. Added expense came in 1922, when the United States agreed to pay Colombia $25,000,000 in order "to remove all misunderstandings" regarding the acquisition of the Panama Canal Zone.

The Treaty of 1903 was revised in 1936, so that now the United States has renounced (1) the guaranty of Panama independence, (2) the right to intervene, and (3) the right to acquire land by eminent domain and is restricted in its right to expand the area of the Canal Zone. Also, the payments of rental to Panama are to be made in gold equivalent, and Panama is granted the right to connect by road the cities of Panama and Colon.

The boundaries of the Canal Zone are drawn approximately 5 miles from the center line of the canal, but in accord with the treaty clause the limits of the zone have been extended from time to time. The Canal Zone includes also such areas outside of the 5-mile limits as are covered by the waters of

Photo by U.S. Army Air Service

PANAMA CITY

The capital of Panama, Panama City, is at the western terminus of the canal, although outside the Canal Zone. The American counterpart is Balboa, which serves as headquarters for American officials. The canal is to the northwest.

Gatun and Madden lakes and the lands immediately adjacent to these lakes which lie below the 100-foot and 200-foot contours, respectively. Although the cities of Panama and Colon are included within the boundaries of the zone as defined by treaty, they have remained, nevertheless, a part of the Republic of Panama. The Canal Zone, however, exercises authority over all sanitation and health measures. The Canal Zone is really a government reservation established to facilitate the maintenance and operation of the canal. Land may not be privately owned but may be leased for approved purposes.

Panama city, the capital, originally a fishing village, which received its name from an Indian word meaning "plenty of fish," is located on hillslopes overlooking the Pacific Ocean. Its population of approximately 75,000 is about one-sixth of that of the whole republic. It is a modern city, dominated by handsome government buildings. Adjoining it is Balboa, an American city which serves as the headquarters of American officials. Colon, named for Christopher Columbus, who always signed his name "Cristobal Colon," is the second largest city of the republic and lies on the Atlantic coast. What is now a modern city of about 30,000 people was a low, swampy, fever-infested island only a few decades ago. Across the street in the Canal Zone is Cristobal, an American city.

At the present the zone comprises 361.86 square miles of land and 190.94 square miles of water, or 552.8 square miles altogether. The population, excluding the personnel of the army and navy, is approximately 52,000, of which normally about 30 per cent are Americans. Of the total population, the canal and the railway employ about 7,500 people. Approximately 700 Americans and 5,000 alien employees are living in the Republic of Panama outside of the Canal Zone.

HISTORIC BACKGROUND

The history of isthmian transit trade divides itself into three periods, according to carrier used: (1) the pack mule, (2) the railroad, and (3) the canal.

For more than three hundred years transisthmian traffic depended upon the pack mule; precious metals formed the principal cargo, and a mule path through the jungle was the highway. At its best the trail was bad, even for a mule; and during the rainy season it was practically impassable in any form. After 1534 the Rio Chagres was improved sufficiently to allow light draft barges to ascend to Cruces and thus supplement the Atlantic portion of the overland route. The terminal ports of the isthmian trail were squalid tropic villages wedged between the sea and the jungle. Porto Bello, especially, with its heavy rainfall and malarial, swampy, Atlantic coast was shunned by all Europeans except for the brief interval when the annual fair was in progress. Old Panama, now in ruins, enjoyed a somewhat better climate and became the entrepôt for the whole Pacific coast. Both villages were commercial communities pure and simple. Their sole *raison d'être* was the transit trade, and they flourished and declined with the ebb and flow of commerce through their gates.

Bad as it was, the isthmian route was preferable in the early days to the long, stormy journey through the Straits. Although steamers now make the passage of the Straits of Magellan in 48 hours, Magellan required 28 days to navigate the narrow water constriction which today bears his name. When the flow of precious metals declined, isthmian shipping languished and by 1750 was of little importance. Meanwhile improvements in ship construction and the increase in knowledge of the southern route led to considerable traffic via the Horn.

Photo by U.S. Army Air Service

THE PANAMA TRAIL IN 1914—THE OLD LAS CRUCES

For more than three hundred years transisthmian traffic followed this trail. The treasures of the Incas crossed here. Not all parts of the trail were this well paved.

In the early sixteenth century Magellan's largest boat was of 150 tons; in 1789 there were thirty-two ships at Callao, Peru, one of 1,800 tons and the smallest of 123 tons. Moreover, by this time most sailing vessels were rounding the Horn rather than following the intricate passage through the straits. For the century from 1750 to 1850 the Cape Horn route was the one most used.

To the builders of the Panama Railway the chief hope for returns lay in the United States intercoastal trade. South American and other commerce was regarded as secondary. This opinion was justified by the fact that during the last twenty years of the railroad period, that portion shipped to or from western South America never amounted to half of the total isthmian traffic. In 1912, after almost half a century of operation, the railroad's total tonnage was equal to but 3 per cent of the trade of Chile alone for that year. It is evident that the supremacy of the southern route in the trade of western South America during the railroad era was never seriously threatened.

The failure of the railroad to divert this trade was due to a series of factors, partly geographic, partly human. Because the trade of western South America was primarily with Europe rather than with the United States, the saving in distance via Panama was not important. The railroad enjoyed a monopoly of the transit trade and used its privilege also to exact high rates for passengers and freight. For example, the following rates are included in its published tariff for the transit of 50.72 miles from deep water to deep water: passenger, $25.00; excess baggage over 50 pounds, 5 cents per pound; coal, $5.00 per long ton; cattle, $5.00–$7.00 each; copper or tin ores in bags, $\frac{3}{8}$ cent per pound; lumber, $10.00–$15.00 per 1,000 board feet; gold, 0.25 per cent, and silver, 0.5 per cent, of its value. Railroad service was usually the basis for much complaint, for in addition to excessive charges there were costly delays, damages to goods, poor connections with boats, frequent theft of goods, and inadequate facilities generally.

Freights via Panama were adjusted to meet the competition of the southern route. In 1905, the cost of shipping 100 pounds of general merchandise from New York to Buenaventura, Colombia, was 75 cents; to Valparaiso, 3,000 miles farther south, only 50 cents. In spite of its efforts, the railroad did little business with western South America except with the extreme northern section; south of Callao, Peru, it was negligible. All the great bulky cargoes making up the major part of the exports of the west coast went via the Horn. In 1884 Chile exported 550,000 tons of nitrate; in 1905, 1,603,140 tons. These tonnages were from twenty-six to thirty times, respectively, the total west-to-east traffic via Panama for the same years.

Turned over to the United States with the French Panama Canal Concession in 1904, the railroad was described as being in a bad state of repair. Little had been done to increase its business or to improve the property. Nevertheless, it was said to be carrying in 1914 more cargo per mile of track than any railroad in the world, and it certainly ranked among the most profitable two or three railroads of its day. It is said to have earned $2,000,000 before completed. From 1853 to 1861 its dividend averaged 16 per cent; from 1881 to 1905 it was almost 5 per cent. In 1868 a single dividend of 44 per cent was paid entirely from earnings. However, with the opening of the canal to commerce in August, 1914, the railroad ceased handling through commercial freight.

Interest in an isthmian canal had been manifested at various times by the different nations of western Europe during even the earliest Spanish colonial times. The Panama site figured prominently in most of the plans. The United States became interested as a result of the addition of Pacific territory after the Mexican War (1848) and the California gold rush a little later. The delay caused during the Spanish-American War by sending the battleship "Oregon" around South America did much to focus attention on the immediate need of a waterway.

The first serious attempt to cut a canal was made by a French company in 1882 under the leadership of F. de Lesseps, builder of the tidewater Suez Canal. Extravagance and corruption, the ravages of tropical fevers, the troublesome floods of the Chagres River, and the inability to realize the magnitude of the task foredoomed the venture to failure. Finally, in 1902 the United States purchased the concession and equipment for $40,000,000. A proposed treaty was rejected by Colombia, but it was subsequently ratified by Panama, which had in the meantime gained its independence. American occupation of the Canal Zone began in 1904, and the canal was opened to shipping August 15, 1914, just at the outbreak of the World War.

THE CANAL

Ever since Balboa in 1513 found that only 40 miles of mountainous terrain prevented ships from sailing from the Atlantic to the Pacific, the commercial world had hoped for a removal of that barrier. Four hundred years were to pass, however, before that dream was to come true, and in the meantime many changes occurred which intensified the need for such a waterway.

The canal, of course, was to provide a short cut between the world's two largest oceans. The intensity of the demand for the undertaking, as well as the particular peoples who would be chiefly benefited, varied much through the four centuries. In the sixteenth century the medieval traders of Europe wanted a better route to the rich Indies. The only available routes were overland across Asia, to the east around Africa, or to the west around South America. The land route was obstructed by the Turks; the other routes were long and perilous. By the nineteenth century, commerce of the world had grown to such proportions as to warrant any reasonable expenditure for the shortening of trade routes. The building of the Suez Canal and the completion of the American transcontinental railway, both in 1869, were an added impetus for a trans-isthmian water connection.

For the United States the need for the waterway became ever more pressing. The expansion of her territory until it reached the Pacific and, later, the acquisition of outlying possessions in it made access to that ocean imperative. For her the Suez route was too long; the transcontinental land routes exacted too high freight rates. Furthermore, the growing realization that the Pacific was not merely a highway to the Indies but had much to offer on its own account served to emphasize the demand. Finally, the United States undertook the task of creating a waterway. The chief objective, it is to be remembered, was to facilitate the intercoastal movement of our own merchant and naval vessels.

At Panama nature left a narrow and relatively low part in the great cordillera extending from Alaska to the Straits of Magellan. In the geologic past the isthmus was a strait, but a crustal movement raised the sea bottom and joined the continents. Long ages of erosion on both slopes have left the isthmus as we find it today. The lowest pass across the divide is 276 feet above mean sea-level; however, the canal actually was cut half a mile east of this point, where the elevation is 312 feet.

Even those who pass through the canal can scarcely appreciate the magnitude of the task. Among man's undertakings which have altered the earth's surface, only the Chinese wall exceeds it in size. Figures expressing the volume of materials excavated, based on the dimensions of its huge locks, are so large as to be all but meaningless to the average person. Approximately enough rock and earth were removed, however, to build a hundred pyramids the size of Cheops. The same amount of excavation would have been sufficient for a canal from Washington to New York, a waterway 228 miles long, 124 feet wide, and 45 feet deep. The cost, exclusive of the fortifications, was approximately $362,000,000.

The canal is of the lock-lake type and connects the Caribbean Sea and the Gulf of Panama. On the Atlantic slope it follows the former valley of the Chagres River, and on the Pacific slope that of the Rio Grande. Dams were built across these valleys, forming lakes upon which ships cross the former divide. The connection between the headwaters of the two valleys was made by an excavation now known as Gaillard Cut and filled by an arm of Gatun Lake. This lake is normally 85 feet above sea-level. Its bottom was excavated to a level 40 feet above sea-level; so the water depth of the lake is about 45 feet. The length of the channel across the lake is about 23 miles, and the cut is about 8 miles long.

Locks are used to raise and lower vessels the 85 feet between sea-level and the surface of Gatun Lake. On the Atlantic side

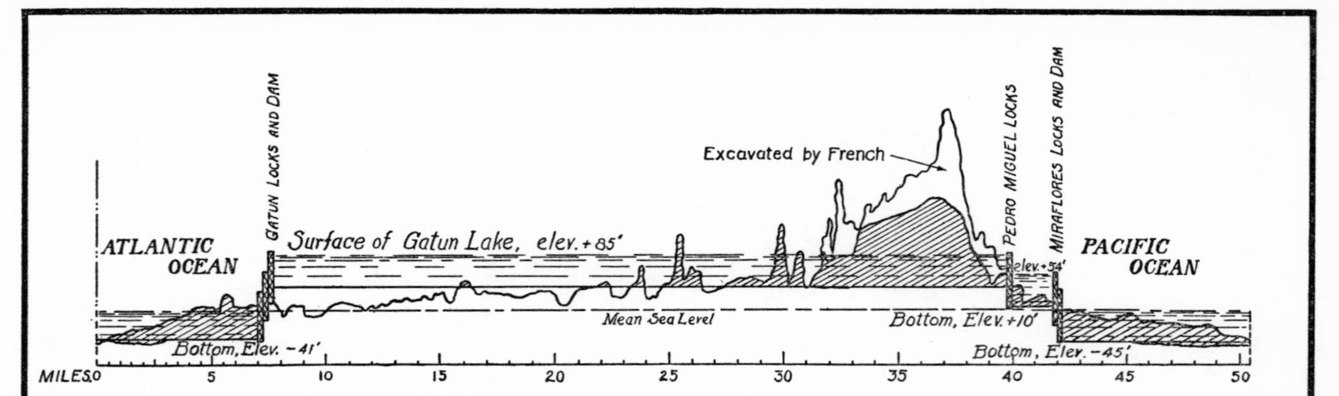

A CROSS-SECTION OF THE PANAMA CANAL ZONE SHOWING VARIOUS ELEVATIONS AND THE PART EXCAVATED BY THE FRENCH

The enormous tonnage passed through the locks places the canal as one of the leading trade routes of the world

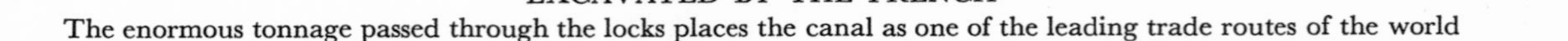

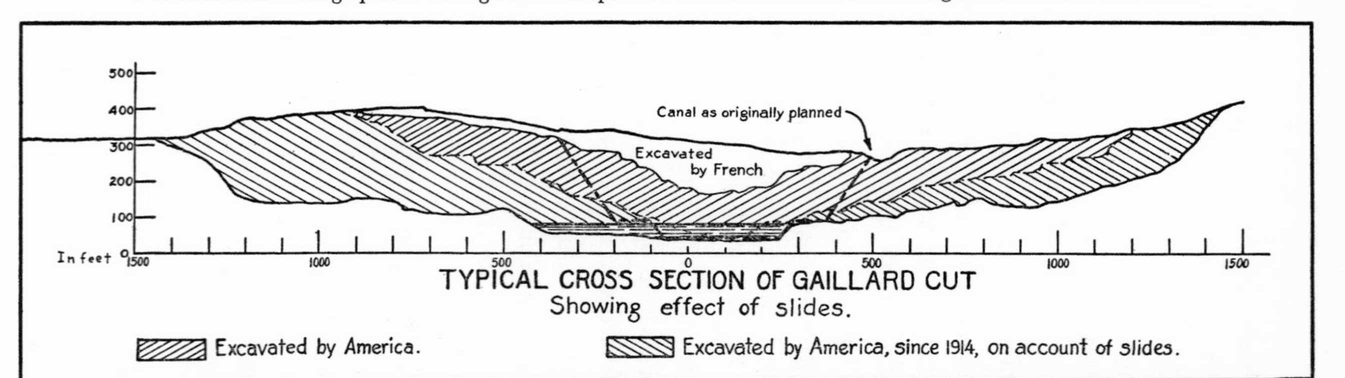

TYPICAL CROSS-SECTION OF GAILLARD CUT SHOWING ALSO MATERIAL MOVED TO CONTROL THE SLIDES

The extra weight had to be removed to keep the bottom of the canal from bowing up, a contingency not thought of when first planned

there are three pairs of steps, or chambers, known as the Gatun Locks. On the Pacific side there are also three pairs of locks. One, Pedro Miguel Lock, is at the Pacific end of Gaillard Cut; two, the Miraflores locks, are about a mile nearer the Pacific. Between Pedro Miguel Lock and Miraflores locks is Miraflores Lake, whose level is normally about 54 feet above sea-level. At each end of the canal, before the locks are reached, is a section at sea-level $6\frac{1}{2}$ miles long at the Atlantic end and 8 miles long at the Pacific end. From deep water to deep water the canal is 50.72 miles long, and it has a minimum width of 300 feet at the bottom of the channels. The lock chambers are 110 feet wide and have a usable length of 1,000 feet. In the sea-level sections the minimum depth is 42 feet.

On the basis of 7,500 net tons per lockage the present capacity of the canal is estimated at from 70,000,000 to 75,000,000 Panama Canal net tons annually. This is nearly three times the tonnage actually using the canal. For strategic reasons, construction of an additional set of locks at a cost of $277,000,000 was authorized by Congress in 1939. The new locks will have a length of 1,200 feet, a width of 135 feet, and a navigable depth of 45 feet. The work will require about six years for completion and will enable the waterway to handle about five times the present traffic. Likewise, the passageway can always be turned into a sea-level canal if that seems desirable. In general, it may be said that the facilities are now ample except that certain navy vessels, like airplane-carriers, are built within the measurements of present locks. According to the engineers in charge, it would even be feasible to fill the locks by pumping water from the sea if the normal fresh-water supply proved insufficient.

Low latitude is a major control in the climate of the Canal

Zone. Although temperatures rarely rise above 90° F., they seldom fall below 70°; they average about 80°, and the seasonal range is almost negligible. Variations are somewhat greater in the interior; but the nearness to the Equator, the close proximity to the ocean, and the humidity prevent any marked fluctuations. The annual temperature range, i.e., the difference between the means of the hottest and coldest months, is only 1° F. in the neighborhood of the city of Panama. Because the relative humidity is high, averaging from 75 to 85, sensible temperatures are moderately high. The maximum temperature recorded in the Canal Zone is 98°, at Madden Dam.

The rainfall is heavy; but, unlike the temperature, it shows marked contrasts, both regional and seasonal. The annual rainfall at the Pacific end of the canal is about 70 inches; at the opposite end it is almost twice as much. Most of the Atlantic slope receives more than 100 inches of rain every year. There are also marked wet and dry seasons. The dry season lasts about four months, from December to April, and on the Pacific slope it is a truly dry season. On the Atlantic side it is dry only by comparison with the rest of the year.

The explanation of the regional and seasonal variation in rainfall is to be found in the fact that the isthmus is mountainous and that it is alternately in the northeast trades and in the doldrums. The northeast trades blow steadily from January to April. Since the Pacific slope is on the lee side, it is dry during this period, whereas the Atlantic slope receives some rain, especially on the upper mountain slopes. During the other eight months of the year convectional rains of doldrum origin bring precipitation to both slopes. The ill effects to man which might be expected to result from the combina-

Photo by U.S. Army Air Service

THE AIRPLANE-CARRIER "SARATOGA" PASSING THROUGH GAILLARD CUT

Already these carriers have reached their maximum width in order to pass safely through the locks.

tion of high temperature and humidity which exists more or less continuously throughout the year are in part mitigated by a high proportion of cloudiness. During the dry season daytime cloudiness averages about 50 per cent, and during the wet season 75 per cent. This natural shield is an effective protection against excessive insolation.

Fortunately, the Canal Zone is not in the path followed by tropical hurricanes. Winds are usually not high enough to have any ill effects. Indirect damage occasionally results from high seas on unprotected coasts and from floods.

In the long struggle to overcome the isthmian barrier, the chief obstacle was the climate. The Canal Zone is situated within the tropics, and the direct physiological effects of heat and moisture have made labor less effective; but the indirect effects resulting from the jungle vegetation, with its pests and diseases, have been even more of a problem. The influence of the climate has always been paramount. The use of pack mule and trail in early times, the seasonal ebb and flow of goods across the isthmus, corresponding to the rainy and dry seasons, the herculean task of building a railroad through the tropic jungle, the choice of the lock type of canal, and the tremendous task of keeping an army of workmen healthy and active for the construction and operation of the waterway were all largely conditioned by the climate. Climate was largely responsible for the failure of the French Canal Company, and it was not until medical research had furnished added weapons that the United States was successful in joining the oceans. It should be noted that, although the humidity and heavy rainfall have been adverse factors in the maintenance of healthful conditions, the present lock-type canal is dependent on a sufficient supply of water from rainfall.

The record of the American sanitary officials is most striking when compared with the experience of the French. Although there are no official records of the number of sick during French occupancy, 1881–89, it has been estimated at about one-third of the entire working force. During the decade of American construction the corresponding rate was 23 per 1,000 per day, with a total force of about 39,000 men, and the death rate was 17 per 1,000, as compared with the French rate of 200 per 1,000. Malaria was rampant in 1906, and 821 out of every 1,000 were admitted to hospitals suffering from it. By 1913 this rate had been reduced to 76; in 1916, to 34; and in 1918 it was 20 per 1,000. Malaria still is the most important cause of the ineffectiveness of labor in the region.

Although much has been done, present conditions are by no means ideal. It is rather surprising to find that tuberculosis is the leading cause of death in the Canal Zone. It affects more of the colored alien population than white Americans. The death rate from all causes in 1918–19 was 20.44 per 1,000; in the United States the corresponding figure was about 16 per 1,000. Malaria has been brought under control; and, in general, it can be said that yellow fever has been eliminated, the last case on the Isthmus being reported in 1905. The work and expense for this accomplishment has been large, and the present status can be maintained only by ceaseless care and watchfulness. The sanitary record is one to which the whole medical world points as an example of what may be done in a tropical area. From a pestilential swamp in which men died like flies from yellow fever and malaria, the Canal Zone was converted into an area in which the death rate was actually reduced below that of some of our large American cities.

Heavy rainfall and high temperature have their natural

consequence in a rich forest cover over much of the isthmus. The Atlantic slope, however, with more abundant rainfall, better distributed throughout the year, has the typical rain-forest of broad-leaved evergreens. The Pacific slope, with less precipitation and a pronounced dry season, has more of a savanna-forest type. As is characteristic of tropical forests, the vegetation of the Canal Zone is extremely varied in composition.

The tidal range at the Atlantic end of the canal is almost negligible; its average is less than a foot, and its maximum is less than 3 feet. As a rule, there is but one high and one low tide per day. At the Pacific entrance there are two high and two low tides daily. The average range here is 12.6 feet; the greatest range recorded for successive tides is 21.6 feet.

An adequate water supply is of paramount importance and is a serious problem. This is especially true for the operation of the lock type of canal, which involves the use of an enormous quantity of water. It is estimated that the average amount of water required for the passage of a single vessel through the canal is about 6,500,000 cubic feet. Water is also needed for hydroelectric power and for the use of the people living within the Canal Zone. The supply is provided by a huge dam across the Chagres River, forming a great reservoir, Gatun Lake, between the dam and the Continental Divide. With the exception of Lake Mead, above Boulder Dam, it is the largest artificial lake in the world, covering about 165 square miles. The creation of this immense reservoir has served to control the floods of the Chagres as well as to furnish water and power.

Provision for increased water consumption was made by building the Madden Dam, completed in 1935, across the river

12 miles above Lake Gatun. It probably will not be needed until the third set of locks is put in but will serve in the meantime for power and added insurance in case of a long dry season. The new lake covers approximately 22 square miles and will increase the water storage for use in lockage about 60 per cent. Added safeguards for a greater water need have been planned by a more economical use of water in lockages and by the availability of steam plants for power use in case of water shortage. A test in March, 1926, showed that the water lockage could be cut to 4,300,000 cubic feet per average vessel. The capacity of the canal is dependent not only upon the speed at which ships can be passed through the locks but more specifically upon the water supply. The present locks are capable of handling forty-eight complete lockages in a day of 24 hours, except during the biennial overhaul period of 90 days, when the capacity is twenty-seven lockages per day.

Silting, slides, and plant growth have been the chief hindrances in the maintenance of the channel. When Gaillard Cut was excavated, the slopes were made approximately uniform. It was anticipated that there might be some sliding or slumping in places, but the engineers felt that it would be easier to dredge the material out after the water was turned in. However, the sliding-down of loosened earth proved to be of minor importance in comparison with other movements not counted on. The removal of such a great mass of material and the exposure of so much fresh rock to air and water for the first time created such great pressure and chemical changes that the equilibrium of the whole region had to adjust itself anew. The sides of the cut at the bottom literally moved inward, and the bottom of the canal moved upward. As a result, these so-called "slides" blocked the channel several times in the early days as more fresh rock became exposed with each dredging operation, and the job of removing the material without causing greater disturbances became a major undertaking. However, with the continued removal of the slides by dredging and with the reduction of the angle of repose above the water the trouble gradually disappeared. Only 2.5 per cent of the entire canal, or 10 per cent of Gaillard Cut, has been affected thus far by these movements.

The primary purpose of the canal is the transfer of ships across the isthmus with safety and dispatch. All the other multifarious activities are subordinate to this one task, and ships go on schedule. Those ready at either entrance may begin at 6:00 A.M., and others follow at half-hour intervals. Those arriving late in the day are held over; or, under certain circumstances, they may make part of the transit and then tie up until the next morning. The traffic does not yet justify night dispatching.

Passage from the Atlantic end begins with raising the boat 85 feet by means of the three Gatun locks. Movement through the locks is under the control of small locomotives. The boat continues under its own power through Gatun Lake, whose channel of 24 miles is marked by lights and buoys, and then passes through Gaillard Cut, a distance of about 8 miles. At the Pacific end the Pedro Miguel Lock lowers the ship to Miraflores Lake, whose elevation is 54 feet. A mile run through the lake brings the boat to Miraflores locks, which lower it to sea-level. The time of transit averages about 8 hours.

Much controversy has centered around Panama tolls. These are not levied on the nature of the cargo carried but on the earning capacity of the ship. The rate is based on the "Panama Canal Measurement," which compiles the net tonnage on the basis of actual earning capacity of 100 cubic feet of interior space per ton. Some commodities need more space and others less, and therefore pay more or less. Commercial

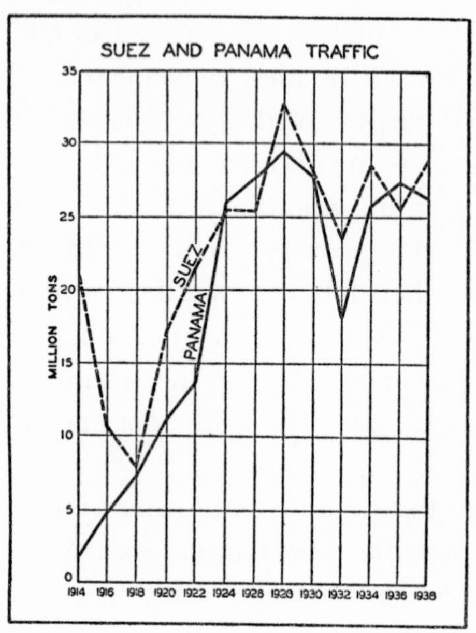

A COMPARISON OF SUEZ AND PANAMA TRAFFIC FROM 1914 TO 1938 IN MILLIONS OF TONS

vessels of all countries pay tolls on the same basis. Since March 1, 1938, a rate of 90 cents per ton on laden vessels and 72 cents per ton on ballast vessels has been in effect. The lowest rate per ton weight is levied on heavy commodities like iron ore. For a vessel carrying iron ore the charge has been as low as 20.67 cents per ton. The average on laden vessels for 1937 was 72 cents per ton.

The Suez system of toll measurement results in a higher levy than at Panama, being approximately 75 cents per cargo ton. An extreme illustration of the difference in tonnage measurement and charges is given in the record of transit of the "Empress of Britain" on her world-cruise, using both the Suez and Panama canals. Suez charges totaled $29,443 plus a charge for each passenger; Panama charges were $18,943, or $10,500 less. Since Suez tolls are collected in gold, or its equivalent, the difference now is even larger than would appear from these figures.

The actual savings effected for ships depends, of course, upon many factors, such as charter rates, the reduction in distance for the particular voyage, as well as the character of the cargo, and the plan of the vessel which may affect the measurement of its tonnage. That the savings may amount to a considerable item is illustrated by a simple case. If the charter rate is assumed to be 10 cents per day per net registered ton, the daily operating cost for a 10,000-ton vessel would be $1,000. An average daily speed for a freighter may be taken as 250 knots. If the vessel were running on the most used route, say from New York to San Francisco, there would be a saving of 32 days in the passage via the canal in preference to the southern route, or $32,000. Tolls at 90 cents per ton would cost $9,000; so there would be a net saving of $23,000.

Although the main business of the canal is to put ships across the isthmus, the policy has always been to make the Canal Zone a service station as well, and therefore only about one-fifth of the total working force is actually engaged in handling the ships, operating and maintaining the waterway, and preserving a clear channel. The various auxiliary activities include repair facilities, bunker stations, sale of food, ships chandlery, miscellaneous supplies, maintenance of hotels, and operation of the Panama Railroad. These facilities and services attract shipping and consequently increase the use of the canal. Other important functions of the government include public health, quarantine, immigration service, customs, post office, schools, police and fire protection, construction of roads, maintenance of water and sewage service, and numerous other activities.

The twenty-five years of canal operation have been characterized by very abnormal conditions in the world of industry and trade. The slides in the canal, the World War, the post-war boom, and the world-wide depression which followed have all operated to disorganize shipping, and their influences have been naturally reflected in the canal's activities. In spite of these abnormal circumstances, however, the waterway has made an impressive record in its service to ocean shipping. Up to June 30, 1937, the total number of transits of ocean-going commercial vessels of over 300 net tons was 92,990; the net tonnage, 450,000,000; the cargo carried, 440,000,000 tons; and the tolls collected, over $406,000,000. During the three-year period ending in 1937, the canal passed 80,000,000 long tons of cargo and collected approximately $70,000,000 in tolls. Not only has the waterway served commercial vessels, but it has also been extensively used by vessels belonging to the governments of the United States, Colombia, and Panama, as well as by vessels transiting solely for repairs. Such annual toll-free passages number about 500, and almost all of the vessels are a part of the American military and naval forces.

Because of the marked difference in the stage of economic development between the Atlantic and Pacific regions, there has always been a marked difference in the character and amount of commodities moving in the two directions through the canal. In general, the Pacific countries contribute bulky products, like lumber, wheat, petroleum, preserved fruits, and fish from North America; nitrates and iron ores from South America; wool from Australia. Silk and tea from the Orient constitute an exception to the general rule, since they are very compact and of high value. The commodities of Atlantic countries, on the other hand, are, in general, manufactured or semimanufactured goods of small bulk and large value. Iron and steel wares have long been the leading items. As a result of this difference, there has been an unfortunate lack of balance in cargo movement. For the whole period during which the canal has functioned, the ratio of the eastbound to the westbound tonnage has been about two to one. This fact places a heavy burden upon shipments westward and, conversely, makes for low freight rates on eastbound vessels. As a result, Europe has become a keen competitor of eastern United States in supplying manufactures to Pacific America. Even such bulky cheap commodities as cement and sand have been carried from Europe to western United States.

A tabulation by nationality of the vessels transiting the canal shows that either British or American ships have led every year thus far. From 1915 to 1918 British ships led; in the next sixteen years American vessels occupied first place. In 1934 the ratio of American transits to British was more than two to one. Based on cargo tonnage, the ratio is about the same. In a recent three-year period there were vessels of thirty-four nationalities; the United States led, with 37 per cent, and Great Britain was next, with 24 per cent. The preponderance of American vessels is to be expected in view of the fact that intercoastal trade is limited by law to American vessels. Great Britain's high rank is due to her pre-eminent position in ocean shipping, as well as to her interest in New Zealand, Australia, and western Canada.

The average character of ocean-going commercial vessels above 300 net tons is a boat of approximately 5,500 net tons. It pays about $4,600 in tolls and carries 4,700 tons of cargo. If only laden boats are counted, the average cargo tonnage would be about 5,600 tons.

With respect to motive power the canal records show a constantly increasing proportion of motorships, as compared with the number of steamers. During a recent year, however, nearly two-thirds of the ocean-going commercial vessels transiting the canal were steamers, and only about one-third were motorships. Of the steamers, about two-thirds burned oil and one-third coal. Since 1934 there has been a distinct tendency away from oil to coal as a motive power.

Aside from the vessels carrying general cargo, tankers have played an important role. These specialized carriers became significant in 1923, when 913 transits were recorded. The peak movement occurred the next year, with 1,704 passages. The number gradually but consistently declined, to only 562 in 1938. In this same period the proportional tonnage carried by the tankers dropped from 39.1 per cent to 11.5 per cent.

An analysis of the records of shipping through the canal for twenty years of its operation shows that the great bulk of the traffic is concentrated into a very few definite routes. As might be expected, the intercoastal routes and the routes along which goods are being sent to or from the United States are the most important. In the movement through the canal from the Atlantic to the Pacific the United States intercoastal route accounts for 33.5 per cent; that from eastern United States to the Far East, for about 21.3 per cent. The two make up more than half of the total traffic in this direction. In the opposite direction, from the Pacific to the Atlantic, the intercoastal traffic of the United States again leads, with 35.6 per cent; from western United States to Europe, 15 per cent; and from western South America to eastern United States, 13.6 per cent. These three routes play the major role and together account for about two-thirds of the total traffic in this direction.

Since the canal joins the Atlantic and Pacific, its main service should naturally be to the lands bordering these oceans. In general it is, but there are notable exceptions. The Atlantic coasts of both South America and Africa have their complementary trade areas in the North Atlantic; consequently, the canal is of little importance to them. The interests of the Far East and Australia likewise are limited, for their trade with Europe goes via Suez or the Cape of Good Hope.

Among individual countries affected by the canal, the United States occupies a unique position. American domestic commerce at present accounts for more than a third of the total canal activity. American foreign commerce can be charged with about two-fifths. Only about one-fourth of the canal traffic remains, and this moves between countries other than the United States. Next to the United States in importance among regions using the canal is Europe, especially in its trade with the Pacific coasts of both the Americas. In the eastbound traffic, that from western United States to Europe ranks next to our intercoastal movement, although it is, to be sure, a poor second. As already noted, the routes from Europe to the two Americas suffer severely from a lack of balance on the two legs of the journey.

Although the canal brought the two coasts of the United States nearer together, at the same time it also placed midwestern industry in a disadvantageous situation with respect to the rest of the country and the world's market as a whole. The Kansas City Chamber of Commerce reports:

> The result of low water-rates from the Atlantic and Gulf coasts give those sections a tremendous advantage we cannot overcome and our Pacific market is largely lost. Prior to the Canal, a large soap plant here served the Pacific Coast trade, but since has found it necessary to open a branch factory in California.

Even as far west as Denver the results are the same, according to the Denver Chamber of Commerce: "At Minnequa is the largest iron and steel manufacturing plant west of Chicago. Formerly this plant marketed approximately three-fourths of its products in the Pacific States. Today this volume has dropped to about one-quarter." Omaha reports that "the Canal route has greatly favored the manufacturers and producers of the East and West coasts, with a corresponding penalty to our producers and manufacturers. Transportation costs by the Canal in many cases are less than half the rail charges enforced by the I.C.C." What is true of these cities is also true of others in the Middle West.

The change since 1914, the year of the opening of the Panama Canal, in the cost of moving a ton of staples via the cheapest route is evident from the following facts: New York, which was 1,904 cents from San Francisco, is now 1,280 cents away; Chicago, which was 2,610 cents from San Francisco, is now 2,946 cents away. Thus, Chicago has moved away by 336 cents, and New York has moved nearer by 624 cents. Furthermore, Chicago has moved 494 cents away from the

Atlantic seaboard and from South America. The change has not been entirely to the advantage of the Pacific Coast. Some of the transshipment business between eastern United States and the Far East that used to go by rail to the Pacific ports now goes direct by the all-water route. Raw silk formerly moved from the Far East to Seattle or San Francisco; now most of it goes to the Atlantic seaboard direct, via the Panama Canal. Spokane, with its inland position, seems to have benefited. "The Panama Canal has not been an injury to the Inland Empire. On the contrary, it has been an asset by lowering freight rates. The Canal has been an important factor in the development of the West and we are a part of the West. We recognize the Panama Canal as a great national asset."

By inaugurating the cheap all-water service between the Atlantic and Pacific coasts of the Americas, the opening of the canal could not help but exert a profound influence upon the transcontinental routes already established. Competition was especially keen with those routes nearest the canal, e.g., the Tehauntepec Railway of Mexico and the Panama Railroad across the isthmus. The Mexican road, which in 1913 carried more than 1,000,000 tons, was in 1915 moving only about 150,000 tons. Traffic on the Panama Railroad declined more gradually, since it was operated as an adjunct of the canal.

The effect on the railroads of the United States of the opening of the new water route was also far reaching. In 1911 it was estimated that these railroads carried between 5,000,000 and 6,000,000 tons between the borders of the Atlantic and Pacific. That portion going via the southern route or via the Panama or Tehauntepec railways was less than 1,000,000 tons. By way of contrast, in the canal's best year, 1929, our intercoastal trade via the canal was about twice the combined rail and water movement of 1911. Essentially all of the water and probably half of the rail intercoastal movement of 1911 was diverted to the new waterway. The loss was a staggering one for the railroads—a blow from which they have not yet fully recovered.

About one-half of the canal's intercoastal business is new, developed because the low rates attracted tonnage that never would have moved without this improvement. Economical transportation was, of course, available only to the immediate hinterlands of the two coasts, within about 200 or 300 miles of tidewater. The average savings on our intercoastal traffic have been estimated at about $10 per ton. In addition, the transportation charges on overland rail routes have been forced down by the potential lower rates of the alternative route, and the result was additional savings to the shippers still using the railroads. It seems altogether possible that the total cost of the canal could be justified on the basis of the average savings in our coast-to-coast traffic alone.

One of the major objects in constructing the canal was to facilitate the movement of our military and naval forces from ocean to ocean. It will be recalled that the voyage of the battleship "Oregon" around South America to join the Atlantic fleet during the Spanish-American War was a powerful factor in arousing American public opinion to the necessity of cutting the canal. In recognition of this military value, the Panama Canal Zone was made a military reservation. The Washington office of the Canal Zone is under the Secretary of War, and the governor reports to that cabinet official. Most of the governors have been chosen from the army, and the canal fortifications have been regarded as a part of our coast defenses. Army posts have been established, and normally a military population of about 8,000 men is quartered there. Both canal entrances are fortified; and flying fields, air-service hangars, and wireless stations have been constructed.

The canal was opened within a few months of the outbreak of the World War. Although it was not found necessary to move the fleet through the waterway during the war, the canal was an important factor in the successful prosecution of the cause of the Allies. Huge quantities of supplies from the Pacific were sent through it. Included in these cargoes were about 3,500,000 tons of Chilean nitrate for explosives. Allied vessels, both merchant and naval, found at the Canal Zone supplies of foodstuffs and fuel, as well as repair facilities, hospitals, and other services. Since the war, our fleet has on several occasions passed through the canal without serious delay or mishap, showing conclusively the value of the waterway as a military asset.

As an engineering accomplishment, the canal ranks among the foremost undertakings of man. In its operation it has profoundly affected world-shipping and quickened the commercial life of vast areas. The sanitary conquest represents one of the greatest triumphs of man over disease, resulting in a health record comparable to that of many American cities. The entire undertaking has been a piece of work of which every American may be justly proud.

The story of a great torrential river made over into a navigable waterway, of a great mountain ridge grooved and bridged by a great artificial lake, of a pesthole transformed into a healthful dwelling place, of all this being accomplished without the least suspicion of graft or corruption—such an accomplishment is one in which any nation may well take great pride. It may never pay in tolls the actual expenditure, but directly and indirectly it has been a most highly profitable investment. In addition, it has been an impressive example of what may be accomplished for peaceful intercourse among nations.

ALASKA

By OTIS W. FREEMAN

FEW AMERICANS HAVE MORE THAN A superficial conception of the real Alaska, and misconceptions about the territory are the rule. To the general reader Alaska suggests little more than a faraway northland of cold and snow, of furs, fish, and gold. The coastal tourists add impressions of totem poles, tidewater glaciers, and snow- and cloud-capped mountains rising abruptly out of the sea. The historically minded may also be able to recall some of the story of Vitus Bering and a century of Romanov control, "Seward's Folly," and the "days of '98." Rarely, however, is this huge territory viewed in its proper perspective. Rarely is Alaska thought of as a place for homes. Nevertheless, Dr. Alfred R. Brooks, the first director of the Alaska Section of the United States Geological Survey, after many years of experience in Alaska, could say truthfully: "Had the Pilgrim fathers settled in Sitka instead of at Plymouth, they would have found milder climate, better soil and timber, and more game, furs, and fish."

Although Alaska has the status of territory in the Union of States, it is far from being a well-integrated part of the Republic. The words "exclusive of Alaska" are only too common in our statistical literature and in general express the normal attitude of the American people. The hopes, the interests, and the problems of the people call forth relatively little understanding or sympathy from the nation as a whole.

Alaska is distinctly a land set apart, isolated from the United States. Located in the far northwest of the continent, its westernmost extent of the Aleutian Islands overlaps easternmost Asia by nearly a thousand miles. A similar arm extends to the southeast, falling short of reaching the state of Washington by a scant four hundred miles. In spite of this nearness to the United States and great extent into Asiatic waters, in spite of its great size (586,400 square miles), and in spite of its rich resources, Alaska is still little more than a name to many. It is, therefore, still a land for the pioneer and frontiersman. For the time being it may be likened to a garret in a well-regulated household, a place with treasures thought of only on special occasions.

Lack of interest may partly account for the small number of people who have made their homes in Alaska. In 1940 the territory had 72,524 people, a gain of 22.3 per cent over 1930, giving the territory the largest number of inhabitants recorded for any census year. The census of 1930 gives 48.3 per cent of the total population as being white; fully half are Eskimos and Indians. Were Alaska as densely populated as Nevada, our most sparsely populated state, it would have more than half a million people, or about eight times as many as it has now. The majority of people live in scattered settlements along the southern fringe, and the vast interior is still most sparsely populated, with little activity other than mining. This paucity of population seems strange, especially when compared with the greater density of population in the Scandinavian countries, which have similar latitudes and positions and are distinctly less favored in natural resources. Perhaps, when the riches of Alaska become appreciated, as Alaska enthusiasts will have it, it will support a larger number of people than are now found in the comparable region of northwestern Europe. The reason or reasons for the present apathy, however, cannot be simply stated, for many interrelated factors seem to be involved.

THE PHYSICAL FRAMEWORK

Both the relief features and the natural resources of Alaska have a geologic background. The history began hundreds of millions of years ago with the birth of a mountainous land in east-central Alaska. Through the ages following, erosion reduced this area to gently contoured mountains, hills, and rolling plains. Erosion also separated the present stream gold from these ancient gold-bearing rocks once deeply buried. The material eroded has again been deposited elsewhere in beds of limestone, shale, and sandstone, hundreds of thousands of feet thick, interbedded not uncommonly with numerous beds of coal. In addition, great masses of molten rock carrying gold, silver, copper, and other minerals have been intruded. Geologically, however, parts of Alaska are still so young that volcanoes are abundant. This is especially true in the southwestern part, where many volcanoes are still active.

The extreme youthfulness has made the coastline exceedingly unstable. During relatively recent geologic time, the entire Pacific coastal section of North America north from Puget Sound has sunk, relative to sea-level. This sinking has caused mountains corresponding to the coast ranges of the mainland states to become offshore islands, and the valleys behind them to be united in one great, quiet "inside" waterway more than 1,200 miles long, extending from Olympia, Washington, to Skagway, Alaska. Coastal plains are absent, and the mountains descend so abruptly into the sea that areas level enough for town sites or farms are rare. The narrow southeastern section from the Canadian line to Mount St. Elias is the Alaskan "Panhandle," with an extremely irregular and rocky coastline.

The mightiest mountain ranges in North America rise in Alaska and extend east-west in three great arcs. Mount St. Elias is the center of a mountain plexus, or huge center of uplift, from which the individual ranges diverge. Of the three successive mountain arcs which trend away to the west, the first includes the Chugach Mountains and the Kenai Mountains, which extend through the Kenai Peninsula seaward to form Afognak and the Kodiak Islands. The Chugachs include many peaks more than 10,000 feet high and several that tower above 12,000 and 13,000 feet. These mountains support very large glaciers, some of which reach tidewater, the best known being the vast Bering Glacier and the beautiful Columbia Glacier, near Valdez. This mountain range, as seen on a clear day, forms a most impressive sight, with its gigantic snowfields and glaciers and towering mountains extending for more than 200 miles along the coast.

Back of the coastal range is an extensive lowland, drained on the east by the Copper River and its tributaries. Next westward is the Matanuska Valley, after which the lowland is drowned to form Cook Inlet and Shelikof Strait, the latter separating Kodiak Island from the mainland.

The second mountain arc, with at least two peaks above 16,000 feet, starts with the high Wrangell Mountains, trending northwest from the St. Elias Range. West of an interruption in the mountain chain occupied by the southward flowing Copper River rise the Talkeetna Mountains, which extend north of Matanuska Valley to the Susitna River, the chief tributary of Cook Inlet. Beyond the Susitna the mountains curve southwestward to form a part of the Aleutian Range in the Alaska Peninsula. The lowland between the second and third mountain arcs is drained mainly by tributaries of the Susitna and Copper rivers, although the drainage of the Wrangell Mountains is northward into the Tanana River and finally to the Yukon River.

The third mountain arc begins near the Canadian border, with the Alaska Range again as the major mountain group. This massive chain is broken in only a few places and consequently forms an effective barrier. The eastern section is relatively low and is cut through by several branches of the Tanana River. The most important break is Broad Pass, utilized by the Alaska Railroad. In this section Mount Hayes (13,940 feet) is the highest peak, but in the more massive part to the west there are many high peaks. All of these, however, are overshadowed by Mount McKinley (20,300 feet), the highest point on the continent of North America and now set aside as McKinley National Park. Since this towering mountain stands above a relatively low region with an elevation of only about 1,000 feet, it probably presents one of the most massive aspects of any mountain in the world. The top is snow- and ice-covered, and great glaciers descend its slopes into the lowland, covering huge areas with ice. On a clear day this mountain is one of the most sublime spectacles on earth, rising higher above the observer at the base than does Mount Everest.

Southwestern Alaska, a continuation of the Alaska Range, is known for its many volcanic peaks, both extinct and active. Among these is Aniakchak, about 24 miles inland from the bay of the same name. Its large crater, nearly 7 miles in diameter and 30 square miles in area, one of the largest known, was discovered as late as 1922. Mount Iliamna, west of Cook Inlet, is one of a group reaching to a height of about 12,000 feet. Of the spectacular eruptions, that of Mount Katmai has been the subject of much scientific interest and study. Its eruption in 1912 was one of the most stupendous in historic time. The whole upper half of the mountain was blown away, and the scattered debris has been recognized 900 miles distant. During the three-day period of severest eruption, several cubic miles of material were blown away, leaving a great 8-mile crater containing a steaming lake. During the eruption a green, forested valley near by with only a few hot springs was transformed, by the red-hot ejecta and subsurface changes, into a lifeless waste from which rise many high columns of steam, charged with minerals. The region has been appropriately named the Valley of Ten Thousand Smokes and is now a national monument.

The Alaska Peninsula continues seaward in the Aleutian Islands that extend in a long, curving course for more than a thousand miles toward Siberia. The Alaska Peninsula and the Aleutian Islands in their long festoon to the southwest are all of recent volcanic origin, so young that little soil has formed. The scarcity of soil and the generally inhospitable climate preclude the growth of timber. Only brush and grasses on the lower slopes seem to survive the fierce gales which sweep this area of cloudiness and fog. The sea is most treacherous, and few natives will brave the difficult landings. Some islands have such steep, high, wave-cut cliffs that landing even under the most favorable conditions is practically prohibitive. This section of Alaska probably constitutes the most active volcanic region in the world. About sixty active volcanoes are specifically known, and new ones are still being discovered as more exploratory work is done. Volcanoes have even appeared only to disappear again below the sea, the best known of these being Bogoslof Island, near Unalaska.

The Brooks Range, or Arctic Highland, has a west-east extent across northern Alaska and ends at the Mackenzie Delta. These mountains are not well surveyed or even entirely mapped, but in general they consist of several ranges or mountain groups more or less connected. Thus, on the west the De Long Mountains rise to the north and the Baird Mountains to the south of the Noatak River, and the central part of the highlands is called the Endicott Mountains. Southward the range in places breaks abruptly to the Central Plateau and elsewhere grades gradually into a dissected plateau.

Northward from the Brooks Range and sloping to the Arctic Ocean is the Arctic Plain, only 10 miles wide at the Canadian line but 150 miles wide at Point Barrow. There is, for the most part, a clear separation between plain and mountains. The Arctic Plain is featureless, consisting of a flat tundra with small streams only slightly incised below the general level. Shallow ponds pit the tundra surface, and in places gravel mounds rise 40 or 50 feet and more to form the chief elevations on the plain. Ground ice lies just below the limit of annual thawing, and in its growth may split the tundra surface into irregular polygons, producing "niggerheads"—grassy hummocks 1 or 2 feet high. The Arctic coast is low, and offshore barrier reefs of sand and gravel inclose lagoons. The winters are long, and ice floes generally block the coast until the middle of July and occasionally line the coast even in August. The short summer brings thousands of eider and other ducks, geese, and other water fowl; but by the end of September the shallow ocean waters freeze over, the birds migrate, and another season of intense cold, semidarkness, and monotony shrouds the region. With the near approach of the continuous sun, the mating and nesting of wild life give evidence of another season.

Interior Alaska consists essentially of a vast plateau, known as the Yukon Plateau, drained by the Yukon River and its tributaries. From an elevation of 3,000 feet on the Canadian line it slopes westward to the sea and also descends from an elevation of approximately 4,000 feet on the north side of the Alaska Range to the river. It has a varied surface of flat-topped ridges, rolling hills, and extensive unglaciated plains. However, vast gravel bars and terraces that rise like giant stairs above the Yukon and other streams record the work done by the flood waters that came from melting glaciers once more extensive than any now existing in the mountains.

Seward Peninsula lies between Bering Sea and Norton Sound on the south and the Arctic Ocean and Kotzebue Sound on the north. At its western end, Cape Prince of Wales on the Bering Strait occupies the most westerly part of the mainland of North America and approaches East Cape, Siberia, to within 60 miles. Of irregular outline, Seward Peninsula is approximately 200 miles long from east to west and 150 miles from north to south. The coastline is low, with offshore beaches and lagoons a common feature on the Arctic coast, except where occasional ridges reach the sea and cause bold headlands. The vegetation is mostly tundra.

Seward Peninsula consists of an ancient and rugged land mass greatly reduced by erosion into gentle, rounded contours. A coastal plain, commonly a few miles wide, gradually rises from the sea to merge into the rolling hills at elevations of one or two thousand feet. The Kigluaik Mountains, an ancient land mass, contain numerous intrusives with which widely disseminated gold deposits are associated. The erosion of these gold-bearing rocks probably furnished much of the gold found in placers. The placer workings at Nome are in both recent and ancient beach gravels now far above the sea. In addition there is placer gold in present stream gravels, as well as in high terrace gravels associated with an ancient river system, of which little can be known at present. The beach sands and gravels in which gold was concentrated by the wave action of centuries have been the area of major activity.

CLIMATE

Climatically Alaska may be divided into two main sections, separated by the high Alaska Range, which extends in a great arc from the southeast, or Panhandle, through the Alaska Peninsula and dies out ultimately in the Aleutian Islands. This magnificent range, the highest in North America, lies athwart the general wind direction and becomes, therefore, a most effective barrier. The part south of this range, including the many offshore islands, has a distinctly marine climate with moderate temperature ranges and a heavy precipitation. The enormous masses of snow which fall in the higher regions throughout the year give birth to the greatest mountain glaciers in the world, any one of several having more ice than is contained in all the glaciers of Switzerland. North of the range the climate is continental, characterized by great extremes of temperature and light precipitation, the latter coming chiefly in the summer. Since the Bering Sea and the Arctic Ocean are covered with enormous ice floes most of the time, their effect is very much like that of an extensive body of land. For this part of Alaska there are no moderating climatic factors.

The climate of the southern and southeastern coastal region

is dominated by its maritime position. Neither extremely low nor extremely high temperatures occur. The average for the winter months is from 20° to 25° F. and for the summer months from 50° to 55° F. Damp, cold winds, frequent storms, fogs, and little sunshine characterize the winter conditions. Although the winters may be classed as mild, with temperatures only slightly below freezing, conditions are, in the main, disagreeable. In the summer, however, the climate is delightful, for the most part, with bright, crisp mornings and long hours of sunshine. The growing season averages about 141 days for the twelve weather stations; and, where soil permits, root crops, grains, grasses, hardy fruits, and flowers thrive unusually well. Back of the low range skirting the coast the climate is less cloudy and humid, but the temperatures reach greater extremes, and the growing season is shorter. To the visitor in Alaska for the first time the luxuriant vegetation along the coast is always a surprise.

The great interior, with its continental climate, is much too large for broad generalizations and must therefore be divided into smaller units. Of these, the Bering Sea section has an earlier and a more severe winter than the southern coast. The water is colder and ice covered for several months each year. The ocean at Nome begins to freeze by the latter part of September, and the long Arctic winter sets in with an average temperature of −10° F. or lower. The land supports a tundra vegetation which is such a good insulator that the mantle rock remains permanently frozen except for a few inches at the top. Over this treeless surface high winter winds whip the light snow into drifts. In the autumn, when the land surface cools more rapidly than the sea, fogs add to the general discomfort.

The Arctic section, with its Arctic Ocean slope, lies north of the Arctic Circle. There are two months or more of continuous darkness in winter and a similar period of continuous sunshine in summer. Winter temperatures not uncommonly fall to −40° or −50° F., and heavy gales make them still less endurable. Maximum temperatures of 90° F. have been recorded at Point Barrow; but, as ice floes last all summer in the Arctic Ocean, an onshore wind may bring freezing temperatures during the warmest month. Some residents find the long, continuous night more endurable than the long day because of the Aurora Borealis and the moonlight and starlight. Even during the long night there are three or four hours of twilight each day. The cold winds are a special menace, and the Eskimos build their houses partly underground. Residents never attempt to grow any plants, and the tundra remains frozen permanently to great depths.

That part of Alaska which includes the Yukon Valley and associated regions has the greatest annual and diurnal ranges in temperature in all Alaska. A winter temperature of −60° F. is not uncommon. A minimum thermometer left by Archdeacon Stuck on top of Mount McKinley and recovered nineteen years later showed that the temperature in the meantime had been down to −95° F. The lowest official record, of −76° F., was recorded for Tanana, in 1886. Fairbanks has an average of 120 days of zero weather annually and 234 days when the temperature falls below freezing at night. Summer temperatures of 90° are not uncommon in the interior, and at Fort Yukon on the Arctic Circle 99° has been officially recorded. Severe "cold waves," however, are infrequent, since the Alaska Range on the south and the Brooks Range on the north act as climatic barriers. With everything frozen, winter is the time for travel. The rivers become smooth highways for dog sleds, and airplanes substitute skis for wheels or pontoons. This season is also one of rare beauty, especially when the whole countryside is clothed in a beautiful, heavy hoar frost.

The interior, however, is less handicapped by the intense winter cold than the extremely low temperatures would seem to indicate. A low temperature is always a "dry cold," with sensible temperatures much higher than those recorded. The interior is relatively dry, with a total annual precipitation of only from 7 to 16 inches, most of it falling in the form of a light, fluffy snow, which, because of its dryness, drifts badly. The ground rarely has a sufficient cover of snow to keep the cold from penetrating to great depths. During the short warm summer, with its many hours of sunshine per day, the surface is thawed out and warmed sufficiently rapidly to make short-season crops possible. The region is favored by lack of rain and cloudiness in summer; sufficient moisture for growing plants, however, is supplied by the thawing subsurface ice. The hours of sunshine amount to 58 per cent of the total, which at its maximum is as much as twenty hours per day. Dead vegetable matter decays slowly and must be removed before the ground thaws out to a depth sufficient for crop growth. Unquestionably, climate is and will continue to be the major controlling factor in the development of the interior.

A possible future in development commensurate with that of the Scandinavian countries and Lapland, because of the similarity in latitudes, is too optimistic. The North Atlantic Ocean is much warmer near Europe than the North Pacific is relative to Alaska. A part of the North Atlantic drift swings through the wide-open passage far to the north into the Arctic Ocean, giving even to Russia some ice-free ports. In the North Pacific, with only a narrow passage through Bering Strait into the Arctic, the warm Japanese current is deflected to the south of the Aleutian Islands and affects materially only the southern coast and the Panhandle section of Alaska. The massive Alaska Range is such a supreme climatic barrier that it effectively limits the marine influences to a very narrow coastal section in the south.

GLACIATION IN ALASKA

Glaciation has profoundly affected the relief of the coastal mountains and the general configuration of the Alaska shoreline. In the Panhandle section of southeastern Alaska glaciers were formerly more extensive, and huge ice sheets occupied the valleys, scooping out debris and deepening them. The ice even crossed the inside passageway in the Panhandle section and rode over the partially submerged mountain range to the west. Along the major courses of the glaciers deep valleys were cut out, some much below sea-level, to form beautiful fiords, locally called "canals," that extend far back into the mountains. This deepening, aided by later sinking, produced many inlets and excellent harbors—a coastal phenomenon in sharp contrast to the unglaciated Oregon coast to the south. The sides of many of the fiords are far too steep for settlements and are devoid of even enough soil for tree growth; but, not uncommonly, at the head of the fiords streams have built deltaic plains sufficiently large to be of economic significance. Many such plains have become sites for settlements and act as connecting links between ocean and land travel. On some of them there is no development other than a fishing settlement with its associated packing plants.

The enormously large, moving ice masses now seen along the coast lead many to believe that this part of Alaska is much colder than it really is. With summer temperatures never high and winter temperatures averaging only a little below freezing, it cannot be cold that produces the great glaciers—the most magnificent mountain glaciers known. Snow will accumulate into great ice fields when more falls than melts. The short, cool summers permit relatively little melting; and the mild winters, during which great masses of warm, moist air from the Japan current are carried inland over the high Alaska Range and coastal mountains, give almost ideal conditions for an abundant snowfall. As year after year more snow falls than melts, great thicknesses pile up and become solidified into ice. In time gravity overcomes friction, and the ice mass moves to lower levels, even to the sea as tidewater glaciers.

These tidewater glaciers are one of the chief attractions to the tourist. The Taku Glacier, near Juneau, has an end face about 2 miles wide and fully 200 feet above the water surface. So vertical, even overhanging, is this great ice cliff that the reverberations of a steamer's whistle may cause huge blocks to break off. When conditions are favorable, even the human voice may act as the trigger to start such a slide. Only 12 miles from Juneau is the large Mendenhall Glacier. A little farther on, ending in Glacier Bay, is the Muir, believed by many to be the most beautiful tidewater glacier in the world. Several other glaciers enter the same bay; and the whole area, covering approximately 1,165,000 acres, has been set aside as the Glacier Bay National Monument. Mount Fairweather and other snow-capped peaks are included in the area, which produces a scenic panorama rarely equaled anywhere. To the west are the great piedmont glaciers, Malaspina and Bering, stretching out over the lowlands between the St. Elias mountain range and the ocean. These glaciers are unique in that enough debris has collected upon their tops to support a

THE TAKU GLACIER NEAR JUNEAU

The end face of the Taku Glacier is about 2 miles wide and fully 200 feet above the water surface. The grounded and polished ridge beyond is good evidence that an antecedent glacier not only filled the valley but covered the higher land as well.

TOTEM POLES AT KASAAN

A genealogical pole commonly stands in front of the owner's house. A totem pole gives the clanship of the family and reads from the top down. The wife's totem caps the top, for the female clan rules the household.

luxuriant forest growth, with trees 18 inches or more in diameter. The Columbia Glacier, on Prince William Sound near Valdez, is one of the tourist attractions, and steamers come within a few hundred yards of the ice mass from which enormous blocks break off to form icebergs.

A curious feature of Alaska is that the Yukon Valley, where the cold is most severe, was never glaciated, although the ground is permanently frozen to depths of 100 feet or more. The explanation is that the Alaska Range acts as a barrier to the moisture-filled masses of air from the ocean and the snowfall is too light to permit its accumulation into glaciers.

THE NATIVE PEOPLES

The native peoples make up more than half the total population of Alaska. Estimates place their number at about 30,000, of which about one-half are Eskimos. The Eskimos occupy Arctic America and have never lived in the central or southern part. Strong Mongoloid features are their chief characteristic. They are stocky of build and possess great strength and endurance. The Indian population numbers about 11,000 and is found along the southern coast and in the Yukon Valley. Of the Aleuts, once much more numerous, there are now barely 2,000. In features they are strongly Mongoloid and resemble the Eskimo more than the Indian. In habits, however, they are more akin to the Indian. Their home is the Alaska Peninsula and the Aleutian Islands.

The Eskimos live in small permanent or semipermanent villages conveniently situated with respect to their fishing and hunting grounds. From time to time a change in village sites is necessary. Birds, caribou, and other land animals supply, in the main, their summer needs; and the marine mammals, like the seal, walrus, and polar bear, those of the winter. Formerly the Arctic coast east of Point Barrow was fairly densely populated, but disease brought by the white man and the indiscriminate killing of animals upon the introduction of firearms have reduced the population greatly. Whalers also are responsible for the excessive destruction of the sea life.

There are, however, still a score or more of small Eskimo villages along the Arctic coast. The center of activities in them is a low-built trading post that supplies traps, guns, hardware, flour, and the like, in exchange for furs. Some neat cabins and, more commonly, crude huts house the families, most of whom are natives. During the winter trap lines in the interior may be run by hunters, but food is secured mainly from the sea. Some domestic reindeer may be kept. Eskimos rarely live away from the coast and rivers from which their food supply comes, except in the season when they follow the reindeer.

Usually an Eskimo cabin, commonly built of stones and chunked with moss, has a storeroom and a living compartment heated by an iron stove. Food supplies are cached on a platform supported by poles high enough to prevent hungry dogs and wolves from reaching it. Snow igloos are built only for dog shelters or by hunters far from home. Tents may serve as shelters in summer. Eskimo dress has not undergone much change, since clothing made of skins and furs is warmer than any other that can be purchased. Native boots are waterproof, whereas imported shoes admit snow water.

The old life of the Eskimos was an excellent adaptation to a harsh environment, now unfortunately upset by the advent of the white man. Few raw materials or food sources existed for them; yet they were happy and healthy. Starvation seldom threatened until after the introduction of firearms and the partial extermination of game. The skin kayak for hunting and the larger uniak for family and freight transport utilized skins with only a framework of wood. Light to carry, such boats could be portaged from one lead of open waters to another or could be easily dragged on a sled over snow and ice by a few dogs. In addition, a uniak, turned on edge, offered (and still offers) shelter from rain and wind and, upside down on poles, served as an acceptable roof for a temporary house. Harpoons, dog sleds, household implements, and other necessities were made of bone, ivory, stone, and driftwood, supplemented by animal skins, hides, and sinews. No crops could be raised and practically no vegetable food was available; yet raw animal food furnished the necessary vitamins in the diet.

The Eskimos learned to keep warm in this cold country; and nothing superior to their dress, which is scientifically utilitarian, has ever been invented for Arctic travel. The coat or shirt extends over the head and has an opening only for the face. At the bottom it comes well down over the trousers, which have no openings except at the top and the bottom. Both these garments may be made of caribou hide, although the men may wear trousers of polar-bear skin with a belt to keep the garments snug. Thus equipped, with a fur-trimmed headpiece to protect the face from the cold winds, seal-skin waterproof boots to keep the feet dry, and an undergarment of bird skin to hold the body heat, the Eskimo was comfortable even in the most severe weather. The winter dwellings were low structures built over a pit for warmth, with roofs of driftwood or whalebone and with the whole covered with turf. Fire, if it could not be borrowed, was started by the rubbing of sticks; and blubber lamps of stone served both for warmth and for preparing the seals and fish secured from holes in the ice.

Today the old ways, unfortunately, are passing, and the younger generation could hardly survive without the articles brought in by the white man. On the whole, the Eskimo's habits of life are changing rapidly, and he is taking up new customs far too readily for his own adjustment.

The Aleuts are very clever hunters but lack the spirit that characterizes the Eskimos. They also live in a treeless environment and secure most of their food from the sea. And, too, they live near the coast and go into the interior only during hunting expeditions. It has been estimated that at the time of the Russian invasion they numbered about 25,000 individuals; but wanton slaughter and cruel treatment, together with the introduction of diseases like smallpox, tuberculosis, and measles, caused thousands of the poor Aleuts to be swept away. Today hardly a thousand pure-blooded Aleuts are left, and these occupy only a small part of their former habitat.

Both the Indian and the Eskimo came from Asia, the Indian probably coming first. Discoveries of kitchen middens and burial places on the Aleutian Islands tend to show that the Indian used this bridge to reach his new home. They may also have entered the New World toward the close of the glacial period by crossing Bering Strait and migrating up the Yukon Valley, which was ice free.

The Indians of the interior formed part of the Athapascan family, the most widely distributed Indian linguistic group in North America. These Indians, called Tinnehs, hunted caribou, mountain sheep, moose, and other big game animals of the interior, trapped fur-bearing animals for clothing, and dried fish during the summer salmon migrations for their winter needs. The villages were semipermanent; but the dwellings were hovels, compared with the large community house of the southern Alaska Indian. Life was such a severe struggle to the Tinnehs that they did not develop so extensive a material culture as the more fortunately situated coast Indians. Today they live mainly along the Yukon River and its chief tributaries.

All the coast Indians were seamen. They lived in community villages along sloping beaches on sheltered bays. Houses were built of cedar beams and planks split by hand implements and were put together at great feasts, called by the whites in the Chinook jargon "potlatch." A common house was about 40 feet square with a pit, perhaps half that distance across at the center, containing a fireplace from which smoke passed upward through a hole in the roof. Around this pit were wooden platforms, which were used by the several families, usually related, that occupied the shelter. Each family had a section of the platform on which the members slept and kept their personal belongings. The Indians made long voyages, sometimes for 1,000 miles, in their cedar canoes, which were as essential to them as the camel is to the Arab. They lived on fish, shellfish, game, and berries. They hunted the sea otter, sea lion, and porpoise along the coasts and gathered furs in the forests. They were active traders and voyagers. They built splendid seaworthy canoes, were clever in wood-carving, worked stone and copper, and made baskets and blankets. Eulachon oil, made from the candlefish, was much used by the coast Indians and was exported to the Indians of the interior, especially over Chilkoot Pass, which, probably because of this trade, became known as the "Grease Trail."

Totemism dominates the social structure, religious beliefs, family names, and ancestral myths of both the Thlinget and Haida tribes. Each tribe is divided into two clans. One uses the eagle as its totem, and the other uses the crow or raven. Each clan in turn is subdivided into numerous smaller groups. The subtotems of the eagle are the bear, wolf, whale, shark, and others; and of the crow, the beaver, frog, salmon, seal, and so on. Each family must contain a member of the eagle and one of the crow totems. If the husband is from the eagle clan or one of its subtotems, the wife must be from the crow or one of its subtotems, and vice versa. A man, however, cannot take a wife from a subtotem of his own phratry even if she is a total stranger and wholly unrelated. For example, an individual having a bear totem cannot marry one with a wolf, whale, or shark totem.

Totems are indications of rank. Certain totem animals have a higher social standing than others, and people are seated in public according to their totem castes. The bear is the symbol of a powerful clan, whereas the mouse and snail groups are the weakest, low-caste divisions. A Thlinget Indian names himself from his native village: Sitka, Stikine, Tongass, Auk, Taku, etc.

Totem poles are of four general types: (1) genealogical, (2) historical or commemorative, (3) legendary, and (4) memorial or mortuary. A genealogical pole commonly stands in front of its owner's house. It indicates the clanship of the family and reads from the top down. The wife's totem is on top, and the husband's is next below, for the female clan rules a household. The historic pole commemorates some important event to the family erecting it, such as a victory in conflict with man or beast, which it is desired to chronicle for the edification of future generations. The legendary pole tells about some especially prized story of importance to the clan or family that erects it. The memorial pole corresponds to a tombstone and is erected at the burial place in memory of the deceased. It generally consists of the single animal totem of the departed placed on top of a cedar pole. Formerly cremation was practiced, and cavities were provided in the back of the totem for the ashes of the deceased. Today burial is practiced, and mortuary poles are rarely erected.

A totem pole is carved from a solid cedar log. Totem carving was a skilled and honored profession, and the workman was paid handsomely. Native pigments consisted of the green-blue of copper carbonate ore, white from lime, red from cinnabar and iron, and black from manganese. These were mixed with salmon oil, and a glutinous substance made from rock-weed gathered at low tide. Today imported paints find general use, but new totem poles are seldom erected by the younger generations.

When a totem pole was erected or a house raised, its owner gave a great potlatch at which an entire community feasted, sang and danced, and received presents from the giver of the potlatch. Such a potlatch was worth while to the Indian giving it, because it raised his importance in a community, which thereafter regarded him with great esteem. Often he might assume a new name after the ceremony. He might impoverish himself so that he had but little property left except his house, but that did not seem to matter. Later on he might expect to receive back in presents from others who gave potlatches the equivalent of his gifts. A potlatch was generally given during the long, monotonous winter. Marriage and death also commonly called for a potlatch.

EXPLORATION AND RUSSIAN SETTLEMENTS

By the beginning of the eighteenth century Russia had extended her influence eastward across Siberia and had explored its eastern shores. Its mariners had learned also of an extensive land to the east beyond a narrow sea, to which Peter the Great then sent an exploring expedition under Captain Vitus Bering, a Dane in the Russian navy. Bering left St. Petersburg in 1725, exploring what is now Bering Strait and the lands bordering Bering Sea. In 1741, with two ships and one hundred and fifty-three men, he started out to explore the coast farther south. Locating a beautiful peak on July 16 of that year, he named it Mount St. Elias, and by the time he returned he had mapped a goodly portion of the Alaskan coast. After many hardships, being much delayed by storms and sick with scurvy, he finally made port on an island off Kamchatka, where he and many of his crew died during a long winter of much suffering.

The survivors of Bering's expedition took back to St. Petersburg nine hundred skins of the sea otter and other furs. The reported abundance caused intense interest, and numerous groups were organized for trade in the land Bering had found, called Alaksu, or "great land," by the native peoples. The inexperienced traders sailed, for the most part, in miserable, poorly equipped boats; and the losses sustained in ships and personnel are almost beyond belief. Many leaders knew so little of navigation that they could merely coast from one island of the Aleutian chain to another. Some of them acted like pirates, treating the natives miserably and even slaying them without reason. Such treatment finally caused the Aleuts to rebel; but, after destroying several Russian ships with their crews, they were defeated and cowed into subjection. With the killing of the animals on the more accessible islands, longer voyages became necessary, and trading companies were organized to finance and handle the fur trade. By 1786 the Pribilof Islands, with their herds of fur seals, were discovered by the company captain whose name they bear, giving a new impetus in the search for furs. In order to maintain better control in the face of the long distance between the colony and St. Petersburg, the government decided to place the Alaska trade as a monopoly under one company. In 1799 the Russian-American Company was organized; and it governed Alaska, with control of the trade, until the sale of the territory to the United States in 1867.

About one thousand Aleut hunters were employed for a half-share of the fur taken. The furs were shipped for sale to Russia and China. Because a new trading capital was needed nearer the remaining sea-otter hunting grounds, New Archangel was founded in 1799 on Baranof Island, now the site of Sitka. The fort was destroyed by Indians in 1802, and most of the persons were killed; but the fort was re-established the next year. Sitka was a thriving trading village several years before there was any white settlement in the Oregon country.

Russia soon realized, however, that she alone could not hope always to control this rich fur country under the handicaps of great distance from St. Petersburg. By 1812 a company of Americans had organized to take part in the trade and to furnish grain and other foodstuffs to the Alaska trappers. To this end Fort Ross was founded in what is now Sonoma County, California, and was sold in 1841 to Captain John A. Sutter for $30,000. The company also controlled a seal-hunting station on the Farallon Islands from 1812 to 1840. It soon became evident that conflicts between fur-trading companies were inevitable, and Russia agreed to limit her territory to regions north of 54°40′, signing the agreement with the United States in 1824 and with Great Britain in 1825. This latitude has held for the southern boundary of Alaska, and for a time was an issue for the northern boundary of western United States. If this boundary line had prevailed, it would very effectively have limited Canada to the east and made Alaska a contiguous part of the United States.

Russia's efforts had been centered upon the beautiful sea otter and the much prized fur seal. Indiscriminate slaughter at all seasons of the year soon thinned the ranks of these to such an extent that it became necessary to go farther into the interior. Here competition became very keen, not only with the Russian-American Company but also with the Hudson's Bay Company. Russia founded Wrangell in 1833 in part to prevent the Hudson's Bay Company from encroaching too far on Russian territory. The great distance from home, however, was a handicap, and the Wrangell post was sold to the Hudson Bay Company in 1840. Fort Taku, 25 miles below Juneau, was built immediately but was abandoned two years later.

Difficulty in securing desired manufactures led to the establishment of a variety of industries, especially at Sitka, where the Russians built a flour mill for grain from California or Chile, a sawmill, a tannery using California cattle hides in part, a shipyard, a foundry, and other factories. The foundry made tools for local use, farm implements for export to California, and engines for locally built ships, and cast bronze bells, some of which were used in the Franciscan missions of California. Ice was also shipped from Sitka to California. The exchange of oak barrels, hides, tallow, and grain from California for ice, furs, and metal manufactures from Sitka has a rather intriguing interest.

With the settlement of the Oregon country and British Columbia by ranchers and miners, the isolation of Alaska from

Russia became more manifest. The territory was impossible to defend during war, and the ordinary returns from the fur industry at the time hardly paid for its retention. With the leasing of southeastern Alaska in 1840 to the Hudson's Bay Company, the tzar's hold on Russian America weakened. Americans had monopolized the Arctic and North Pacific whaling industry for more than a generation, and a few American ships had traded for furs in Alaska. Russia was loath to sell Alaska to Great Britain because of the Crimean War and preferred to dispose of it to the United States. She consummated the sale in 1867 for the sum of $7,200,000, which included payment also for certain goods received by United States war vessels from Russia during the Civil War; the actual cost of Alaska, therefore, was hardly 2 cents per acre. The purchase of Alaska was opposed by many as unwise at the time, but more than $50,000,000 in value of fur seals has been secured since 1867. The value of minerals produced since the purchase exceeds the cost nearly a hundred times, and each year the fishing industry alone has a value of output four or five times the entire purchase price.

WHITE SETTLEMENTS

For the purpose of this study Alaska can conveniently be divided into seven sections, based on location and relief: (1) Panhandle Alaska, from Mount St. Elias and the Malaspina Glacier to the border of British Columbia (Lat. 54°40′ N.); (2) southern Alaska, between Mount St. Elias and the Kenai Peninsula, inland to the Alaska Range and including the coasts of Cook Inlet and Prince William Sound; (3) southwest Alaska, including Kodiak Island, the Alaska Peninsula, and the Aleutian Islands; (4) the Yukon-Kuskokwim interior lowland; (5) the Arctic Highlands, or Brooks Range; (6) the Arctic Lowland, sloping from the Brooks Range to the Arctic Ocean; (7) Seward Peninsula.

The variations in landscape of Panhandle Alaska are well reflected in the towns along the coast. Ketchikan, the southernmost city, has no level land but clings to the mountain side; parts of it, including the main business streets, are built on piles over the water. Flights of stairs are necessary to reach some houses perched on slopes so steep that the first floor of one may stand above the roof of its neighbor. The town has about 4,000 permanent inhabitants, but boasts are made that during the salmon-canning season it is first in population in Alaska. As in most towns along the coast, the life of the community centers around the salmon.

Famous for its totem poles is Wrangell, of about 1,100 people, near the mouth of the Stikine River in a beautiful setting of forest slopes, bare rock, and green meadows framed in eternal snows. John Muir characterized the Stikine as "a hundred miles of Yosemite." He counted a hundred glaciers within view of the river and two hundred more within close range. In addition to fishing, the town has the benefit of mining activity in the upper river, which is navigable for small steamboats and launches. Petersburg, in a setting of ice- and snow-covered mountains, is another interesting fishing center.

Skagway and Dyea were "gold-rush" towns. Dyea was the more important at first because it was better located with reference to the Chilkoot Pass, but it was handicapped by extensive mud flats and high tides. With the discovery of White Pass, somewhat lower (2,888 feet), Skagway, with better landing facilities, became the outfitting post. With the completion of the railway in 1899 over the pass, Skagway's place seemed

KETCHIKAN WITH ITS TROLLING FLEET AT ANCHOR AND DEER MOUNTAIN IN THE BACKGROUND

Life centers about the salmon fisheries, and during the runs the town claims to lead in population.

THE MAIN STREET OF KETCHIKAN

Ketchikan clings to the mountainside or is built on piles over the water, including the major business district. Flights of steps are necessary to reach some of the houses shown in the upper right. The relative cheapness of lumber is evident in the various types of construction.

assured, and the town prospered greatly while the boom lasted. What the population was in 1898 is not known, but records seem to indicate that it was between 15,000 and 30,000. There were daily changes in the population. By 1900, however, the number had dropped to 3,117, by 1910 to 872, by 1920 to 494, by 1930 to 492 people, and the preliminary data for 1940 gives 634. There is little hope now for Skagway, as the route to the Yukon must pass through Canadian territory.

Sitka, with nearly 2,000 people, the old Russian capital of Alaska, was founded in 1799 on an island named after its founder, Baranov. The town has only about a thousand people but is picturesquely located along an isle-dotted coast. One part is the Indian section, with wooden structures, brown and weather-beaten, some of them erected on piles over the water; the other is the "white man's" Sitka, with better homes, a Russian Orthodox church, an Indian school, and a home for pioneers.

Juneau, the present capital and a most picturesque city, is built along an inlet called Gastineau Channel and has a population of nearly 6,000. When founded, wheeled vehicles were unknown to the region, and even pack horses were uncommon. The streets, therefore, twist and wander unexpectedly up and down steep grades. Today most of these streets, originally laid out seemingly without reason, are paved, and an improved highway extends out from the town to near-by places. Gold caused the founding of Juneau, but it was an important center long before the "days of '98." Across Gastineau Channel at Douglas was the once famous Treadwell mine, which operated profitably until the ocean waters broke in and forced its abandonment. The chief operating mine is the

Alaska-Juneau property within the city limits, which produces each year over $4,000,000 in gold from low-grade ores. The big mill and tailings dump are a waterside landmark.

Outside the cities in Panhandle Alaska, several mines, perhaps two dozen salmon canneries, and many fox farms support isolated groups or individuals. Whenever possible, homes are located on the waterways, and communication between the towns and the isolated settlers is almost wholly by water. Instead of an automobile the common conveyance is a motor boat.

In southern Alaska the principal towns are Cordova and Valdez on Prince William Sound, Seward on the Kenai Peninsula, and Anchorage at the head of Cook Inlet. Seward is the terminus of the Alaska Railroad, and the carshops and headquarters of the line are located at Anchorage. Both the railroad and highways connect Anchorage with Palmer in the Matanuska Valley. Valdez has a curious site in that it is built on the outwash material deposited from a melting glacier, and underneath the debris there is still stagnant ice; so Valdez is really built on top of a glacier. Valdez is the ocean terminus of the Richardson Highway to Fairbanks, which in an extent of nearly 300 miles is not joined by a single side road. From the port of Cordova the Copper River and Northwestern Railway, the construction of which is described in one of Rex Beach's novels, is built inland. A little dairying and gardening are carried on near all the larger settlements; but as none of the towns contains a thousand people, the available markets are obviously small. Numerous salmon-canning towns along the coast are busy during the summer and lie deserted during the off season.

In interior Alaska, Fairbanks, a town of 3,500 people, is the largest center. Since the town has a sales territory covering nearly 100,000 square miles, its business section is relatively larger than that of a city of similar population in the States, and even a daily newspaper is supported. Although founded as a mining-supply town, Fairbanks has more elaborate buildings and modern conveniences than are usually expected in a community that lies within 2° of the Arctic Circle. Outside of Fairbanks the scanty population resides in a number of little trading centers along the Yukon River, in a few missions established for the natives, and in numerous mining communities that usually operate only in summer. All the settlements are widely separated, and not many of them contain more than a few hundred persons or even more than a few families or groups of single men.

With the discovery of gold in the Seward Peninsula in September, 1898, and the resultant gold rush, Nome's history is inseparable. Its name, it is said, came by accident. A surveyor put "Name?" on the map; and, in transposing, the word became Nome. Once a boom city of 15,000 people madly mining the bonanza beach placers, the town now has a population of only 1,500. Although there is no harbor and navigation is possible only during the short summer, Nome is still the largest city in Alaska west of Fairbanks and is the headquarters of all the business of the Seward Peninsula. Goods and passengers are landed in small boats from ships anchored offshore, or in rough weather are taken over the surf by cable to a tower on the shore. Although much of the business section of Nome was destroyed by fire in 1934, it is nevertheless a busy place, especially in summer, when mining and the tourist trade are most active. Each winter a famous dog derby is run to Candle and return, a distance of about 410 miles, with a record of less than three days for the round trip. In addition to gold, Nome exports nearly all of the frozen reindeer meat sent out of Alaska. Most food, except reindeer meat and a few garden vegetables, has to be imported, along with other supplies.

There are no towns and practically no inhabitants in the Arctic Highlands. Point Barrow, the most northern postal station in the United States, has few permanent white residents, aside from a missionary and a school teacher and about 400 natives. The region has no future outside of a mere living for Eskimos, who are not self-supporting.

In southwest Alaska, very sparsely populated and containing 1,100 people, the largest center is Unalaska, with its 300 people. The larger part of the white population is there for limited periods only, as officials, teachers, missionaries, and the like. Unalaska is the headquarters for the revenue cutters which patrol the Bering Sea for the protection of the fur-seal colony on the Pribilof Islands, and adjacent Dutch Harbor has been considered for a new submarine and airplane base.[1] Recently a revenue cutter discovered on one of the islands a small colony of sea otters which may become the nucleus of an important industry. The sea otter, for a time thought to be extinct, is literally worth its weight in gold on account of its most highly prized fur. The inhospitable Aleutian Islands, long known to possess almost ideal conditions for raising foxes, may have some future in the development of this industry, as the long, dark, cool season produces a fine, long, silky fur. Since the fox is naturally timid, isolation is particularly desirable; and, as the waters are ice free, the animals may roam half-wild over an entire island. A number of fox farms have already been established and are, for the most part, fairly prosperous.

[1] Construction of a naval and airplane base began in 1940.

THE DEVELOPMENT OF TRANSPORTATION

The development of less costly transportation to and from the interior of Alaska has caused much concern since the discovery of gold. Until the late 1890's only a few white prospectors and fur-traders visited the Yukon Valley. Early in 1897 reports came from the Yukon of the discovery of rich gold placers on Klondike Creek just within British territory. In July of that year the steamer "Portland" arrived in Seattle with her gold cargo, and the mad "rush" for the new Eldorado was on. Various routes were taken by different groups, each hoping to reach the diggings first. Some went up the Yukon to Dawson, 1,600 miles by steamer; some followed the Stikine River from Wrangell to Telegraph Creek; others even went up the Copper River from Valdez or tried to cross the trailless, snow-clad mountains. The greatest influx, however, was from Dyea, at the head of Lynn Canal, via the Chilkoot Pass and from Skagway via the White Pass. Skagway, having the better landing, however, soon became the center of hope and tragedy, a boom town of tents and wooden shacks with stores, warehouses, saloons, dance halls, and gambling dens. The story has been told and retold, and many a living "sourdough" still can give his version. Sufferings were intense, as many prospectors were ill equipped for the hazardous journey over the Pass and down the Yukon. Inexperienced men attempted to transport goods with pack horses and mules over a steep, rocky trail that defied even the most able. In Dead Horse Gulch probably 3,000 horses died from hardship and starvation, leaving their bones as a monument for the present-day tourist. Skagway is still the point of departure for tourists. The White Pass and Yukon Railway starts at its wharf, runs up Main Street and over the summit of White

Pass to White Horse and beyond. From White Horse, river steamers provide summer service to Dawson, a distance of 480 miles, and in winter dog sleds make the journey on the frozen Yukon.

The Yukon is one of the great rivers of the continent and drains 330,000 square miles of land. Its source in British Columbia is less than 25 miles from the Pacific; yet its waters flow 2,300 miles before they reach the ocean. The stream is navigable for about 2,000 miles from St. Michael on the delta to White Horse rapids in Yukon Territory. The river, however, is open to navigation only for about four months of the year, and the steamboat service has declined greatly since the opening of the Alaska Railway. Nevertheless, some service by river is maintained for the scattered trading posts and small towns along this waterway, as well as the Tanana River, which provides water connection for Fairbanks.

At the present time the Alaska Railroad from Seward on the Kenai Peninsula to Fairbanks on the Tanana River, 486 miles, is the chief route into the interior. It is government owned; it was begun in 1915 and completed in 1923. A second port, at Anchorage, on an upper arm of Cook Inlet, has been developed to improve the service, but it is handicapped by its 40-foot tides. From Anchorage the line follows the Susitna River and its tributary, the Chulitna, to Broad Pass; then it continues down the Nenana to the Tanana and Fairbanks. A branch line has been extended into the coal fields of the Matanuska Valley, where now there is also the agricultural colony sponsored by the government. In spite of high passenger and freight rates—two to four times those in the States for similar service—a large deficit has accumulated, and the expected development of bordering areas has not materialized.

Competing with the railway is the Richardson Highway between Valdez and Fairbanks, only 370 miles long. On it busses run on regular schedule during the summer and carry passengers for about half the railroad rate. During winter months mail service is maintained by dog sled. The building of more such highways may provide a partial solution to the transportation problems of Alaska. A highway to Alaska from the States has been proposed and, with Canadian co-operation, may in time be constructed. Such a highway, located between the Rocky Mountains and the Coast Range, would necessarily be expensive and would have little or no value except from a military standpoint.

The principal private railway in Alaska is the Copper River and Northwestern, a standard-gauge line 196 miles long, built at a cost of $23,000,000 from Cordova to the rich Kennecott copper mines for the purpose of bringing out the ores for the Tacoma, Washington, smelter. Exhaustion of the known ore reserves at Kennecott caused the mine and railroad, both of which were once large money-makers, to discontinue operations in 1938, and the future of the railroad is problematical.

The development of aviation has greatly lessened the isolation of interior Alaska. Fairbanks and Juneau are connected with regular airplane service and are the leading aviation centers. From Juneau there is also airmail service with Seattle. For several years planes have flown on schedule from Fairbanks to Nome, McGrath, Wiseman, and other centers. In 1938 twenty-five aviation companies were operating about a hundred planes in Alaska, and 130 recognized landing fields had been constructed. Between 20,000 and 25,000 passengers are carried per year, besides over 3,000,000 pounds of freight and 500,000 pounds of mail. The saving in time by airplanes, when compared with other means of transport, is remarkable. For example, the flight from Fairbanks to Nome takes only a few hours, whereas the journey by dog team requires weeks. Via the Tanana, Yukon, and Yokuku rivers it is 1,400 miles from Fairbanks to Wiseman but only 200 miles by plane. Planes fly to McGrath from Fairbanks, 300 miles, in less than two hours but the journey requires seventeen days by dog sled. Airplanes have displaced many dog teams for carrying mail and transporting sick to hospitals. The number of passengers carried is increasing rapidly. Green vegetables, eggs, fruit, and other foodstuffs are regularly delivered to many communities by airplane.[2]

MINERAL RESOURCES

Alaska contains a great variety of mineral resources. Coal, petroleum, building materials, and base metals have a wide distribution but can profitably be mined only where favorably situated near water or rail transportation. Only gold possesses sufficient value to permit its profitable production in remote regions, and only along the main arteries of traffic have large and stable mining enterprises been developed. With further exploration and prospecting other substantial mining camps are bound to develop, especially when higher prices and improved and cheaper transportation furnish the needed incentive.

Gold and copper are the leading minerals, together accounting from 1880 to 1939 for about 95 per cent of the total of nearly $800,000,000. Of this total, gold accounts for about 63 per cent, copper 32 per cent; and the other minerals, such as silver, coal, tin, lead, platinum, aluminum, for about 5 per cent. The value of all minerals produced in Alaska in 1939

[2] In 1940 construction began on government airports at Anchorage, Sitka, Kodiak, and other southern and central Alaskan localities, including several on the Seward Peninsula. These were a part of the national defense program. New army and naval bases were also under construction.

was approximately $28,000,000, nearly $475 per capita for the residents of the territory. Not many countries, if any, have such an export record. Nearly 5,000 men are employed in the mining industry, practically one-fifth of all wage-earners. Alaska may be looked upon as a great mining country, although by no means is mining to be regarded as the leading industry.

GOLD

The Russians knew that gold existed in Alaska; but production was negligible, even under America's rule, until in 1880, when a $20,000 output was recorded. Gold comes both from veins, or lodes, and from placers of sand and gravel that carry concentrates of gold dust and nuggets derived from the weathering and erosion of gold-bearing rocks. For the years 1880–1938 placers account for nearly two-thirds of Alaska's output of $511,000,000. In 1938 placers produced $13,580,000. The first production of gold, however, came from very large deposits of low-grade ore near Juneau, averaging only between $1.00 and $2.00 gold per ton; however, by handling thousands of tons daily under efficient management the mines proved very profitable.

Juneau owes its beginning to the discovery of gold in its vicinity in 1880. The Treadwell mine at Douglas, across Gastineau Channel from Juneau, was once the largest gold mine in North America. After producing in a small way for a few years, it built a huge stamp mill in 1887 and operated with large profits until 1917, when the deep workings that extended below sea-level caved in and salt water flooded the mine beyond the capacity of the pumps. After milling the ore from upper levels, the mine had to close. Several other mines have operated on the mainland near Juneau. Of these, the Alaska-Juneau, located on the water side at the south edge of the town, operates the largest gold quartz mine and mill in Alaska, one that ranks with the largest gold mines on earth. From 1893 to 1938 the Alaska-Juneau has produced nearly 40,000,000 tons of ore, from which metals, mostly gold, have been extracted to a total value of nearly $60,000,000. There are many other low-grade mining properties in the vicinity, and the district has by no means been worked out. In all, approximately $150,000,000 in gold has been produced from the vast low-grade quartz lodes in the Juneau gold belt.

Gold-bearing veins are widely distributed in Alaska; but because the cost of transporting both supplies and ore mined is high, only very high-grade ore can be profitably marketed. Although the production of gold thus mined is only about $2,000,000 annually (a third of the value coming from the Juneau district alone), yet, in view of the difficulties encountered, it indicates something of what the future has in store.

Rich gold placers were first found on Klondike Creek near Dawson City in the Yukon Territory of Canada. In 1897 at least $2,500,000 in gold came from there, and the next year $10,000,000; the resulting gold rush has been unequaled in intensity. Prospectors who were unable to secure ground in the Klondike crossed the American border and located placers within the Yukon Valley of Alaska. This exploration has gone on even to the present day. The most productive placers were found in the interior of Alaska and in the Seward Peninsula. Previous to 1898 the output of placer gold was inconsiderable, with an average value of only $280,000 per year from 1880 to 1898; but from 1898 to 1938 a total of over $300,000,000 in gold dust and nuggets has been recovered from placers.

The history of Nome on the Seward Peninsula is typical of Alaska placer developments. After the original discovery, the

JUNEAU, ALASKA

Gold started Juneau, but the town was an important mining center even before the "days of ninety-eight." Across Gastinean Channel is Douglas, where was located the famous Treadwell mine, which operated most profitably until the ocean waters broke in and ended the extraction of gold ore.

A HOMESTEAD NEAR FAIRBANKS

Cabbages, root crops, and flowers, especially pansies and sweet peas, grow most luxuriantly in the short summer but in the long hours of sunshine. In the foreground there is barley, grown for grain and forage. The lone crosses in the middle background mutely tell their own story.

first steamer from Seattle arrived at Nome in June, 1899. There was no harbor, and goods and people were landed on a sandy beach littered with driftwood from Yukon floods. Back of Nome lay the frozen, treeless tundra. In addition to placers on higher land, there was gold in the beach sands, and more than $2,000,000 was quickly taken from them. In 1900 probably 1,800 more persons arrived at Nome, and nearly $5,000,000 in gold came from the placers. Then ancient high beach gravels containing gold were found back of Nome, and in 1906 more than $7,000,000 in gold was washed from them. After the richest placers that could be worked by hand were exhausted, giant dredges were installed. At present nine big dredges mine most of the $2,500,000 in gold coming from the Peninsula. During the forty years following the first gold discovery at Nome, over $100,000,000 in gold and several hundred thousand dollars in silver have come from the region. Geologists estimate that nearly $200,000,000 in gold remains to be mined near Nome, and the increase in the price of new gold to $35 per ounce will permit working of some of the low-grade placers that were formerly considered unprofitable.

Placer mining in interior Alaska has many difficult problems to solve. All placer methods require much water, and in some cases water is brought scores of miles. Gold-bearing gravels are almost always solidly frozen, even to depths of from 100 to 200 feet. Since the greatest concentration of gold lies just above bed rock, the removal of a useless thick overburden of frozen gravel may be very expensive. The working season is short and is limited by the quantity of water available. Dry summers seriously handicap placer mining.

Special methods for thawing the gold-bearing gravels have been developed. At first miners built fires over the ground to be thawed or on the face of the drift. Fairly satisfactory for shallow deposits, this method proved useless in gravels containing pure ice in quantity. Then hot stones were used; but they proved too heavy, too slow, and too expensive to handle. Steam pipes driven into the gravel had moderate success. Today the thawing of frozen ground is accomplished by means of large quantities of ordinary, unheated stream water.

In the main the gravel is overlain with muck, peat, and other organic debris which very successfully insulates them from normal thawing during the summer. After the organic material has been removed, iron pipes are forced into the gravel down to bed rock at intervals of from 20 to 30 feet, and cold water is forced through them. The process generally requires from two to four months for the thawing at Nome and Fairbanks. The success of the venture is entirely dependent on large-scale production. One company at Fairbanks employs 500 men for the summer, removes 8,000,000 or more tons of muck annually, and then moves as much as 9,000,000 tons of gravel. Water is brought from a distance of about 90 miles, and some 200 miles of pipe are used at the mines. Under these conditions the cost of operating is great, about 20 cents per cubic yard, or twice that in California. Should the price of gold be raised again, huge quantities of gravel could be worked that are now worthless.

Since the placer-mining season in Alaska lasts only from five to seven months, wages are high in order to attract and hold labor. Freight rates on machinery, foodstuffs, and everything else consumed by miners and operators make the cost of operation so high that some low-grade placers that would be profitable if located in the States cannot be worked at present. It is estimated that the known placers near Fairbanks will last for twenty-five years at the present rate of production. Probably $500,000,000 in gold remains to be produced from Alaska placers, which is equal to the entire production for the past sixty years. The trend of placer mining in Alaska during the last few years is toward the use of dredges and other machinery requiring larger and larger capital investments. By such methods large low-grade deposits can be worked when carefully and efficiently managed. Small rich placer deposits that do not require such large amounts of capital for machinery will probably continue to be found and developed by individual prospectors for many years to come; but as time goes on, the big operators will likely produce most of the gold dust.

COPPER, COAL, AND OTHER MINERALS

The value of copper produced in Alaska up to the end of 1938 approximates $227,300,000. This is 44 per cent of the value of the total gold production during this period and greatly exceeds all other minerals combined. During the World War and for several years thereafter the value of the copper greatly exceeded that of gold. In 1916 nearly 120,000,000 pounds of copper, valued at $29,500,000, and from 1900 to 1938, 1,364,000,000 pounds, came from Alaska. The greatest production has come from the mines at Kennicott, although other copper mines are worked in southeastern Alaska, and doubtless other deposits remain to be discovered. From 1911 to 1938 the Kennicott, an extraordinarily rich mine, produced more than $200,000,000 worth of copper. This mine is now closed, apparently worked out.

Sixty miles east of Cordova, at Katalla, is the only producing oil field in Alaska. The production is small and is used only locally. Far north, along the Arctic near Point Barrow, are believed to exist important deposits of petroleum, but at present the region is too remote to permit profitable development. Favorable prospects for petroleum exist in other localities, and the northwest part of Alaska has been placed in a naval oil reserve.

Alaska is fairly rich in coal, the deposits of which are widely distributed, although none is located particularly favorably for export. Production, therefore, has been limited to supplying local demands, chief of which have been those of the railroads and as fuel for heating. When a sufficient outside demand arises, the development will increase manyfold. At present only two fields have much activity: the Matanuska field furnishes most of the coal for the Alaska Railroad; and the Nenana, or Healy, field ships coal to Fairbanks for power and domestic use. The Alaska coal varies from low-grade bituminous to anthracite, depending on the degree of metamorphism. In general the lower grades of coal are in nearly horizontal beds, whereas the higher grades are in strata that have been faulted and crushed, a fact which adds distinctly to the cost of mining. The annual production in recent years has been less than 150,000 tons, worth about half a million dollars. This is by no means the maximum limit of production.

One of the notable mining developments of recent years in Alaska has been the large increase in production of platinum and other metals of similar properties, like osmium, iridium, and palladium. The production now is more than a million dollars annually. The largest output comes from the Goodnews district of southwestern Alaska, between the bays of Bristol and Kuskokwim. Here the platinum is recovered from placers by a dredge and dragline equipment. Platinum is also secured from ores near Kasaan, on Prince of Wales Island, and as a by-product from some placer operations on the Seward Peninsula.

Tin has been mined since 1902 in the Seward Peninsula, which is the only district with an appreciable production in United States territory. The quantities produced have not been sufficient to warrant equipment for smelting in the United States, and consequently ores thus far have been shipped to Singapore for reduction. Nearly all the ore comes from placers, much of it as a by-product from gold placers. Tin lodes are known, but the price of the metal has not warranted entering strongly into competition in the American market with Bolivia and the Malay region. Up to the present a total of about 1,500 tons of tin ore, roughly valued at $1,500,000, has come from the Seward Peninsula.

More than $12,000,000 worth of silver has been produced in Alaska, all of it as a by-product from copper and gold lodes or gold placers. More than 70 per cent of it has been a by-product from copper mines alone. Also about $2,000,000 worth of lead has been produced; but, like the silver, it has been recovered as a by-product mostly in the course of gold mining, principally from the Alaska-Juneau district. Antimony, quicksilver, gypsum, limestone, and other mineral deposits are widely distributed. There is no lack of rich and varied mineral deposits, most of which will sometime become available for use when transportation and mining costs can be materially reduced and outside demand or prices are increased.

FISHERIES

The fisheries of Alaska are the most important source of wealth. From 1880 to 1938, inclusive, there was sold over $1,170,000,000 worth of canned salmon, fresh and cured fish, shellfish, fur-seal skins, whale oil, and other aquatic products. This exceeds the value of minerals produced during the same time by nearly one-half. From 20,000 to 30,000 persons are annually employed in the fishing industry, including 5,000 Indians, one-sixth of the entire native population, and about as many more white residents of Alaska. This leaves about 15,000 or 20,000 seasonal workers to be imported for the fishing industry alone.

The catching and canning of salmon stands first among all industries. Under intelligent control it is a resource scarcely ever fully appreciated, ever perpetuating itself without effort on man's part. The annual value of canned salmon alone exceeds the combined value of all minerals, furs, and other products of Alaska. The maximum output to date occurred in 1936, with 8,455,000 cases of forty-eight 1-pound cans each, and it represented 94.1 per cent of the total American production. The industry, of course, is a coastal one, extending from Bristol Bay and the Alaska Peninsula to the Panhandle section of southeast Alaska.

Five species of salmon live in the coastal water on both sides of the Pacific Ocean, and each differs from the Atlantic salmon. They are the chinook, sockeye, humpback, coho, and dog salmon. The average weight of the chinook, usually called "king salmon" in Alaska, is from 20 to 25 pounds, but there are occasional monsters two to three times as large. The flesh is usually deep salmon red, although a rather large proportion of the king salmon in southeastern Alaska has white flesh and is then not canned but is frozen or salted for market. The king salmon feeds in the coastal waters, and large quantities are caught by hook and line in addition to those taken during the runs up river in their fourth year. The sockeye, or red salmon, average about 8 pounds for male fish and $5\frac{1}{2}$ pounds for females, and they spawn also at the end of four years. The humpback, or pink salmon, spawns at the end of two years; hence it is not such a large fish and averages only 4 or 5 pounds in weight. It attains its greatest abundance in southeastern Alaska, where the runs last from June until September. The coho, or silver salmon, spawn normally in their fourth year and average about 6 pounds in weight, but many attain a maximum of 30 pounds. Since the runs of the cohos come later than for other species, and the flesh is light in color, the fish is rarely canned in quantities. Canned, it sells under the name of "medium red salmon." The dog, or chum, salmon average about 8 pounds and may reach 16 pounds in weight. The flesh is light yellow, and the canned product does not sell well; consequently, the fish are frozen, salted, or smoked. In central, western, and arctic Alaska, natives dry this species for winter dog food; hence its name. The steel-head trout is treated like a salmon by fishermen, but it does not die at the end of a spawning migration and may enter streams more than once for breeding purposes. Most steel-head trout are sold fresh or frozen as salmon.

During their life-span the five varieties of true Pacific salmon spawn once only in shallows at the headwaters of freshwater streams. The infants secure nourishment from the yolk sac until they are about an inch long, and then they leave their home in the gravels to feed on insects and other water life. When several months old, they migrate to the open sea. During the two to four years that salmon live in salt water, they feed within a few miles of the coast, mostly on small crustaceans that float in incredible numbers in the shore waters. At maturity, reached at different ages for the various species, they return to the fresh-water streams in which they had their origin and ascend in vast schools to the spawning grounds. Once started upstream, they struggle against all obstacles, swimming up swift rapids and "jumping" considerable falls, in their unreasoned urge to reach their spawning grounds. It is at this time that man takes them by the hundred thousands, and even bears and other animals feast on them. The spawning grounds consist of clean, sandy gravels in shallow water, in which the female scoops a hollow and deposits her eggs, which are then fertilized by the male. The life-work of the adult Pacific salmon ceases after the gravel is scraped over the eggs by the tail of the female. The emaciated fish, which have not eaten since they left the ocean, float slowly in the water, tail downstream, and perish either from starvation or from the attack of parasites before they reach the ocean. Since a certain percentage of breeding stock must be allowed to reach the spawning grounds in order to maintain salmon fisheries, the fishing season is closed during part of the migrations, and limitations are placed on the length of nets and traps which block streams. So far, not a great deal of artificial salmon propagation has been attempted.

During 1936 and 1937 a controversy arose between the United States and Japan in regard to the sending of floating canneries and other vessels to Bristol Bay. The Japanese were supposed to be engaged in crab-fishing but had gear on board for taking salmon and presumably had caught the fish in shallow water, although more than 3 miles offshore. As a protective measure, salmon caught contrary to regulations cannot be landed even if secured beyond the 3-mile limit. Since the Japanese used ships for canneries, they could disregard these conservation measures and in the end might destroy the Bristol

Bay salmon industry in which Americans have invested some $20,000,000. Bristol Bay fishermen threatened to forcibly expel the encroaching Japanese. As a result of much agitation, the United States government made strong protests to Japan, which in 1938 gave provisional assurance that licenses for salmon-fishing in Alaskan waters would no longer be granted, and Japanese vessels were withdrawn before the fishing season began. Recognizing that this is not a permanent arrangement, the Alaskan fishing industry continues to urge that American jurisdiction be extended over waters adjacent to Alaska in order to curb possible encroachment by alien fishermen in the future.

Fishing methods include seines, traps, and hook and line. Seine traps take more than half the Alaskan fish catch, although the proportion declined from 61 per cent in 1930 to 55 per cent in 1932 as a result of the government's discontinuance of many trap locations, to allow local residents to catch more fish with other gear. Permanent traps are erected where the ground permits; but on a rocky bottom, floating traps must be used, since piles cannot be driven. In salmon traps a barrier, or "lead," of floating logs supports wire or nets in place from the bottom to above water-level and deflects the fish into a pass leading to the trap proper. This consists of two V-shaped "hearts." The larger, 30–60 feet across, opens into a smaller one, which in turn leads to a square pot through the "tunnel." On both sides of the pot are square compartments, called "spillers," which store the fish that enter through tunnels from the pot. Fish are removed from spillers by a net called the "brailler," operated by a power capstan on the boat or scow, into which the fish are dumped. Several tons of salmon are loaded quickly by this method. Traps are placed near stream mouths and on points near shore where migrating salmon pass. Floating traps consist of logs 18 inches to 2 feet in diameter, bolted together in the same arrangement as that described for the fixed traps. From the floating logs a barrier of nets fastened to iron rods descends 30 feet below the surface. Wire netting is generally used in trap construction, about sixty rolls being needed for each trap. A fish trap may cost several thousand dollars. Purse seines, handled by power boats, are another important method of fishing in Alaska. On sighting a school of salmon, a dory with a seine 1,200 feet long and 100 feet deep encircles the fish. A power winch hauls in both ends of the seine, narrowing the circle and at the same time drawing the bottom of the net together by the purse line running through iron rings in the bottom of the net. After the net is pulled alongside the vessel, the fish are dipped from the bunt, or "pocket," of the seine into the hold. Only the king salmon are caught in quantity by hook and line.

Alaska canneries are always on tidewater. A location is chosen near some stream toward which the salmon migrate during the runs to the spawning grounds. At the cannery the fish are unloaded from the purse seiners and scows with an automatic elevator, which eliminates hand pitching, and workmen separate the catch into the different species. Fish are allowed to shrink from eighteen to twenty-four hours before canning, to eliminate the danger of packing light-weight cans with an excess of juice.

Canning machinery is arranged on a "line" and performs all the important operations with great economy of time and labor. Formerly many Chinese workmen were imported; now the "Iron Chink" does the work of a score of men, cutting off head, tail, and fins, taking out entrails with wedge-shaped knives, removing the scales with stiff brushes, and cleaning with strong jets of water. Revolving gang-knives then slice the fish to fit the can, into each of which $\frac{1}{4}$ ounce of salt has been dropped. A rotary filling-machine forces the salmon into the cans, which are carried by an endless belt over a weighing machine, which shunts those underweight to the side for special attention. After the sealing in a vacuum closing-machine, the cans are placed in iron crates and run into retorts for cooking. Steam at a temperature of 240° F. cooks the salmon sufficiently from 90 to 120 minutes to soften the bones and make them edible. The cans are then cooled, labeled, and packed for export. Formerly a large crew came in the spring to make the cans; now companies import flattened tins, which are reamed out as needed.

A typical Alaskan salmon cannery is located near supplies of fish along the shore where waters are sufficiently quiet and deep to permit boats to dock. A generous source of pure, fresh water is required; but since southern Alaska is a very rainy region, this is not difficult to obtain. The cannery is usually built on piles with a short wharf in front. Refuse is dumped through the floor of the building, to be carried away by the high tides, which here average nearly 20 feet. Besides the cannery building, there are a storehouse for the cases of canned salmon and a combination store, office, and boarding-house for the workmen. Some men prefer to board themselves, and shacks or huts are provided for them. Some canneries use oriental labor, chiefly Filipinos; others employ considerable numbers of Indians, and white men only for positions of authority. Traps are usually operated by the canning company itself. Independent fishermen operate many of the trollers and purse seiners and sell their fish to canneries as opportunity offers. In the summer a good-sized cannery, with a seasonal output of from 50,000 to more than 100,000 cases, is a busy little community of a hundred people or more. In winter only one or two watchmen remain. The catch of salmon may vary considerably from day to day; and when big catches are made, employees must labor long, sometimes from twelve to twenty hours during the twenty-four, to care for all the fish, since the salmon deteriorate rapidly and must be canned before they are thirty-six hours out of the water.

Although the majority of Alaskan salmon are canned, considerable quantities are frozen for sale during the winter; and some are salted, smoked, or mild cured. Only the finest and freshest halibut, salmon, and other fish are chosen for freezing. After freezing, they are dipped in water and covered with a glaze of ice to protect them, after which they are piled up like cordwood in storerooms kept at a temperature of about 15° F. There are twenty-five cold-storage warehouses in Alaska, the largest plants being located in Ketchikan, Juneau, Petersburg, and Sitka. For mild curing 15,000,000–20,000,000 pounds of king and silver salmon are used annually. Fish, generally caught by trolling, are carefully cleaned, split into halves, and packed in large wooden casks holding about 800 pounds of fish and 100 pounds of salt. Chief buyers of mild-cured salmon are the makers of smoked salmon, Germany being the largest consumer.

The value of output of halibut fisheries in the Pacific coastal waters is equal to that of the rest of the world combined. Halibut are caught from the Oregon coast to Bering Sea, a distance of 2,000 miles. Although some boats take their cargoes direct to Seattle or Canadian ports, the Alaskan waters account for fully one-half of the total catch, which in value is next to salmon. The annual catch of halibut along the Pacific Coast is about 50,000,000 pounds, of which Alaskan shipments are credited with about $2,500,000 annually. None is canned; it is all sold fresh or frozen. Eastern United States offers the best market. When caught, halibut are packed in crushed ice or kept in refrigerator compartments in the holds of ships. After freezing and glazing with ice at the shipping center, they are sent east in refrigerator cars or are placed in cold-storage plants, to be marketed during the off-season months.

The Pacific coastal waters are an especially favorable habitat for halibut. Along the coast there are extensive shallow banks with sand and gravel bottoms less than 150 fathoms below the surface of the sea. These banks support a rich marine life on which the larger forms feed. The waters are also clear and cool, about 40° F. As the more accessible grounds have been overexploited, seaworthy power-boats, capable of remaining at sea for several weeks at a time, have taken the place of the small dories. Overkilling is still taking place, and the supply of fish is rapidly diminishing. Conservation measures have been introduced recently, after an agreement with Canada, whereby a three months' closed season on halibut is provided. It has been hoped that these measures will be sufficient to insure the perpetuation of the industry.

Other fisheries, although not as important as either salmon or halibut, are nevertheless of real significance. The catch of herring of about 80,000,000 pounds annually is, strangely enough, on the increase. Some of the catch is salted, but much of it is reduced to oil and meal by five companies in southeastern Alaska. Shellfish, like crabs, clams, and shrimp, are also a considerable item. Bristol Bay and the embayments of Panhandle Alaska are the leading centers of activity. By international agreement the catch of whales is limited, but the value of the annual catch in Alaskan waters is between $300,000 and $400,000. The walrus and hairy seal add considerably to the native needs.

FURS AND GAME

The Alaska fur seal and its relatives were once widely distributed in the Pacific area, with breeding grounds in both the North and the South Pacific Ocean. In 1786, when Pribilov discovered the islands that bear his name, the herd of fur seals using the group as a breeding place were estimated at from 4,000,000 to 5,000,000 animals. During the Russian period the killing was a government monopoly, and the animals were fairly well protected. However, by the time the United States purchased Alaska, their number had been reduced to about 1,500,000. Other fur seals of a slightly different species resort to breeding grounds on the Commander Islands, near Kamchatka, and to one or two of the Kuril Islands belonging to Japan; but these herds have been reduced to insignificant numbers. Formerly millions of fur seals lived also in the southern oceans, along the shores of Patagonia, Falkland Islands, Galápagos Islands, and other isolated spots. Sealers have nearly exterminated these in spite of their inferior fur. The only large herd of fine fur seals left alive is that of the Pribilof Islands.

The Pribilof group lies more than 200 miles northwest of Unalaska and consists of two main islands about 30 miles apart—St. Paul, 13½ miles long with an area of 43 square miles, and St. George, 12 miles long, covering 30 square miles—together with a few islets, the largest of which has an area of only 100 acres. The islands are of volcanic origin, have no harbors, and landing is possible only in calm weather. There are occasional open winters, but generally the coasts are blocked with ice floes several months of the year. During April winter changes into summer, and at this season dense fogs shroud the islands most of the time.

The nomenclature used for the seals is peculiar. The old males are called "bulls" and may exceed 6 feet in length and weigh from 400 to 600 pounds or more. The females are called "cows," are about 4 feet long, and weigh about 75 pounds. The young are not called "calves" but "pups," possibly because they play together as happily as puppies. The young males, who are excluded from the breeding grounds, are called "bachelors" and commonly live alone until they are about seven years old. The immature females play with the newborn pups rather than live in special quarters like the bachelors. Since the seal is polygamous, a large proportion of the bachelor seals can be killed each year without injury to the normal increase of the herd. Bachelors have prime fur at the age of three years and may easily be driven in bands to the slaughtering pens.

In return for an annual payment, Congress in 1870 gave a monopoly to the Alaska Commercial Company for taking 100,000 male seals a year during a period of twenty years. After 1880, however, pelagic sealing became a serious threat to this seal herd. The sealers cruised outside of the 3-mile limit or followed the herd during its migrations and speared or shot the seals while they slept on the water or swam toward their feeding ground. Probably half of the seals which were shot sank and were never recovered. Since from 70 to 90 per cent of the seals taken were females, the death of one seal was doubled, because the pup perished of starvation without its mother. The attacks of the pelagic sealers caused such destruction to the herd that in 1911 its number had declined to about 150,000 individuals, and the vast rookeries were the site of only a few scattered harems, where formerly the whole coast had been black with animals. The fur seal was definitely doomed if the killing continued. It was in 1911 that the United States negotiated treaties with Great Britain, Russia, and Japan prohibiting pelagic sealing in return for certain annual payments. These treaties expired after fifteen years and have been renewed for a second term.[3] All has been accomplished that was expected, and the number of seals is now estimated at about 2,000,000. This is probably the largest single herd of wild mammals that collects in one spot on the earth's surface. An average of about 55,000 skins, worth $250,000 or more, are taken each year, mostly from St. Paul Island. Practically all of the killings are of three-year-old male seals. The government seal skins are prepared for market in St. Louis, Missouri, where they are sold at two annual public auctions. Additional income is secured from the manufacture of some of the seal carcasses into meal and oil, and from the sale of about 2,000 blue-fox skins per year, the foxes being fed on some of the seal carcasses. About 300 natives have been transferred to the islands and do most of the manual labor of killing and skinning. In the summer the ceaseless pounding of the surf, the weird cries of the sea birds, the roaring of the bulls, and the bleating of the cows and young pups form a striking contrast to the calm of winter, when ice floes may block even the pounding surf.

The Russians first entered Alaska because of the lure of the furs, and the fur industry still produces two or three million

[3] In 1940 Japan notified the United States that this treaty, expiring in 1941, would not be renewed, claiming damage to fisheries by the fur seals. What will result from this cancellation of the treaty is not yet clear.

dollars per year. The climate favors the growth of superior pelts; and because of the small population, there are great areas suitable for fur-bearing animals. Hence, the output of furs should continue indefinitely, especially as the animals may be trapped only in the open season, between November 15 and March 1, when the pelts are in prime condition. Besides the trapping of wild animals, thousands of foxes and mink are raised in a semidomesticated state by fur farmers who have located generally on islands in southeast and southwest Alaska. Fox skins come first in total value, followed in order by mink, beaver, muskrat, lynx, and other fur-bearing animals.

Wild-life resources have a distinct value both to tourists and to permanent residents. In some parts miners and other settlers largely depend on caribou, mountain sheep, and other game, together with fish, to supply their needs for fresh meat. In addition, natives and many whites prepare dried meat and fish for winter use. Hunting and fishing are good in Alaska, and hundreds of men come to the territory to enjoy these sports. The wild sheep and other animals in Mount McKinley Park are always an attraction to visitors. Thirteen bird and game refuges, aggregating over 4,000,000 acres, have been established to protect the breeding grounds of birds or to afford safe homes for big-game animals.

FORESTS AND WATER POWER

Although most of Alaska has been listed as forest covered, only about 3,000,000 acres have trees of commercial value for lumber or pulp. Fortunately, fully three-fourths of this timber lies within a few miles of the sea and rarely at altitudes above 2,500 feet. The Forest Service estimates the Panhandle section alone to have 80,000,000,000 board feet and southern Alaska another 6,000,000,000. Farther inland there is another

1,000,000 acres of limby spruce, birch, and cottonwoods, with possibly 500,000,000 cords of wood. Such scrub stands are highly prized locally for their use as fuel, mine timbers, construction purposes, and the like. Unfortunately, the growth in the interior is extremely slow, and near some settlements large areas have been deforested or badly damaged by fire. In the far north large areas of brush, tundra, and muskeg have little or no value at present.

The commercial forests are composed of a mixture of hemlock and spruce with scattered groves of red and Alaska cedars. For the most part, there is a dense undergrowth, making exploration difficult. Many trees are of huge size. Hemlocks and spruces may be 3–5 feet in diameter at the base and cedar trees 6–8 feet, with corresponding heights to lower limbs. Dead tops show that much of the timber is overripe, and cutting operations have not kept pace with the growth. Sitka spruce makes the best lumber, red cedar is preferred for siding and shingles, and hemlock is cut for ties, piling, flooring, and rough lumber. Both the spruce and hemlock make excellent paper, and, according to the Forest Service, they can yield an annual crop of some 2,000,000 cords of wood. The two national forests, the Tongass in the Panhandle and the Chugach in the Prince William Sound region, have 21,346,000 acres in reserves, parts of which contain some of the finest timber in Alaska.

The commercial forests are also the regions of the greatest hydroelectric possibilities, although trees are of less importance in protecting the watershed in Alaska than they are in lower latitudes. In the Panhandle section alone, with its unusually steep slopes and very heavy precipitation, there are possibilities of developing at least 1,000,000 horsepower of hydroelectric energy, an output much greater than the region probably will ever be able to consume. A normal pulp industry, it has been estimated, would furnish an outlet for about one-fourth of the amount, and mining another fourth. Some of the mining properties, notably the Alaska-Juneau mine, have developments of their own, and small plants locally furnish electricity for some communities. Unfortunately, in the placer-mining districts, where enormous quantities of water are needed for power, hydraulicking, and thawing, the amount only too commonly is very limited.

AGRICULTURE AND LIVESTOCK

In comparison with Scandinavian and Baltic countries in similar latitudes, Alaska will always have only a small production of crops and livestock. The physical conditions underlying the two regions are very different and really not comparable. Under certain limitations, crops may be grown in Alaska, as has been proved long since; but agricultural lands and grasslands, for one reason or another, are limited in extent and quality. Although estimates give 65,000 square miles, an area larger than Illinois or Iowa, as being capable of some form of cultivation, there are, almost everywhere, one or more unfavorable factors which make such an estimate largely meaningless. In central Alaska the long, cold winter and the short growing-season rule out most crops. The general lack of flat lands in the parts more favored climatically rules out agriculture except patch farming. The only sections with fair opportunities are the Matanuska and Tanana valleys, together with some others of minor importance in the south and southeast.

In view of the handicaps, it is evident that Alaska can never hope to compete with more favored regions in the markets of the world. The isolation of one section of Alaska from another and the great distances intervening will also set a very definite limitation on the integration of the various parts, owing to the necessarily high transportation charges. Crops, if grown, must be consumed in the place of origin; and, on the basis of such sustenance farming, agricultural progress necessarily must be slow. These limitations, in large part, account for the fact that only 5 per cent of the persons gainfully employed make their living primarily from farming, and that over a million dollars worth of agricultural commodities are imported annually, many of which could be produced at home were transportation facilities more favorable.

At present, and presumably in the future also, Alaskan agricultural production is, and will be, of those products which are more or less perishable and which may be adapted to the short growing-season. Vegetables, eggs, and dairy products are at present the most profitable farm products, although potatoes, rutabagas, carrots, beets, and other root crops, peas, and many other garden vegetables of high quality are produced also. Even some hardy small fruits, like strawberries, currants, and gooseberries, are successfully grown; but tree fruits usually winter kill and are not commercially successful.

The agricultural possibilities of chief interest lie in the Panhandle, southern Alaska, and the central interior. The decidedly mountainous character of Alaska naturally limits agriculture. Furthermore, the entire Arctic plain is too cold; and the Seward Peninsula, the Aleutian Islands, and other coastal areas bordering the Bering Sea are too cold, cloudy, or wet for crops, although grazing for reindeer is available. Extensive grasslands on Kodiak Island and some other sections in southwestern Alaska, little used as yet, have some prospective value for hardy cattle or sheep in spite of the stormy climate. Not all of coastal Alaska is mountainous or ice field, but the flat lands are very limited in extent. Where soil conditions are favorable, grasses and root crops, such as potatoes and turnips, grow luxuriantly. Near some settlements, such as Juneau, small farms supply vegetables, fresh milk, and cream for the limited local market, their owners making, in the main, a good income.

The most publicized area in Alaska for agriculture and probably the most favorable for development is the Matanuska Valley, located about 125 miles inland from Seward, at the head of Knik Arm of Cook Inlet. The area under cultivation is about 15 miles long and nearly as wide and is tributary to the town of Palmer, about 40 miles northeast of Anchorage. In the Matanuska Valley are fairly extensive, well-drained terraces which possess somewhat acid but reasonably fertile silt-loam soils of fluvioglacial and aeolian origin. In its virgin state the land is covered with a thick tangle of spruce, aspen, birch, and undergrowth. The high latitude of the region makes a climate with long winters, short summers, and a great contrast in the duration of sunshine between summer and winter days. Winds from Cook Inlet and the warm Pacific somewhat modify the winter cold. Because the heaviest rainfall occurs in July, August, and September, hay must be cured on racks or poles. Snowfall is rarely heavy, and the ground is often swept clear by the wind, thereby causing winter killing of susceptible plants. Fine-quality strawberries are grown, but only as annual plants, because of winter killing. Potatoes of early-maturing varieties yield well but are somewhat watery when harvested and require curing for several weeks in heated cellars to become of good quality. Yields of potatoes of from 300 to 400 bushels per acre are not uncommon, and the present production may be increased considerably, since over 1,000,000 pounds are imported from the States each year.

Although the Matanuska agricultural colony was founded only recently, farming there has been carried on for a generation. Several men located farms in the Matanuska Valley about thirty years ago and since then have successfully raised hay, grain, and root crops; and in 1915 a United States agricultural experiment station was located at Matanuska. In May, 1935, the Federal Emergency Relief Administration sent to the valley 200 families from Michigan, Wisconsin, and Minnesota, who had been on relief, to start an experimental farm colony. Some of the men, however, were found to be physically or mentally unadapted to pioneer conditions and returned to the States. In part, these failures have been replaced by Alaskans. In 1938 about 180 families resided on settlement farms, and they should succeed if they can find a market for their products. The farms average 40 acres, and each is improved with a house, a barn, and other buildings. Most of them have cows, poultry, and pigs as the farm animals. The land was cleared by tractors and other machinery; and in two years, after clearing, from 4 to 6 tons per acre of hay was cut. Other crops include some spring wheat and barley, raised for poultry and hog food, and peas that yield well and are used in part in a canning plant at Palmer. Root crops, strawberries, and garden vegetables are supplied to Anchorage and other towns, but the steady farm income is expected to come from the sale of dairy produce made in a co-operative creamery at Palmer. It is hoped that much of the food now imported by the people along the Alaska Railroad can be supplied from the valley.

The Matanuska and other settlers will be able to sell their produce to advantage only as long as production does not exceed the demands of the few thousand possible customers. The entire population of Alaska, including all the Indians and Eskimos, totals less than half that of the city of Spokane, a limited outlet indeed. Obviously, not many agricultural colonies are yet needed to supply the needs of the territory, although, if Matanuska succeeds, the development of one or two more similar areas would seem to be justified. Distances are so great in Alaska that homesteading pioneer farmers will have a lonesome life, and their children will have small chance of an education except in sponsored farm-colony enterprises. The development of manufactures, such as the wood-pulp industry, may help to increase the local market and to encourage farming. For the most part, the pioneer farmer's life in Alaska is by no means simple and easy. However, he can commonly, if so minded, add to his income by working for a time in a mine or forest or by raising foxes for their fur. Fish for food and timber for fuel or buildings may always be had for the effort. Life is less complex and, in a measure, less strenuous than in the poorer sections of our larger cities, and many colonists live better with fewer days of labor.

In interior Alaska agriculture is still in the pioneer and experimental stage. The natural handicaps of the farmer include a growing season of less than a hundred days; generally poor soils; frozen ground; low precipitation; vegetation such as moss, timber, and brush; high cost of transportation; small available market; and last, but not least, the necessity of wearing nets as protection against mosquitoes. On the other hand, the farmer generally receives fair prices for his crops; long hours of summer sunshine in a measure compensate for a short growing season; and, after the land is cleared of its plant cover, the ground thaws deep enough in a few years so that ground frost is not injurious to the growth of crops. The most favorable region is in the Tanana Valley, north of the Alaska Range, where a fairly fertile sandy or silt loam covers 10,000 or more square miles of land, varying from level bottom-land to slightly rolling upland country. Other areas of tillable soil are tributary to the Yukon River. Although farm land is tax exempt in central Alaska, hardly 200 people obtain a living from farming or dairying in the whole interior.

The means of making a living on farms are varied and abundant. Oats and hay are the leading crops, with potatoes, vegetables, strawberries, and raspberries in varying amounts. Wheat matures near Fairbanks, and several years ago a flour mill was built; but the grain was found unsuitable for milling and could be used only for feed, and so the mill never operated. Two good-sized dairy farms supply Fairbanks with fresh milk, but all butter is imported. Dairymen must feed their cows for at least seven months; and, since most of the grain fed is imported, it is impossible for interior Alaska to build up an export of any surplus dairy produce. Producers receive good prices for milk, eggs, and vegetables, since the supply does not equal the demand. Moreover, considerable free goods are available for Yukon farmers. Fish from the rivers and game like caribou and mountain sheep can be secured without much difficulty. The birch and spruce forests provide a near-by source for fuel, posts, and building material for the mere cutting. Men may earn some cash by mining and trapping in their spare time. Given the right kind of settlers, those who are willing to work and who can endure pioneer conditions, Alaska has much in its favor.

Some possibilities for grazing livestock occur in Alaska, although cattle and sheep are of less importance than the reindeer. Natural grasslands suitable for grazing occur on Kodiak Island and its close neighbors, on part of the Aleutian chain, in portions of the coast of Cook Inlet, on Kenai Peninsula, and elsewhere, including part of the Healy Plateau in the interior. The Kodiak area supports at present about 700 cattle and more than 12,000 sheep; and as the winters are generally open, the animals need little or no shelter or stored food during the winter. Elsewhere the animals require winter feeding, and the difficulty of curing hay forms a decided handicap to expansion of a sheep or cattle industry.

On the tundras of the interior, the Bering Coast, and the Arctic plains the introduced reindeer, requiring no hay and but little care, has become the important source of food and hides for leather and greatly outnumbers all other domestic animals combined. The introduction of the reindeer to Alaska was brought about by white men interested in helping the natives, and the effort has proved very successful. After white traders supplied the Eskimos with firearms, large game animals on both land and sea were rapidly killed off, and the natives were threatened with starvation. In an attempt to better their condition Dr. Sheldon Jackson secured private contributions amounting to $2,146 and in 1862 imported 16 reindeer from Siberia. Soon after, Congress was prevailed upon to appropriate money for the importation of others and the maintenance of the industry. Altogether, between 1892 and 1902, 1,280 reindeer were imported into Alaska. These have now increased to herds that number upward of a million, and through them the well-being of the natives has been immeasurably improved. Reindeer are comparatively easy to herd, two men and several dogs being able to care for several thousand animals. Although both Eskimos and whites now engage in raising reindeer, the former own approximately two-thirds of the entire stock. Where available, reindeer meat is widely used for food by both natives and whites; and in some years 1,000,000 pounds of frozen reindeer meat, prepared in a refrigeration plant at Nome, have been exported to the States.

Reindeer are wonderfully well adapted to the Arctic environment. They herd together well and are easy to domesticate. Brothers to the caribou, but somewhat smaller than their wild relative, they can be improved by crossing with the native caribou. They can withstand intense cold, are excellent swimmers, and their wide, flexible hoofs enable them to travel over deep snow and muddy tundra without difficulty. The only climatic condition that affects them seriously is the formation of a hard crust on the snow, through which they are unable to reach their food. During spring, summer, and early fall they graze on grass, sedges, and herbaceous vegetation and browse freely on willows and other shrubs. During the winter they prefer lichens, chief among which is the reindeer moss. As this plant is a very slow grower and may take from fifteen to twenty years to recover completely after thorough grazing, large areas of land are needed for the winter range, especially since 33 acres of grazing land is allotted officially for each reindeer. Mosquitoes and various kinds of flies greatly harass the animals, and the favored summer pasture land therefore is along wind-swept coasts and in the higher regions.

Since the skins of reindeer are too delicate to survive branding by a hot iron, ownership is determined by slitting the ears or by inserting disks in them. Such owner's earbrands are then recorded. At annual roundups, held at convenient points, fawns are marked, and animals are selected for slaughter. Reindeer are polygamous; and, as in the cattle industry, the principal production of meat comes from steers, which dress on an average of 150 pounds of meat, exceptional animals furnishing 200 pounds.

The government estimates that 350,000 square miles of grazing land exists in Alaska, of which 200,000 square miles are particularly suited for reindeer. In these pastures three or four million reindeer could yield about 1,000,000 hides and 150,000,000 pounds of meat annually. Although reindeer and caribou freely interbreed, the domestic reindeer industry cannot be carried on in a wild-caribou range because of the straying of the domestic animals. Eastern Alaska has great herds of wild caribou, which serve as a food supply to Indians, Eskimos, and whites, and here the grazing might well be left to the undomesticated caribou. It is reasonable to expect that 2,000,000 reindeer could be accommodated in Alaska on the northern and western tundras without injury to the native caribou and with decided profit to owners.

GENERAL CONCLUSION

In the past Alaska has been a land of adventure and romance, a place where the chance existed for a poor man to gain wealth quickly from placer gold and the fur trade. At present Alaska is primarily a region of exploitation, where men go for a time to earn a living or to win independent wealth from fish, minerals, or forests. The future must lie with those hardy souls who still possess the pioneering spirit, a love for the wild, and a willingness to labor far from the bright lights and gaiety of cities, in order to subdue the wilderness and create farms and settlements for trading and industries in Uncle Sam's beautiful but unpeopled great northland.

Recent studies undertaken by the Department of the Interior foreshadow a possibility of a self-supporting population of 5,000,000 or more for Alaska. In view of a white population, normally about 30,000, this, if true, indicates remarkable possibilities. The hope seems to lie not in the coming of the individual colonist but in the development companies, like the Hudson Bay or Plymouth companies. It is hoped that proper legislation may be enacted to permit the migration of various alien groups already interested. A report of the National Resources Committee makes Alaska potentially richer than Sweden and Finland together. Alaska is larger by two-thirds than these two countries, with only one-one hundred sixty-fifth as many people. The primary need would seem to be the development of a cheaper transportation. This would help to lower the present fantastically high cost of living and also to provide Alaskan industries a means of reaching a market. Such development is not thought feasible for the isolated colonists.

That Alaska has reached its final stage in its economic evolution is quite certainly not true. Whether organized group settlements like that of the government-sponsored Matanuska Valley is a solution remains yet to be proved. It is, however, certain that Alaska will never become an exporter of agricultural products on a major scale. The major development must be along other lines, but agriculture can support other industries by keeping down the cost of living. Considerable hope lies in pulp and paper manufacturing, lumbering and woodworking, salting and pickling herring, fur and leather working, and, especially, the mining of ores and coal. The time may not be far distant when Alaskan coal will fill a real need on the West Coast in place of a waning oil supply.

At present, as it was in the past, Alaska is a land of exploitation. Conservative estimates place the wealth thus far siphoned off at $2,000,000,000, and only an infinitesimal amount has flowed back in for local development. Very definitely the development of Alaska has been based on an absentee landlord system, for few have gone there to make it their home and to take part in an expanding frontier. At present there are 228 white males for every 100 white females, and only 35.4 per cent of the white males over fifteen are married. The birth rate is only a little more than half that in the States and not nearly enough to maintain the present population. Such is not a healthy state of affairs for any territory, no matter under whose control.

The hidden riches of Alaska are of no immediate commercial significance. The distance from world-markets and especially the inadequacy of local transportation facilities make individual commercial development impracticable. Any federal aid in fixing groups of people in permanent homes is apparently entirely justified. This seems to be the first step in establishing a new Alaska. Growth of population in a newly opened territory creates markets for local products. Through the growth of population and trade, improved transportation facilities inevitably develop. Very few areas warrant the development of transportation facilities in uninhabited areas. The need in Alaska is unquestionably for a resourceful people willing to lead a pioneer life. It is no place for those who expect to be pampered and supported for the sacrifice they think they have made. To the young and vigorous with a spirit like that of their forebears, Alaska offers much.

THE TERRITORY OF HAWAII

By JOHN WESLEY COULTER

MARK TWAIN ONCE DESIGNATED THE HAwaiian group as "the loveliest fleet of islands that lies anchored in any ocean." This estimate has not been reversed with the years, and the islands deservedly are renowned for their scenic beauty, for their music, and for their coral strands bathed in surf and sunshine. The islands, too, are semitropical, with a May-day climate throughout the year. The visitor is impressed also by the good will shown on every hand, and in the more densely populated sections the American spirit prevails. On the whole, the people are loyal and patriotic. Children of the foreign born even resent being classified under any other heading than that of American citizens. Modern transportation has reduced the distance from San Francisco to a little over four days by boat and to about eighteen hours by commercial air liner. Early settled by a brown-skinned Polynesian people, the islands became organized as a kingdom, then as a republic, and now are an integral part of the United States, with the status of territory.

The natural beauty, the profusion of flowers, and the hospitality of the people are conceded by all who know the Hawaiian Islands. The islands, however, are not without their scientific interest. The great variety of phenomena resulting from vulcanism and the spectacle of continuous volcanic activity give to the scientist a natural laboratory rarely equaled anywhere. There is abundant evidence even of an ancient period of intense glaciation, correlated with the glacial period on the North American continent. Also, the continuous beating of the trade-wind waves on the northeast coast has cut off the lower ends of valleys, leaving a veritable panorama of waterfalls plunging directly into the sea, always an object of interest from the decks of the passing ships. These falls are of different heights, and the streams that come over the old lava flows are abundantly supplied with water from the heavy precipitation on the upper slopes of the windward side of the great volcanic cone of Mauna Kea.

THE TERRITORY OF HAWAII

The varied hues of a cosmopolitan population are among the visitor's first impressions. In Hawaii, East and West min-

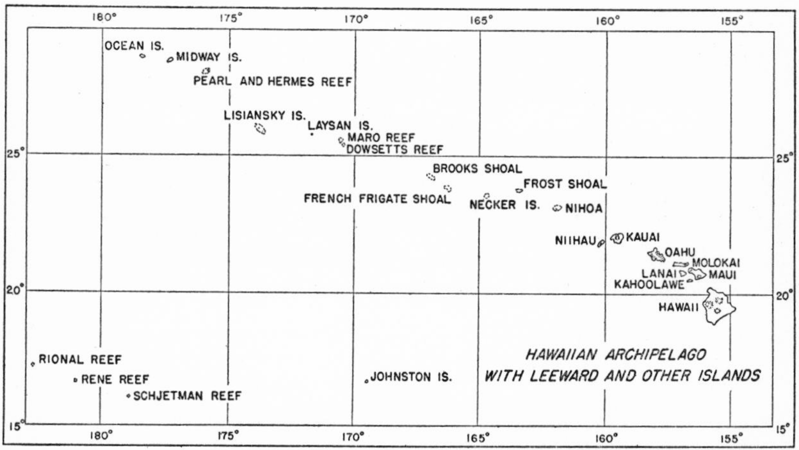

HAWAIIAN ARCHIPELAGO WITH LEEWARD AND OTHER ISLANDS EXTENDING FOR ABOUT 45° OF LATITUDE

gle in business and pleasure—Chinese and Portuguese, Japanese and Caucasians, Filipinos and Puerto Ricans, and all of them rub elbows with the hospitable Hawaiians, friends of the world. To the colorful background of the land of their adoption the immigrants have added a tinge of their own native land. In all, about 425,000 people are permanent residents of the territory.

The Hawaiian Islands comprise a large archipelago in the Pacific Ocean about 1,400 miles north of the Equator and some 2,000 miles from the mainland of the United States. The inhabited islands lie between 18°55′ and 22°15′ N. and between 154°50′ and 160°30′ W. Their area, 6,435 square miles, is a little more than that of the states of Connecticut and Rhode Island together. The island of Hawaii, nearly twice as large as all the other islands combined, contains 4,030 square miles; the other seven range from about 700 to 45 square miles. Oahu, on which Honolulu is situated, has an area of 604 square miles.

Big differences in relief and consequent gradations in temperature from lower to higher levels, the constancy of the prevailing winds, and great variations in rainfall at different locations combine to give the islands a wide variety of climates. Many areas on the leeward sides have weather throughout the year somewhat similar to that of the Mediterranean summer. Between altitudes of about 2,000 and 4,000 feet the climate is like that of the temperate land of Central America. In this zone lies the "coffee belt" of Kona, famed for its salubrious atmosphere. At the tops of the highest mountains subpolar conditions prevail.

The relief of the main islands varies within wide limits. Built upon the ocean floor by volcanic eruptions, the islands have grown above the sea to various heights by further outpourings of lava and accumulations of other volcanic ejecta. Mauna Kea and Mauna Loa on the island of Hawaii are cones with altitudes of 13,784 and 13,653 feet, respectively. Even in summer snow flurries occur on their tops, and water freezes. On the slopes of these volcanoes are hundreds of square miles of barren wastes. Haleakala, on the island of Maui, reaches an elevation of 10,025 feet. On the island of Oahu, Puu Kaala stands 4,025 feet above the Pacific.

The surfaces of the original mountain slopes have been modified in various degrees by weathering and erosion. Older domes—for example, Waialeale on Kauai—have highly dissected surfaces of alternating ridges and valleys. Into some of these lava masses erosion has carved great gulches, leaving between them steep, sharp-topped divides. In contrast, however, Mauna Kea and Mauna Loa on the island of Hawaii, more recently formed mountains, have been little affected by erosion. The slopes of Mauna Loa are covered by a recent outpouring of lava which preserves the wrinkled and jagged forms in which molten rock came to rest. Those of Mauna Kea are interrupted by steep cinder cones, which still maintain much of their original shape.

The islands are not wholly mountainous, however. There are many plainlike surfaces widely distributed at varying altitudes. For example, a broad coastal plain skirts the southern shore of Oahu. Western Molokai and central Maui are made up of extensive areas of little relief. Waimea Plateau stretches between Mauna Kea and Kohala, and Humuula Plateau between Mauna Kea and Mauna Loa. Taken by and large, there is a remarkable variation in the relief of the territory. Only two states on the mainland exceed the island of Hawaii in range of elevation, and only four exceed it in maximum absolute elevation. Even the city of Honolulu is built on land varying in altitude from sea-level to approximately 2,300 feet.

Although the islands lie relatively near the Equator, their position in the northern part of the trade-wind belt gives them a cooler climate than their low latitude would seem to indicate. The trade winds blow regularly from the northeast and east. The sensible temperature for the islands is relatively low. Places on the windward or northeast slopes are cooler than those on the lee side. In Honolulu the August, or highest,

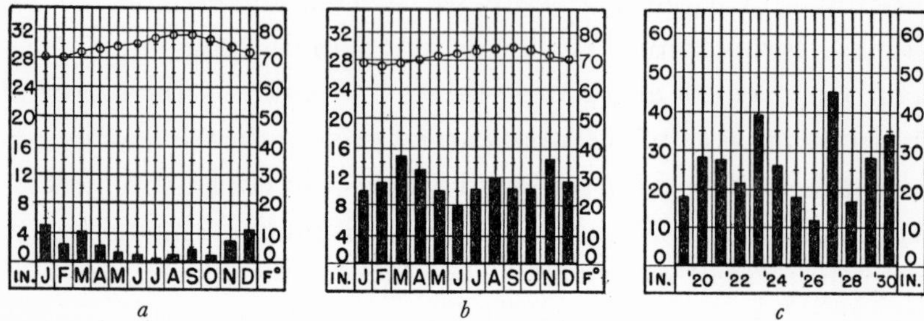

VARIATION IN RAINFALL IN DIFFERENT PARTS OF HAWAII

a) Average annual rainfall and temperature for Honolulu; typical of the leeward sides of the islands.

b) Average annual rainfall and temperature for Hilo; typical of the windward sides of the islands.

c) Variation in annual rainfall from year to year at Honolulu; typical of the variation in the territory.

mean is 78.4° F.; the January, or lowest, mean is 70.7° F. At Hilo on the island of Hawaii, the comparable figures are 75.0° and 69.9°. The mean temperature of the ocean at Waikiki beach in Honolulu is 74.1° F. at eight o'clock in the morning for January.

The lee slopes of mountains receive a moderate or scant rainfall. Honolulu, on the south side of Oahu and on the lee side of a mountain mass, has an annual rainfall of only 26.84 inches. Hilo, at a similar elevation but on the east or windward side of Hawaii Island, has an annual rainfall of 139.43 inches. Much of the rain that falls on lee slopes is the result of

"Kona" storms which occur with southerly winds; these storms generally occur in the cooler months of the year.

The maximum rainfall occurs on the windward slopes at elevations somewhere between 2,000 and 5,000 feet, depending on conditions. Thus, near the summit of Mount Waialeale on Kauai Island, the annual rainfall reaches the surprising total of 440 inches, an amount nearly as great as that of Cherrapunji in India, with its 456.95 inches, the greatest known.

An almost infinite variety of relationships between wind, topography, and altitude brings about a similar variety of rainfall conditions in remarkably close proximity. For example, Puu Kukui, on the island of Maui at an elevation of 5,000 feet, has an annual rainfall of 370.07 inches; and Kihei, at sea-level 10 miles away, has only 11.29 inches. Similar sharp contrasts are also found on leeward sides, and people in Honolulu sometimes speak of "one-shower" and "two-shower" streets because showers are more numerous on the one than on the other.

There are also great variations in rainfall from year to year at the same places in all parts of the islands. In 1926 at the United States Weather Bureau station in Honolulu the precipitation was 11.27 inches; in 1927, 43.52 inches, or nearly four times as much; in 1928, only 15.34 inches. Records of precipitation at other stations in the islands show similar annual variations. There are also great variations from month to month; no single month or season can be designated as the rainiest for any period of successive years.

Such great variations in rainfall and in other conditions of the environment result in great differences in natural vegetation. The middle slopes of the mountains of the territory are characterized in general by dark-green forests—thin stands in areas of moderate rainfall and dense, leafy growth in wet zones. In a few highlands there are patches of typical bog vegetation. In contrast, some areas at medium elevations are deserts of lava, like Kau on the island of Hawaii.

The higher parts of the islands vary from forested mountain ridges to desolate lava-covered wastes. The mountains on Oahu and Molokai are forested to their summits. The higher areas of the volcanoes of Mauna Loa and Mauna Kea, on Hawaii, reach far above the timber line.

Besides an extremely large number of native species, there are thousands of ornamental trees, shrubs, and flowers, introduced from various parts of the globe. In Honolulu parks the handsome Indian banyan tree with its great branches is propped by its stout, aerial roots. In the gardens of that city the beautiful Mexican golden cup adorns fences and arbors. Norfolk Island pines and Japanese cedars flourish in the cool uplands. The rose, national emblem of England, is an adopted flower of the island of Maui. The lilac, carnation, and many orchids have also come from abroad to enhance the natural beauty of these sunny islands of the Pacific.

The landscape of Hawaii is noted for its great variety of form and color. On some of the islands narrow coastal plains are backed by gentle slopes which end abruptly against steep precipices. On others a gradual slope extends from the ocean waters to the very summit of the more elevated parts. Gray, parched areas of semiarid vegetation contrast sharply with the dark green of the luxuriant rain forest or with that of sugarcane fields and other crops. Some shorelines, like those of Hawaii and Lanai, are very regular. Others—for example, those of Oahu—are indented with bays and inlets.

The cultural development is confined almost entirely to the narrow coastal fringes of the islands. The development starts even within the bordering ocean, where artificial fishponds are constructed among the coral reefs. The inclosing walls are 4 or 5 feet high, built from boulders of lava and coral. Their construction goes so far back in Hawaiian history that folklore attributes the first to the *menehunes*, or Polynesian fairies.

The lower slopes and the narrow coastal plain are given over very largely to sugar cane. On the east coast of the island of Hawaii, sugar-cane fields stretch out continuously for 60 miles or more. On the other islands the cane fields are less continuous. In all, about 250,000 acres are used for this crop. From an interisland steamer or from an airplane such areas appear like great carpets of green, marked off into huge rectangular patterns by the various roadways. Within these areas stand the mills, with their shining roofs and tall smokestacks and with the usual cluster of houses adjoining. In some parts the grayish-green slopes of semiarid brushwood and a stunted forest growth stand out against reddish-brown soil entirely devoid of vegetation. Then there are areas of low, rolling country cut by gulches extending from the mountains to the sea. Here on the gentler slopes are clumps of broad-leaved banana and dome-shaped mango trees or the rows of some truck crop outlined in an irregularly shaped field. In the still flatter areas are the symmetrical patches of light green with their taro and rice. This cultural landscape of crops is broken on the island of Oahu by the occasional barracks of soldiers or sailors. The naval base at Pearl Harbor, Oahu, has its appurtenances of machine-shops, oil tanks, dry docks, and the like, giving the appearance of a small town. On some of the lower plateaus great fields of pineapples are outlined in blocks by dirt roads.

At the edges of these areas there are groups of frame houses, the homes of the workers. At various altitudes in some of the more level sections are extensive tracts of grasslands.

The urban settlements of the islands are outstanding features on coastal plains and lower slopes. Hilo on Hawaii, Lahaina on Maui, and Honolulu on Oahu are ports which serve near-by agricultural sections. The hinterland of Honolulu, however, actually includes all the islands in the group. The city stretches for about 14 miles along the ocean and extends 4 miles up Nuuanu and Manoa valleys and lesser distances into smaller valleys. Wharves and adjoining warehouses are confined to the harbor, which is small and in part artificially constructed. The larger and more attractive business houses in the city are headquarters of sugar and pineapple companies and two banks. Two large buildings on Waikiki beach are commodious hotels. Beautiful parks and other recreation grounds are situated in the downtown district, along the ocean, and in the suburbs.

LAND UTILIZATION

The great majority of the people of the Hawaiian Islands earn a living directly or indirectly from agriculture. The territory is pre-eminently a land of sugar cane and pineapples. Many other forms of agriculture are represented: corn, cotton, coffee, rice, and taro are raised. Vegetables of both the subtropical and temperate zones are produced; and tropical fruits, like bananas, papayas, coconuts, mangoes, guavas, and breadfruit, grow abundantly. Stock farming has been an important industry in Hawaii for decades, and the huge Parker Ranch on the island of Hawaii, with its 500,000 acres of land and 30,000 head of cattle, is world-famous. Sheep and goats range at the higher elevations, and hogs and poultry thrive on farms in the lowlands. The sugar-cane and pineapple plantations depend on the local breeders to supply them with their horse and mule draft animals. The average annual value of agricultural products is about $100,000,000, of which about $60,000,000 represents sugar, $34,000,000 pineapples, $4,500,000 animal products, and $1,500,000 coffee, vegetables, and fruits.

Throughout the islands there is a marked tendency for crops to be grown in belts or zones related to altitude and moisture conditions. Rice and taro grow mainly on flood plains and river deltas; bananas and vegetables on the next higher lands. Sugar cane is dominant on the lower mountain slopes, although some is grown at an altitude of 2,000 feet. Pineapples, for the most part, occupy the lands above the cane fields; coffee and cotton are raised in the middle altitudes. Many of the higher slopes have no agriculture except in favored places where cattle find some grazing. Thousands of acres in the highlands are in government or private forest preserves. The acreage that ultimately may be put under the plow is unknown, as conditions may change greatly. There are many favorable areas widely scattered throughout the islands that may add their quota to the agricultural land; but with present markets, cost of production, and standard of living there is little hope of increasing the acreage.

The crops are unevenly distributed among the various islands. Oahu has the most land in cultivated crops, in large part because in the city of Honolulu there is a ready market for a wide variety of products of the soil. Although the growing of bananas, various types of market gardening, and the production of dairy products are important locally, the two

ARABLE AND NONARABLE LAND IN THE TERRITORY OF HAWAII

About 8½ per cent of the area of the islands is used for tilled crops

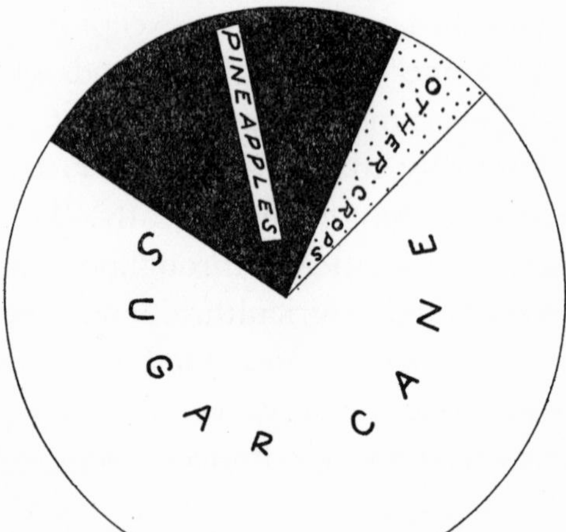

AREA DEVOTED TO MAJOR CROPS

Of the total cultivated land in the territory, about 72 per cent is used for sugar cane, 22 per cent for pineapples, and 6 per cent for other crops.

great money crops are sugar cane and pineapples. On Hawaii, sugar-cane fields are common, but there are no pineapples; this island also produces all the coffee that enters commerce from the territory; nearly 1,500,000 acres are in pasture. On Maui there is a relatively large acreage in sugar cane and pineapples, with a fairly large area devoted to mixed farming. On Kauai sugar cane and pineapples are the leading crops, although the island produces almost all the rice grown in the

TABLE 1

LAND UTILIZATION, 1930

Crop	Acres	Classification	Acres
Sugar cane	252,128	Total cultivated land	351,719
Pineapples	78,750	Pasture	2,076,347
Coffee	5,498	Forest reserves (private)	354,796
Rice and taro	2,741	Forest reserves (government)	667,018
Vegetables	2,319	Roads, city, town, and village sites	42,144
Fruits and nuts	2,862	United States military and naval reserves	24,556
Other crops (including fodder)	7,421	Wasteland and unaccounted for	601,820
Total cultivated land	351,719	Area of the islands	4,118,400

territory. On Kahoolawe and Niihau there is grazing only; these two islands and Molokai are without sugar cane because of the aridity and the lack of suitable water for irrigation. Although agriculture is the chief industry, only 8.5 per cent of the entire surface of the Hawaiian Islands is used for tilled crops. On Hawaii, the largest island, only 4.8 per cent is in crops; and on Kahoolawe there is no agricultural development because the rainfall is inadequate. Of all the islands, Oahu is most favored, for it has 21.6 per cent of its area under cultivation. Of the total area cultivated in 1930, 71.69 per cent was used for sugar cane, 22.39 per cent for pineapples, and only 5.92 per cent for all the other crops. This distribution may be considered normal, although more recently the sugar lands have been reduced 8–10 per cent under the quota system of the Agricultural Adjustment Act.

POPULATION

The origin of the native people of the islands has been established as Polynesian, but the exact place from which they came will probably never be known, for the story of their migrations is lost in antiquity. It has been fairly definitely established that they came to the islands a long time ago in at least two distinct migrations; the first occurred prior to A.D. 500; and the second, during the eleventh and twelfth centuries of the Christian Era. When the archipelago was discovered by Captain Cook in 1778, the number of inhabitants was probably not more than 250,000. Contacts in subsequent years with foreigners—sandalwood-traders, whalers, and others—resulted in the introduction of diseases which so decimated the natives that by 1853 their number was only 71,000 and was still diminishing. At this time there were about 2,000 foreigners in Hawaii, more than half of whom were Caucasians of American and European origin. There were also nearly 400 Chinese, representing the first of many different racial or national groups which came to the islands from time to time.

The history of the coming of the later racial groups reflects the history of the sugar industry. Sugar cane was under cultivation by the natives at the time of the discovery of the islands, but it is believed that the earliest manufacture of sugar did not take place until 1802. In that year a Chinese who came in one of the vessels engaged in the sandalwood trade manufactured a small quantity of sugar on the island of Lanai.

The first effective sugar plantation was established at Koloa, Kauai, in 1835. A decade later there were a score of sugar enterprises operating, but only in a small way. The discovery of gold in California in 1848, with the consequent increase in population, brought about a considerable demand for sugar there and resulted in a marked expansion of the area used for sugar cane in Hawaii. By 1850 the amount produced was 750,238 pounds. Inevitably there arose the need of an abundant supply of cheap and dependable labor in order to produce profitably more and more sugar.

The resources of the Hawaiians were such that it was not necessary for them to accept plantation employment in very great numbers. Their physical, psychological, and cultural traits had become nicely adjusted to the natural environment of their country long before the white man disrupted their whole social and economic order. Perhaps another factor in the situation was that the white foreigners did not give any demonstration that manual labor of any kind was a desirable thing. Business men and others, including some of the leading Hawaiians, who were anxious to make money quickly, believed that the natural resources of the islands could not be fully exploited unless there could be brought about the immigration of a large number of people accustomed to hard work and willing to work regularly. To any sugar-planter who could meet the expense involved, the advantages of an introduction of foreign laborers were believed to be many.

In 1852 a shipment of Chinese laborers was brought to Honolulu, and others soon followed. In 1859 South Sea Islanders were landed on the island of Kauai to work on a plantation. In 1869 cargoes of laborers arrived from the Caroline Islands, Humphrey Island (Manihiki), and Danger Island

(Puka-puka). In 1870, 30 white men from the United States came to Hawaii to work on sugar-cane plantations.

A duty on sugar imported into the United States worried the planters and militated against the highest development of the industry. Aid was obtained in 1876 by the government of Hawaii in a reciprocity treaty with her great neighbor which provided for the reciprocal free admission into the United States and the Hawaiian Islands of certain commodities, among which sugar was the only considerable article of export from Hawaii. The resulting expansion of the industry called for more and more laborers for the plantations.

In 1878 a number of Portuguese arrived from Madeira, followed soon afterward by many more. In 1896 there were 15,191 Portuguese in the islands, including the Hawaiian born. In the same year the number of Chinese residents reached 21,216. In 1881 two vessels with Norwegians arrived. In 1885 the introduction of Japanese laborers began on such a large scale that by 1896 there were 24,407 Japanese in Hawaii. During the 1880's and 1890's a thousand Germans came to the Hawaiian Islands, adding another element to the racial and national groups.

In order to regulate the supply of labor and to prevent competition for laborers between plantations, the Hawaiian Labor and Supply Company was formed in 1882, consisting of representatives of the various plantation owners. In 1895 it was reorganized into the Hawaiian Sugar Planters' Association. Until the annexation of the Hawaiian Islands to the United States in 1898, nearly all foreign unskilled labor came indentured or under contract to serve for a term of years at stipulated rates of wages and hours of labor. The picture was changed in 1900, when all such labor contracts were made void by terms of the Organic Act, which provided for the government of the islands as a part of the United States.

With annexation the Chinese exclusion laws of the United States effectually shut out further immigration of Chinese laborers, already much restricted by Hawaiian laws. However, between 1903 and 1905 more than 7,000 Korean emigrants came to the Hawaiian Islands. The so-called "Gentleman's agreement" of 1907 prevented skilled and unskilled Japanese laborers from obtaining passports to go to the United States and therefore to Hawaii, and in 1924 an act of the United States ended the immigration of Japanese except under very stringent conditions.

Between 1906 and 1931 the Hawaiian Sugar Planters' Association turned almost entirely to the Philippine Islands as a labor reservoir. An organization in the Philippines was built up under arrangement with the insular government, which by advertising and other means had little trouble in getting thousands of young men of the poorer agricultural classes to emigrate. With the recent granting of independence to the Philippine Islands, effective in 1946, the immigration of Filipinos to the United States has been restricted to 50 a year. The average number of Filipinos that arrived in the Hawaiian Islands from the Philippines each year between 1921 and 1929 was 8,190. The greatest number in any one of those years was 12,578, in 1928; and the smallest, 4,995, in 1926. In 1931 their number was 66,049; since then it has decreased, as a result of excess of departures over arrivals, to 52,810 in 1938. Filipinos are the most numerous workers in the cane fields today and form nearly 13 per cent of the total population of the territory.

A great many immigrants from Europe had come as family units within their group, whereas most of those in the early groups from Asia came as men without wives. Later many Japanese procured wives from their native land. Many Chinese, Koreans, and especially Filipinos remain in the islands to this day mainly a body of men without families. These in-

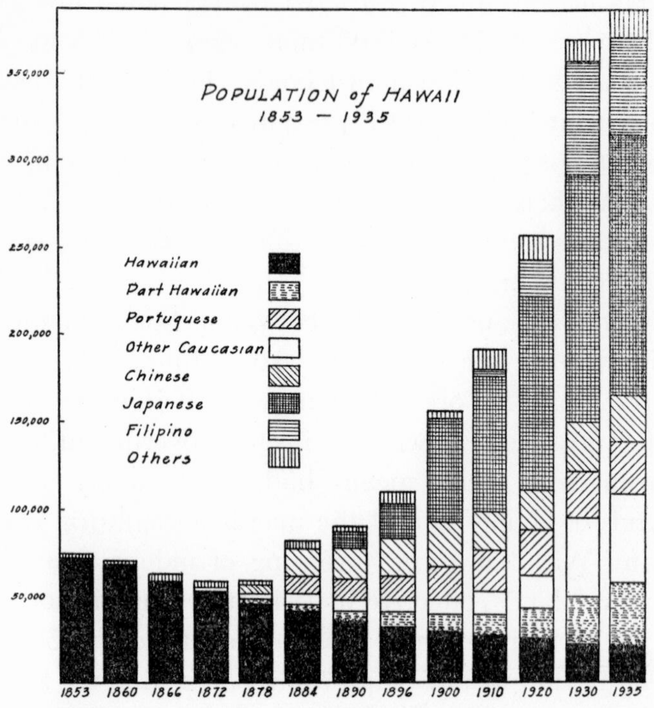

GROWTH OF THE POPULATION OF HAWAII, 1853–1935

To be noted is the marked decrease in the native people and the marked increase in the Japanese.

equalities of sex ratios and various other social and economic factors have brought about many interracial marriages in Hawaii. The sanction of such unions by law and public opinion means much to a people of mixed blood so far as social status, economic opportunities, and general character as citizens are concerned.

All Hawaiians and part-Hawaiians are citizens of the territory and of the United States. A large number of Portuguese immigrants who did not migrate to the mainland of the United States when their labor contracts expired have become naturalized citizens. Puerto Rican immigrants were granted citizenship by Congress through the Jones Act of 1917. Many

TABLE 2

POPULATION OF THE TERRITORY OF HAWAII
JUNE 30, 1938

Race	Number	Percentage of Total Population
Hawaiian	21,268	5.2
Part Hawaiian:		
Caucasian-Hawaiian	20,507	5.0
Asiatic-Hawaiian	20,360	4.9
Caucasian:		
Portuguese	30,406	7.4
Puerto Rican	7,639	1.9
Spanish	1,248	0.3
Other Caucasians	67,706	16.5
Chinese	28,380	6.9
Japanese	153,539	37.3
Korean	6,707	1.6
Filipino	52,810	12.8
Others	915	0.2
Total	411,485	100.0

Chinese and Japanese are barred from naturalization by laws of the United States. More than two-thirds of the Filipinos are aliens. Children of all races born in the islands since annexation are citizens of the United States.

Tables 2 and 3, compiled by the Bureau of Sanitation, Board of Health of the territory, give the composition of the population and the number of citizens and aliens estimated as of June 30, 1938. The race names, taken from the United States census, correspond to distinctions formerly made in the kingdom of Hawaii. Hawaiians are the supposedly full-blooded descendants of the old Polynesian inhabitants of the islands. Caucasian-Hawaiians are mixed-blood descendants of the Hawaiians and Caucasians; the Asiatic-Hawaiians are of mixed Hawaiian and Asiatic ancestry. The Asiatic ancestry is commonly Chinese; but Japanese, Korean, and Filipino blood also enter into the mixture. About one-third of the Asiatic-

TABLE 3

Citizen and Alien Population, June 30, 1938

Race	Citizens	Aliens
Hawaiian	21,268	....
Part Hawaiian:		
Caucasian-Hawaiian	20,507	....
Asiatic-Hawaiian	20,360	....
Caucasian:		
Portuguese	28,898	1,508
Puerto Rican	7,639	....
Spanish	1,069	179
Other Caucasians	66,382	1,324
Chinese	24,097	4,283
Japanese	116,584	36,955
Korean	4,355	2,352
Filipino	16,201	36,609
Others	825	90
Total	328,185	83,300

Hawaiians have Caucasian blood also. The terms Portuguese, Puerto Rican, and Spanish are applied only to those who are not known to be mixed with each other, or with "Other Caucasians." The term "Other Caucasians" refers to all Caucasians who do not belong to the Portuguese, Puerto Rican, and Spanish groups. They range from descendants of early missionaries to the service men of the military and naval establishments, and represent a variety of nationalities besides American. The total of 67,706 today may be contrasted with the corresponding numbers of 8,547 in 1900 and 1,262 in 1853. "Other Caucasians" are commonly referred to in the territory as the *haole* population, a Hawaiian designation originally applied to any foreigner.

The density of population for the eight inhabited islands is nearly 64 per square mile, but its distribution is very uneven. Hawaii, the largest island, has 20 people per square mile; Oahu, 378. Kahoolawe has 2 people for 45 square miles, its total area. Hundreds of square miles in the higher portions of the larger islands are uninhabited. In contrast, many areas along the peripheries are densely populated. Honolulu, the capital of the territory, has 153,073 people—37 per cent of the total number of people in the islands; Hilo, the second city, has 16,459.

THE SUGAR-CANE INDUSTRY

Thirty per cent of the people of the Territory of Hawaii live on sugar-cane plantations upon which they depend directly for their livelihood. A large number work in subsidiary industries: on railroads connecting the plantations with the seaports, on the wharves as stevedores and clerks, in machine-shops and fertilizer factories, for oil companies and other business concerns—all dependent entirely, or to a large extent, upon the business of producing sugar. Approximately 39 per cent of the property taxes paid to the territorial treasurer and a substantial portion of income taxes, customs duties, and internal revenues come directly and indirectly from sugar.

There are 38 sugar-cane plantations in the islands: 16 on the island of Hawaii, 10 on Kauai, 7 on Oahu, and 5 on Maui. Olaa Sugar Company, on the island of Hawaii, the largest plantation, has 15,087 acres in sugar cane. Waimea Sugar

Mill Company on Kauai, the smallest, has 660 acres. Many sugar companies have considerable areas of unused, nonarable land or land used only in connection with the conservation of water. In addition to their own cane acreages, a few have contracts with small farmers from whom cane is bought and ground in the company mills.

The amount of land used for sugar cane on each of the four producing islands depends upon the existence of large tracts of adjacent lands suited to cane production by relief, by rainfall, and by opportunities for irrigation. Several factors handicap the sugar industry in Hawaii: a scarcity of labor resulting from the isolation of the islands, cool winters which retard the growth of cane, and scant annual rainfall in otherwise favorable places, necessitating costly irrigation. The period of growth necessary for sugar cane ranges from about fourteen to twenty-two months, depending in part upon the altitude of the fields and the amount of water available.

The unusual conditions of the environment in Hawaii call for highly specialized varieties of cane. There is probably no other place in the world where science has been so intensively applied to the growing of a crop. Varieties of cane from many lands have been planted in experimental plots and crossbred, producing hundreds of thousands of hybrids. Of the many, only a few strains have proved to be very valuable.

Land used for sugar cane is prepared for seeding by thorough plowing. The seed consists of pieces of stalks 1–2 feet long, usually cut from the tops of ripe cane before harvest. About one-tenth of the area of a plantation is planted each year. Five or six crops are raised from one planting; crops subsequent to the plant crops are termed "ratoon crops." The invariable practice of raising sugar cane continuously necessitates the application of a large amount of fertilizer; that commonly used is composed of nitrogen, phosphoric acid, and potash. The amount used is about 1 ton per acre and is determined by careful analyses of the soils of the different fields.

It requires approximately 2,000 tons of water, equivalent to about 125 inches of rain a year, to mature enough cane to furnish a ton of sugar. The farther below that amount the available water falls, the more hazardous is the use of the land for this crop. The rainfall on most plantations on the windward side of the islands is sufficient, but the scant rainfall on the leeward side necessitates costly irrigation systems.

The irrigation water is surface runoff from the mountain ranges and ground water from wells and tunnels. The task of procuring water for irrigation is complicated by the absence of large rivers. Furthermore, nearly all the streams in the islands are very irregular in their flow, rising suddenly to great volume during heavy rains and dwindling to insignificant streamlets or drying up entirely during periods of fair weather. Because the streams have steep gradients, there are few basins in which much water could be stored, and in them only by the construction of very high dams.

Perhaps the most important factor is the pervious nature of the soil, which allows surface water to seep quickly to a ground-water level, which in many places is too far below the surface to be valuable.

Water, the life-stream of the islands, is costly. A plantation on Oahu has irrigation equipment valued at $5,750,000, and the operation of the pumping system requires an annual outlay of $365,000 for power alone. On irrigated plantations the capital invested in waterworks, the cost of their maintenance, and the expense incurred in applying water to the fields make up a large part of the total expenditure of the production of sugar. Although irrigation is costly, the cost is warranted by increased yields. The average return of irrigated plantations is about $8\frac{1}{2}$ tons of sugar per acre of sugar cane, and that of unirrigated plantations is $5\frac{1}{2}$ tons of sugar per acre. Although irrigated plantations use only 53 per cent of the cane acreage,[1] 66 per cent of the sugar produced annually in the territory comes from them.

Each district has its individual problems. The diversity of soil and climatic conditions, even on adjoining plantations, makes it necessary for each manager to devise his own best system of production. On some plantations fixed schedules of planting and replanting are followed; on others, fields are ratooned as long as they yield a profitable return.

The time of harvesting is related to the peculiar environmental factors of the territory and the distribution of labor. Harvesting generally begins in November and ends the following August or September. The optimum ripening period is from the latter part of February until the end of June. However, if all the cane to be harvested were cut during that period, a temporary reinforcement of the labor staff would be necessary, and one of the important objectives of plantation

[1] The figures for 1934, a representative year, are:

	Acreage		Production of Sugar		Tons of Sugar per Acre
	Acres	Percentage of Total	Tons	Percentage of Total	
Irrigated	131,789	53	688,350.7	66.6	8.6
Unirrigated	117,032	47	345,388.1	33.4	5.5

management is to give employment throughout the year to a permanent labor force.

In order to make cutting cane less arduous, cane fields are "burned" before harvesters begin operations. Because of the large amount of juice in the stalks, they do not burn; the dry leaves, however, which would cut and irritate the workmen, are totally consumed. As the burning destroys the eyes or buds of the cane, some of it is "topped" for seed before the burning takes place. Green tops are cut for mule fodder.

Cut cane is transported to the mill in railway cars run on portable and permanent tracks, by trucks, overhead cable, or, where water is available and the topography suitable, in flumes. The process of extracting sugar from sugar cane is divided into five steps: crushing the cane and extracting the juice, clarifying the mixed juice, condensing the clarified juice into a thick syrup, crystallizing the syrup, and separating the crystals from the mass. The last process at the mill is bagging for market.

The total yearly output of raw sugar in Hawaii is about 1,000,000 tons, one-seventh of the amount consumed annually in the United States. From 1921 to 1931, inclusive, the amount produced in the territory increased approximately 82 per cent, although the acreage increased only 15 per cent. Among the more important factors contributing to the increase were the introduction and propagation of new varieties of cane, improved cultural practices, and more efficient methods of extracting the juice.

With the exception of from 20,000 to 30,000 tons consumed annually for domestic purposes and about 20,000 tons refined locally for use in the pineapple industry, the sugar produced in Hawaii is shipped to two refineries near San Francisco and to one on the Atlantic seaboard. The refined sugar is sold by the brokerage system, the Pacific Coast states and the area from the Rockies east to the Mississippi River now absorbing about three-quarters of the output.

There are five large agencies or sugar "factors" in the territory, all of which have headquarters in Honolulu: American Factors, Ltd.; C. Brewer and Company, Ltd.; Alexander and Baldwin, Ltd.; Castle and Cooke, Ltd.; and Theo. H. Davies and Company, Ltd. They look after the interests of stockholders; arrange for the shipping of raw sugar from the plantation ports, or landings, to the refineries; and buy machinery, provisions, and other supplies for their plantations. They look after the matters involving land titles, leases, taxation, and insurance, and supervise all expenditures. The directors of these agencies appoint their plantation-managers, and the managers are responsible to them for the conduct of all plantation employees.

Plantation-managers and their employees and dependents live on the plantations in villages. The larger villages are situated near the sugar mills. Homes are one-story frame buildings with *lanais*, or verandas. The larger houses, neatly painted and set at the back of closely mown lawns separated by trim hedgerows, are the homes of plantation executives. Smaller buildings a short distance away, ranged along both sides of well-kept streets, are business districts with establishments similar to those which serve rural communities on the mainland.

Stretching away from the urban settlement, sugar cane to the extent of thousands of acres in hundreds of fields undulates in the vigorous breezes of the trade winds. A field of full-grown cane resembles somewhat a similar area of standing corn. Stalks, 10–15 feet high, with pendant leaves, grow near to-

OAHU SUGAR COMPANY MILL AND PLANTATION "CAMP"
AT WAIPAHU, ISLAND OF OAHU

Note the fields of sugar cane and also the area devoted to market gardening in the immediate vicinity of the village.

gether in rows and form what looks like an impenetrable jungle when viewed from a short distance. Fields of tasseled stalks, ripe for harvest, are interspersed with fields of cane in various stages of growth. Here and there are areas of mottled brown which mark fields in which remain the stumps of harvested cane, and reddish brown patches indicative of soil recently plowed. Adjoining fields are separated by tracks of permanent railway, by dirt roads, or merely by furrows.

When viewed from a sufficiently high elevation, a plantation scene generally presents small groups of houses at outlying points within its confines. They are the villages where laborers live in proximity to the fields in which they work. They are situated at crossroads on a plantation, at the junction of two routes, or at other strategic points. On irrigated plantations the cultural landscape also shows here and there reservoirs and conspicuous concrete buildings which house pumps.

Among the many problems to be solved on plantations are those concerned with the recruiting of laborers, methods of employing them, and the effective distribution of their work throughout the year. The labor problem has always been a serious one in the Hawaiian Islands. Among the inducements held out to Filipino immigrant laborers has been a free passage back home provided a man works 720 days on any plantation or plantations of the Hawaiian Sugar Planters' Association during three consecutive years. Most of those who return take with them from $500 to $1,000 in wages saved during their term of labor. Extraordinarily large sums of money are sent home yearly, amounting in some years to approximately $3,000,000. In addition to saving money, these people have returned home considerably influenced by the American standard of living and otherwise broadened in experience.

Japanese workers rank second in number on sugar-cane plantations. Having lived in the islands longer than the Filipinos, they have in general moved up to more skilled work and higher wages. Many of them are contractors or foremen under one of the systems of labor employment. The nature of the work on plantations is such, and the necessity for efficiency so great, that systems of employment of labor are practiced which put as much responsibility as possible on the laborer, pay him wages in proportion to the value of his work, and increase his contribution to the success of the business venture. The two methods of employment commonly practiced are called "long-term contract" and "short-term contract."

The short-term contract merely means that wages are paid to laborers on a piece-work system and generally at the end of each month. Laborers employed in cutting cane are paid by the ton of cane cut; those who load cane on railway cars are paid by the ton loaded. Hoeing, irrigating, fertilizing, planting, and other work of a similar nature are sometimes paid for by the row, acre, or other unit of measurement. Employment on a short-term contract is particularly adapted to unskilled or inexperienced labor.

The long-term contract is used to encourage laborers to do their best in positions assigned to them and because of the difficulty of supervising labor in fields where cane has reached a height of more than 4 or 5 feet. Long-term contracts are made by the plantation-manager with a number of laborers, under a foreman or field boss, who agree to do the work necessary to raise a field of sugar cane. The number is generally from six to twelve according to the size of the field, the ratio being one laborer to about 10 acres. The contract usually begins at the time a field of cane is planted or ratooned and ends when the cane is ripe for harvest. The contract specifies a rate of payment per ton of cane harvested from fields the employees have tended. During that period the laborers are paid an "advance" on their contract of $1.50 a day. When the sugar cane is harvested, a settlement is made whereby employees are paid the value of contracts less "advances." Men permitted to enter into long-term contracts are the more experienced, efficient, and reliable members of the labor force—the backbone of the labor supply.

Since the demand for labor is greatest during the harvesting season, and since harvesting operations are carried on for only seven or eight months of the year, whereas all labor is employed on a yearly basis, an "off season" remains during which the labor force must be kept busy. The maintenance of equipment provides many laborers with employment during that season. The machinery of the mill is entirely overhauled; plows and tractors are repaired. Work in connection with the maintenance and repair of roads and permanent railways also provides employment for a considerable number of men. Old sheds are torn down and new ones are built; laborers' homes are also renovated or rebuilt. All "odd jobs" which can be saved for the "off season" are postponed until then. Off-season work is generally done on short-term contract or piece-work system.

Laborers have free houses, fuel, and water. The houses are built and kept in repair by the plantation companies. Dormitories are provided for unmarried workers. Plantations have hospitals with resident physicians and nurses, which provide free medical service for workers who earn less than $100 per month and their families. Employees earning $100 or more receive medical and hospital service at cost. Nurses visit the homes of laborers and, among other things, advise mothers on the care and nurture of children. Most companies provide plots of ground free of charge for laborers, where they can raise vegetables for their households.

There is a highly developed organization of the man power of plantations in an effort to secure the largest returns possible under the difficult environmental conditions of operation. The manager is accountable for the business success or failure of the organization and for the morale of his workers and is directly responsible for the general welfare of the thousands of people who live on the plantation. The pressure of economy makes it necessary that junior officers think and plan also. Field *lunas*, or foremen, are required to make reports and to use their judgment and experience in the best interests of the plantation and of the laborers under their immediate supervision. The chief engineer, the field experimenter, the chief chemist, and other heads of departments form a cabinet on whose judgment and opinions the plantation manager can rely. Each is an executive in his own restricted sphere, and each has an opportunity to advance to a higher position in accordance with his education, experience, and ability.

Although the business of raising sugar cane demands a worker's best and most intelligent efforts during the working day, and notwithstanding the fact that the work of a field laborer is arduous, the employees of sugar-cane plantations have time and opportunity for recreation and social activities. The employees have literary clubs and societies, with headquarters in clubhouses furnished and maintained by the plantation companies. Books from public libraries or their branches may be borrowed from the club librarian.

Baseball and soccer teams are organized to compete in intramural and interplantation games. Trophies for tennis champions draw forth the best efforts of devotees of that sport. Sunday is a day of rest and recreation on a plantation. In the morning, services are held in the various churches or other religious centers. The afternoon is generally devoted to recreation; at that time the population of the villages turns out to cheer for the home team.

In the primary schools on the plantations, children have opportunities to complete standard school courses. In addition, Japanese-language schools are supported by the parents of children in attendance. On the Oahu Sugar Company plantation at Waipahu, a company of the Hawaii National Guard provides the drill and discipline which membership in such a unit entails, and inculcates something of the spirit of American citizenship and the duties and responsibilities which it involves. That unit of the national guard is composed almost entirely of young American citizens of oriental parentage.

The successful continuation of the sugar industry in Hawaii is dependent upon an assured future supply of labor. The general trend in plantation leadership is to turn to the locally born children growing up in the islands. Today 30 per cent of the labor in the cane fields is done by citizens of the United States, nearly all locally born youths. However, the majority of young men wish to live in the towns and cities and to have "white-collar" jobs. Just how the labor in the future will be adjusted to the necessity of the situation remains to be seen.

Another factor of critical import to the production of sugar in Hawaii is the tariff, the importance of which cannot be overestimated. The tariff is regarded by the people in the territory as the *sine qua non* of the sugar industry. A prominent attorney in Honolulu stated the situation succinctly in the words: "Our islands are necessarily agricultural; the very existence of our agricultural enterprise depends upon the tariff wall which Congress has erected around them, and the prosperity of our islands depends largely on whether or not our agricultural enterprises prosper." The history of tariffs as they affected the sugar industry in Hawaii shows the overwhelming importance of that factor in the use of the land for sugar cane.

A reciprocity treaty with the United States by the government of Hawaii in 1876 by which sugar was admitted into the United States free of duty was of signal importance in the expansion of the area used for sugar-cane production in the islands. The annexation of Hawaii to the United States in 1898 made the prosperity of the sugar industry more secure and resulted in its further expansion. Since then, increases and decreases in the tariff have resulted in corresponding booms and depressions.

Summing up the factors responsible for the success of the sugar industry in the Territory of Hawaii: (1) sugar cane is adapted to a large part of the arable land at the lower elevations in the islands; (2) sugar is a staple commodity for which there is a large market on the mainland of the United States; (3) great scientific knowledge and business ability are used in the industry; (4) a supply of labor has been maintained by immigration and by all-year employment; and (5) a protective tariff and a quota system enable the growers of cane and beet sugar in the United States, including Hawaii, to supply an appreciable part of the sugar consumed there.

THE PINEAPPLE INDUSTRY

When and from where the first pineapples came to the Hawaiian Islands is a matter of conjecture. That it was early is certain, for a Spaniard, Marin, wrote in his diary on January 11, 1813, that he had made various attempts to grow them as a crop. At this time, it seems, the plant was growing in a semi-wild state, flourishing best, evidently, where the conditions were most favorable. The plants produced some fruit, which was gathered and sold to whalers. Production as a commercial crop, however, was long delayed, and not until 1880 did some farmers have sufficient faith in this half-wild plant to put it under cultivation. In 1885 new varieties were imported in the hope of getting a better strain. As a result of much study and experiments, the improved "smooth cayenne" is grown commercially in the islands today.

The modern history of the industry is an account of pioneers in a new field of agricultural endeavor who, for the most part, employed the method of trial and error. During the course of adjustment to the natural environment it has been necessary to determine by experimentation the fertilizer requirements, soil preferences, and reaction of the plant to rainfall, drainage, winds, and sunshine. Methods of handling the fruit in the canneries have been worked out, the length of time required to sterilize it, and the temperature that must be maintained in the cookers. Finally, the industry is one in which competing companies have been forced into a co-operative system.

The first company of importance established for the production of pineapples was organized in 1891. During the early and middle nineties the industry was carried on with indifferent success. Enterprising pineapple farmers who in 1900 took up homesteads at Wahiawa, on Oahu, successfully marketed several crops. In 1907 provision was made for the disposal of the entire crop of the Hawaiian Islands before it had matured. During those early years the main interest of growers was the raising of fresh fruit for markets on the mainland of the United States. Canned pineapples were hard to sell, for there was little uniformity in the quality, and markets had not been created for them.

Among the homesteaders at Wahiawa were James Dole and John Whitmore, men to whose efforts and initiative the development of the industry has been largely due. They realized that a big business could be built up only by creating a large market for canned pineapples. Their efforts were so remarkably successful that near the end of the first decade of the twentieth century the tendency was for the industry to double each year the output of the year preceding. Land suitable for raising the fruit seemed plentiful, and expansion went on apace. About 1911 there was an overproduction, and the market failed to absorb the output.

The decade following was a time during which outstanding improvements in canning machinery were made, and the mechanization of the industry proceeded very rapidly, both in factory and in field; all of this progress increased the output. In 1912, for the first time, the number of cases of canned pineapples exceeded a million. Between 1911 and 1913 Henry Ginaca, employed by the Hawaiian Pineapple Company, evolved and perfected the "ginaca" machine, which peels the fruit and removes its core, preparatory to slicing and cooking. In 1915 the market was again oversupplied, and leaders in the industry adopted a more conservative policy.

The post-war period of the Hawaiian pineapple industry was one of further and further expansion. During the third decade of the century, the discovery and use of "mulching paper" to inhibit the growth of weeds and to conserve moisture resulted in greatly improved methods of cultivating the crop. In 1922 an experiment station was established at Wahiawa, on Oahu; and in 1924 a research association was organized. Carefully planned advertising stimulated the demand for the canned product. Although there was co-operation in research work and in advertising, keen competition existed for land to raise the fruit, and great rivalry arose in selling the canned product. Many small farmers also specialized in pineapple-growing, and they either sold their product to the canneries with whom they had contracts or else built and operated co-operative canneries of their own.

For several years of the third decade of the twentieth century the industry remained on a high level of production. Near its end, three circumstances were largely responsible for a further expansion. First, it was found that pineapples flourished in semiarid areas; consequently, growers utilized thousands of acres of such land for the crop. Second, the agriculturists in the industry developed and practiced a more intensive system of planting. The increased number of plants per acre produced much larger yields. Third, experiments successfully solved the problem of controlling wilt, a disease caused by mealy bugs. The greatest expansion took place on the islands of Maui, Molokai, and Lanai, where thousands of acres were put under cultivation.

In 1929 the pack of canned pineapples amounted to 9,211,376 cases; and in 1930 it reached 12,672,296 cases—about 80 per cent of the world's output. During the first three decades of the twentieth century the land used for pineapples increased from a few hundred to more than 78,000 acres. It was unfortunate for this expanding industry that the buying-power of the American people was so drastically curtailed by "the depression." A huge surplus accumulated as the markets of the world failed to absorb the product. The companies became convinced that they must co-operate in the output of their product in order to protect their interests. Negotiations were so successful that in 1932 seven companies signed articles incorporating the Pineapple Producers Co-operative Association.

There are seven large pineapple companies: the Hawaiian Pineapple Company; the Hawaiian Canneries Company; the Maui Pineapple Company; the Baldwin Packers; the Kauai Pineapple Company; Libby, McNeill and Libby; and the California Packing Corporation. Their organizations are somewhat similar to those of the sugar-cane plantation companies. The agent for the Maui, Baldwin, and Kauai companies is Alexander and Baldwin, which is also the factor for five sugar-cane plantations. The Hawaiian Pineapple Company is the reorganized company of which Dole was president and which faced serious financial difficulties during the depression. Approximately 60 per cent of the pineapple production is in the hands of agencies which also control a large part of the sugar-cane production of the territory. The Hawaiian branches of Libby, McNeill and Libby and the California Packing Corporation deal with pineapples only. In addition, there are a number of small growers who, however, raise less than 1 per cent of the total. Some of the large companies have contracts with small farmers from whom they buy fruit. Japanese planters near Kapaa, Kauai, have a co-operative organization and a cannery of their own.

The pineapple has a marvelous adaptability to various natural environments. It is raised commercially on Oahu in places where the rainfall is only 20 inches a year; in northern Kauai, where the rainfall is 70 inches; and on Maui, in an area of 120 inches. Nearly all the pineapples are raised on plateau-

HARVESTING PINEAPPLES IN THE HAWAIIAN ISLANDS

Workers are cutting off the tops, preparatory to packing the fruit in boxes to be taken to the cannery.

like lands at elevations between 500 feet and 1,000 feet. On Molokai all the pineapple land lies above the 450-foot contour, and on Lanai between 1,000 and 1,700 feet.

Pineapple fields are thoroughly prepared for planting by repeated plowing and disking until a deep, mellow seed-bed is established. Lanes 300 feet apart are laid out in the fields. Mulching paper is spread on the ground, usually a 36-inch asphalt-saturated paper, through which are set in rows crowns from the tops of the fruits, slips borne on the fruit stem, or shoots arising lower down on the main stalk of the plant. Crowns, slips, and shoots are left exposed to sun and wind for weeks or even months before they are planted in order that a layer around the part which is placed in the ground may be hardened and toughened as a protection against injurious organisms.

Planting usually takes place in the early fall, and produces the first yield the second summer, following a period of from eighteen to twenty months of growth. Of four or five shoots which spring from the main stalk of the plant, two are generally allowed to remain to produce fruit the following summer. Thus the plant crop yields one fruit per plant for harvest; and the ratoon crop, two. A second ratoon crop is harvested one year after the first, the fourth year after planting. During growth, the spaces between the rows are thoroughly cultivated and fertilized. Sulphate of iron is applied directly to the leaves of plants because the iron in much of the soil is chemically unavailable. The yield is about 60 tons per acre for each five-year cycle; for three yields in each cycle the proportion may run 30–15–15 tons per acre. Pineapples from the plant crop are the largest, averaging between 5 and 6 pounds per fruit.

The ripening season for nearly all the pineapples raised is from the middle of June to the beginning of September. Eighty-five per cent of the annual crop ripens and is picked, sorted, delivered to the canneries, and canned at that time. The fruit generally matures only in those months, no matter when it is planted. If, for some reason, fruit does not mature in proper season, it may wait over for a whole year. The harvesting is by hand; pickers pass up and down the rows, breaking ripe fruits off at the stem with a twist of the wrist and putting them into bags slung over their shoulders. The filled bags are carried to the nearest field lane, where they are emptied. The crowns are cut off, and the pineapples are graded into three sizes and packed in boxes for transportation to the canneries. Nearly all the grading is done in the field by the harvesters, who, if they are not sure of the sizes, use rings to measure the fruit.

Harvested pineapples are carried from the fields to canneries located on the islands where they are raised or to ports from which they are shipped to Honolulu, the most important canning center in the territory. At ports of shipment great cranes transfer, a truckload at a time, tiers of skips weighing about 9 tons, to barges which, when full, are towed by tug to the port of Honolulu. There reversing the process, cranes lift the skips to railway cars, which transport them to the canneries.

In the cannery the fruits, segregated according to size, are shelled and cored in ginaca machines. Long belts convey them past women and girls, who deftly cut out any deep eyes that may not have been removed by the machines. The fruit then goes through a slicing machine and is packed in cans according to grade. Broken pieces, diverted on sidetracks, are collected for canning as crushed or grated pineapple. Cans of the perfect product are taken on small, wooden trays in trucks to the syruping machines, which automatically supply each can with the requisite amount of syrup. A conveyor then carries the cans to the steam cooker for sterilization before they are capped. After passing through a second cooking machine, the cans are set out in a cooling-room and lacquered to preserve the tin. They are then sent to a warehouse, labeled, and packed in cases; and finally they go on their way to various parts of the world.

Until the restriction of Filipino immigration, pineapple-planters recruited part of the necessary field labor in the Philippine Islands. A far larger number of laborers is required during the summer harvest, June–September, than at other times of the year. As these months constitute the "off season" on many sugar-cane plantations, both industries use in common a small proportion of the total labor supply. The two mainland pineapple companies without cane connections make special arrangements with managers of sugar plantations for the transfer of labor. The labor for the canneries, operated at capacity only during the summer, is enlisted from housewives and daughters, schoolboys and schoolgirls, who earn pin money and school expenses during that season.

The months from February to May constitute the slack season on the plantations, and at the beginning of this period growers lay off many laborers. In years past, workers have found employment during those months on sugar-cane plantations, coffee farms, or in other fields of work or have migrated to the mainland of the United States.

About half of the field laborers are Filipinos, and one-fourth are Japanese. The rest are representatives of the other races in the islands except "Other Caucasians." Nearly all the *lunas*, or field bosses, are Japanese, men who have the ability to direct and to supervise the work of subordinates. About 50 per cent of the mechanical work—driving tractors and trucks, and mending plows, cultivators, and other agricultural machinery—is done by Portuguese, old settlers who have advanced from the field-labor class.

Ten years ago the island of Lanai was a wind-swept waste. Forty-three people lived there, tending 400 cattle and a few patches of taro. With an investment of about $6,000,000 the island was transformed into a modern pineapple plantation. A port was developed at Kaumalapau on the southwest side by dredging and by the construction of a breakwater and a concrete wharf. A winding, asphalt road was built into the higher lands of the interior. To accommodate the laborers, the town of Lanai was laid out, a model pineapple settlement with neat houses among pines and cypress trees, equipped with electricity and running water. A motion-picture theater, ice, cold storage, electric-light plants, a hospital, a bank, a post office, stores, a machine shop, garages, warehouses, offices of the company, a church, a police force, and a fire department—all constitute complete units within the town itself, built for the laborers.

Research by a staff maintained by the Pineapple Producers Co-operative Association and by the University of Hawaii has contributed much to the knowledge about pineapples and their cultivation. Among the fields which scientists have investigated are the destruction of pests and the combating of diseases, the introduction of new varieties, and the control of soil erosion. Since producers are faced with the possibility that the one variety raised in Hawaii might sometime be seriously attacked by disease, experiments are being carried on as a protective measure to produce new varieties free from threatening pests.

Thousands of acres of good pineapple land are still available and will be planted as the demand for the canned product increases. It is estimated that the total acreage where the natural environment is suited to the production of the fruit may sometime yield a pack of 20,000,000 cases of canned pineapples a year.

FORESTRY AND STOCK-RAISING

The primary consideration in Hawaiian forestry is the protection of watersheds for the conservation of water, such a vital item in the sugar industry. The practice of forestry, therefore, consists chiefly in the prevention of overgrazing in the reserves through fencing and by planting trees on denuded areas. Before the first forest reserves were set aside in 1904, many important watersheds had already been ruined, largely through overgrazing by both domestic and wild cattle. About one-fourth of the island area has been placed in the following reserves: Hawaii, 562,271 acres; Maui, 149,074; Kauai, 143,938; Oahu, 120,492; Molokai, 46,524.

There are about one and a third million acres of grazing land in the territory, or about one-third of the total area of the islands. Much of this, however, is rough and broken country of little value for raising stock. On the island of Hawaii there are large areas of lava flows on which, at times, cattle are permitted to range. In the main, the lands given over to pasture cannot be used for the raising of pineapples or sugar cane either because they are too high and, therefore, too cold or because sufficient water is not available. Some land formerly used for sugar cane and pineapples is now used for grazing. The pasture value of many acres of grazing lands has been greatly improved during the last twenty years by the introduction of Bermuda, Napier, and Natal grasses and other forage crops. Such improvement is of special significance, for cattle in Hawaii are marketed directly from pasture without the feeding of corn or other concentrated feeds.

Nearly all the cattle ranches are owned by "Other Caucasians" employing Hawaiian cowboys; they vary in size from a few thousand to the half million acres of the Parker Ranch. Each of 11 of the 45 ranches in the islands has more than 3,000 head, and the Parker Ranch has about 30,000. Of the total number of 140,000 head, the greater number by far are Herefords. Although livestock is the third agricultural industry, representing 4 or 5 per cent of the total agricultural income, the local products supply only about three-fourths of the local needs. The other fourth comes mainly from California and supplies the army whose specifications call for more fat than the native meats can furnish. It is believed by many that the territory could become independent of imported meats should local stock be finished on a feed of molasses mixed with pineapple bran or bagasse.

There are at present 160 dairy farms in the territory and 10,000 dairy cattle, mostly Holsteins and Guernseys, producing annually about 40,000,000 pounds of fresh milk. The demand for fresh milk is increasing faster than the population. Many residents of oriental ancestry, formerly not accustomed to use milk, have come to appreciate its value in maintaining health and promoting the growth of children. The consumption on the island of Oahu, where Honolulu is situated, has doubled during the last fifteen years, although the population has increased by only about 60 per cent. The consumption for the island, however, averages only 0.4 pint per day per person.

Among other livestock raised in Hawaii, horses and mules hold important places. On cattle ranches light horses are raised for home use, and on some there is a surplus for sale. Mules are the common work animals on cane and pineapple plantations.

SMALL FARMING

Coffee farming, cotton production, and the raising of rice and taro are associated in Hawaii with people of various racial extractions. Coffee farming is carried on almost entirely by Japanese, and cotton is raised by them to supply a local demand for specialized commodities which they use. Rice-growing, engaged in almost exclusively by the Chinese for about fifty years, is now carried on in part by Japanese. Taro, formerly raised by Hawaiians, is now produced largely by Chinese.

Coffee farming in the territory represents a type of agriculture in contrast to the regimentation of plantation life. The farmers are, for the most part, former plantation laborers who now enjoy the independence of leasing land and working it as they choose. Coffee farms are situated in two districts on the island of Hawaii: about 700 acres on the northeast, windward coast, and 3,800 acres in Kona in the central part of the west or leeward coast. Both areas lie between approximately 1,500 feet and 2,500 feet above sea-level. There are about 600 farms altogether, ranging from 5 to 15 acres in area, nearly all leased for periods of from ten to twenty years; a few are held in fee simple. They are operated by the tenants or owners and their families, except during the picking season, which, for most of the area, is in October and November. At that time extra labor is furnished by Filipinos who migrate to the coffee lands at the beginning of the harvest and return to pineapple fields or sugar-cane plantations when the harvest is over. The average production of green coffee is less than 10,000,000 pounds, of which about 90 per cent reaches the mainland of the United States for use in blending. Since coffee does not seem to be so well adapted to the islands as some of the other crops, an increase in production is doubtful.

Only about 400 acres in the territory are used for cotton, nearly all in North Kona, on Hawaii. There the plant, raised as a perennial on small farms, is pruned to the stump in the fall and sprouts a new growth following the spring rains. The ginned product is made into batting, which is used as padding for *futon* and *zabuton*, bed covers and cushions commonly used by Japanese.

Rice farming in Hawaii, at one time second in importance to the raising of sugar cane, has declined markedly because of the successful competition of rice raised in California and seems to be doomed. About 5,000,000 pounds are produced annually in the islands, and 85,000,000 pounds a year are imported from California. About 1916 the Japanese began to displace the Chinese, who at one time had 10,000 acres under cultivation. In that year 4,757 acres of paddy land were cultivated by Chinese and 1,659 by Japanese. By 1932, out of a total of 1,126 acres, the Japanese had 711, and the Chinese 415. In more recent years a few Filipinos have taken up rice-growing, and their interest may, in part, revive a dying industry. Today, as in the past, seedlings are raised in beds and transplanted to paddy fields by hand; the crop is cut with sickles; and the grain is trodden out under horses' hoofs and winnowed by the trade winds. Under such conditions it is hardly to be expected that the islands can meet the competition of California.

It is difficult to turn abandoned rice land to profitable use, for most of it is at, or close to, sea-level and is hard to drain. Some former paddy fields are being used for fodder crops; others, for vegetables. Near Honolulu some old rice land is being used as a bottom for fishponds, in one of which there is an old rice-threshing floor, a submerged tablet to the passing of the industry.

Less than 2,000 acres of land is now used for taro, a remnant of a much larger area of earlier days. Raising taro by wet-land farming, the most important agricultural occupation of the Polynesians, is now carried on for them by Chinese. The large fleshy roots, or more properly corms, of the plant are cooked, pared, pounded, and mixed with water to make *poi*, a food eaten by Hawaiians and by orientals and Caucasians who have developed a taste for it.

Truck farming and other small farming are carried on mostly at higher altitudes in small, scattered, inland areas in nearly all of which the economies of large-scale production are impossible. The more important areas are the Kaneohe district on the island of Oahu, the Kula slopes of Maui, and the Waimea and volcano districts on Hawaii. In all, there are some 4,000 diversified crop farms in the territory. The products are cabbages, peas, potatoes, tomatoes, and other commodities similar to those raised generally on the mainland, as well as oriental vegetables not commonly found there.

The main difficulty which besets truck farmers is the hazard of weather. As already stated, the rainfall of the islands is very irregular in amount and in time. For a period of five or six weeks it may be ideal for truck farming; there may then be a downpour with floods down the slopes which wash out the vegetables, or there may be a drought lasting two months. Another difficulty which harasses both vegetable and fruit farmers is the control of numerous insect pests, which not only attack growing plants but eat stored produce as well. The warm climate enables insects to multiply throughout the year and to produce from six to twelve generations annually.

The great majority of commercial small farmers are orientals on small holdings. They have little knowledge of Western types of farming, although they have behind them a useful tradition of intensive agriculture. They do not appreciate the standardization and grading of agricultural products commonly practiced on the mainland of the United States. Small farmers harvest and ship to Honolulu on Oahu, the main market, a considerable amount of low-grade produce. Commission merchants there charge from 15 to 25 per cent of its retail value for sorting and grading the produce after they get it. The freight rates on such produce from other islands may make the total cost to the grower prohibitive.

More than half of the fresh vegetables consumed in Honolulu, the only big market for them, are imported from California. Nearly all the fresh fruits used in Honolulu are also imported from the mainland. The total value of the imports of these commodities amounts to about $1,500,000 a year.

There are semiarid districts in the islands where truck farming and fruit-growing could well be carried on if irrigation facilities were available. The Waianae and Mokapu districts on Oahu, Kihei on Maui, and lower Kona on Hawaii could all be developed if water were available. Surveys have brought out the fact that water could be provided. The initial investment, however, would be great, and would be forthcoming only with help from the federal government. With irrigation water available, farmers would not be subject to the vagaries of weather; furthermore, the areas available are large enough to practice the economies of production on a large scale.

FISHING INDUSTRY

Fishing in the Hawaiian Islands is distinguished from that off the coast of mainland United States in several respects. Very little net fishing is practiced, for, near shore, coral and rough lava tear the nets and, a short distance offshore, ocean depths drop to several thousand feet, too deep for using nets successfully. Nearly all the catch is taken by hook and line. A small amount of fish is obtained by aquiculture from the fishponds formerly used by the Hawaiians. These ponds, fringing the coasts of various islands, vary from 10 to about 300 acres in area and are stocked with young mullet caught in hand nets.

Although the Territory of Hawaii is an archipelago surrounded by thousands of square miles of water, the number of fish readily available is not great. Their food supply is restricted because of the depth of water and the absence of banks, like those off the northeast coast of America and in other great fishing grounds. About 10 per cent of the fish consumed in the islands is imported, mainly from northwest United States and Japan.

About 750 species of fish are found in Hawaiian waters, but not more than 150 reach the market in any one year. Several hundred varieties, some of them brightly colored, are caught in small numbers by amateur fishermen, including schoolboys. About three-fourths of the catch consists of two varieties: *aku*, the Hawaiian name for a species of tuna; and *ahi*, a Hawaiian name which includes another species of tuna as well as albacore. The annual catch of the commercial fisheries during the past ten years has averaged 11,800,000 pounds, valued, as landed, at about $1,000,000.

There are 2,670 licensed fishermen in the territory; they use 1,000 licensed fishing boats, exclusive of canoes. Commercial fishing is almost entirely in the hands of Japanese, most of whom learned the business in their own country. Hawaiians, using spears, throw nets, and other native methods, get a little money from the occupation. All the fishing boats except row-boats are of Japanese design, and all the equipment is of American manufacture. About 80 per cent of the catch is taken within 3 miles of the coasts of the islands, although a few big boats make long voyages to the faraway leeward islands. Honolulu is by far the most important fishing port, and Hilo is second.

A significant development in the industry in the future is not anticipated. Older Japanese are retiring, and it is difficult to induce their sons to take up fishing. There will be an increase in demand with an increase in population, and perhaps larger boats than those generally used at present will be built which will make longer voyages. Some mourn the loss of the knowledge and expertness of the old Hawaiian fishermen. None of the agencies of the commercial fisheries have tried systematically to utilize or conserve the skill that was the peculiar endowment of the native. Much of his intimate knowledge of fishing grounds, weather, seasons, habits of fish, and methods of fishing has been lost forever.

MANUFACTURING

Nearly all manufacturing in the Territory of Hawaii is directly dependent upon its agriculture or on products of the bordering ocean. The making of raw sugar is carried on in the plantation mills, and in one of them the sugar is also refined.

The Honolulu Iron Works, employing about 500 men in the main plant, is the most important manufacturing establishment in the Hawaiian Islands. Founded in 1853 by David M. Weston, inventor of the Weston method of drying and cleaning by centrifugal force, it has been a principal factor in the primary industry of Hawaii in that through its agency nearly all the sugar mills in the territory have been erected. This company has erected also most of the sugar mills in the Philippine Islands and four similar mills in southeastern China. The establishment has also a merchandising business dealing in engineering supplies and machinery, structural steel, and electrical and hydroelectrical machinery. A branch in Hilo looks after the mechanical interests of plantations on the island of Hawaii.

During the peak of the pineapple season hundreds of people work in the canneries—tending ginaca machines and revolving knives, packing the fruit, and engaging in all the other activities peculiar to canning. A subsidiary of that industry is the manufacture of cans, during the height of the pineapple season. A large factory in Honolulu with a capacity of 2,500,000 cans per day has branch plants in Kahului, Haiku, in Lahaina on the island of Maui, and in Kalaheo on the island of Kauai.

Wallboard from bagasse, the residue of crushed sugar cane, is manufactured in Hilo, where a plant is capable of producing 100,000,000 board feet annually. Because competition from the mainland is keen, only about one-tenth of the bagasse available is used for this purpose. Processing coffee berries, ginning cotton and manufacturing *futon* and *zabuton* from it, milling rice, and making *poi*, both fresh and canned, are all carried on in a small way in the islands. A new fish cannery, built in Honolulu in 1933, with a branch at Hilo, presages some development in that industry.

A few plants manufacture products which neither involve the use of much machinery nor incur appreciable overhead cost and which would be expensive if imported from the mainland because of freight charges. Half a dozen concerns make mattresses, mainly from cotton; a paper-box factory uses material obtained in bulk from southern California; and a concrete business manufactures pipe for sewers, culverts, and storm drains. The manufacture of ukuleles is a small industry in the territory which has helped a great deal in advertising the islands all over the world.

Some 200 Hawaiians, mostly women, engage in making *leis*, or garlands, a unique and colorful industry of legendary and historical associations, and one which reflects the hospitality and good will of the people in general. Beautiful flower *leis*, tokens of friendship and *aloha*, are made from *ilima*, ginger, *lehua*, and other native plants and from many varieties of introduced flowers.

ATTRACTIONS FOR VISITORS

The climate and scenery of the territory make it an ideal holiday spot among the world's playgrounds. Vacation travel to the Hawaiian Islands has reached such proportions that the business of catering to visitors is regarded as the third industry of the territory, ranking next after the production of sugar and pineapples. On the four islands of Hawaii, Maui, Kauai, and Oahu there are forty tourist hotels, ranging in size from small country inns to a luxurious hostelry at Waikiki beach in Honolulu, the Royal Hawaiian Hotel. Some 45,000 tourists a year visit Honolulu; a little more than half of them are one-day visitors from steamers passing through the port.

Besides the climate and scenery, there are the volcanoes of Kilauea and Mauna Loa, which, when active, are never ending sources of wonder to residents and visitors alike. Kilauea was active almost continuously from 1823 to 1894, intermittently from 1894 to 1906, and continuously from 1906 to 1913. Again, after a few months of quiet, it erupted from 1914 to 1924, and intermittently from 1924 to 1935. It is easily reached from Honolulu by steamer or airplane. A good trail is now being made to the crater of Mokuaweoweo at the summit of Mauna Loa which will make the crater accessible from Kilauea by foot or on horseback. Haleakala, on the island of Maui, has one of the largest volcanic craters in the world. Kilauea, Mokuaweoweo, and Haleakala are all in Hawaii National Park.

THE MODERN HUMAN SCENE

Although the various races in the Hawaiian Islands earn a living, side by side, with similar machinery, tools, utensils, and other implements of material culture, some of them still preserve in large degree the cultural, religious, and social institutions and traditions of their homelands. Each of several groups has characteristics which distinguish it from others. There is, however, abundant evidence that the people of the territory are in the process of becoming a homogeneous group. That is not strange when it is considered that thousands of immigrants have proudly adopted Hawaii as their home and are bringing up their families under the democratic influence of the United States. Even the grandparents of many of the children of Asiatic ancestry who are now attending the public schools were born in the islands.

Among many individuals of nearly all the races represented, the process of Americanization has gone so far that the ancestral culture has been almost entirely forgotten. The degree to which they have entered into the inheritance of America depends on several factors, the more important of which are the size of their group, the cultural traditions of the ancestral homeland, the length of residence, and the character of the opportunity presented.

A racial harmony has been achieved in the territory largely because of education and an unusual equality of economic opportunity. Since annexation, forty-two years ago, education has been entirely along American principles. Children of all races have grown up side by side in the same public schools, using the same American textbooks, and participating in the same games. The tremendous economic development in the islands has enabled the immigrants to better their economic status in the meantime. The great business expansion has given a unique economic, as well as social, mobility and has reduced interracial competition thus far to a minimum.

At least two other factors have counted in lessening racial and nationalistic distinctions in the islands, namely, missionary idealism and the unbounded hospitality and friendly spirit of the Hawaiians. A group of Protestant missionaries arrived in Hawaii from New England in 1820 and were followed in subsequent years by eleven more groups and some independent arrivals. The scope of their early evangelistic efforts among the natives was later enlarged to include work among immigrant peoples. Missionary work is still carried on under the auspices of the Hawaiian Board of Missions and various

Christian churches in the islands. Roman Catholic and Mormon missionaries have also played a significant role in Hawaii. Largely as a result of such missionary work, permanent Caucasian residents of the islands are tolerant to an extraordinary degree.

The nature of the Hawaiians themselves has been a gentle and civilizing influence. These descendants of the original inhabitants of the islands have been exceedingly hospitable to all peoples alike. They have acted as a sort of flux or welding medium not only physically through intermarriage but also in a cultural sense. The cultural and intellectual contacts of the Hawaiians have for so long been with America that in some ways they have come to think and feel much like citizens on the mainland of the United States. Their ordinary medium of communication is English, although in some parts of the territory the older people still speak Hawaiian.

The ancient color of Hawaiian life may be observed each year when Hawaiians celebrate Kamehameha Day in honor of Kamehameha I, who, between 1795 and 1810, conquered the islands and became king of the whole group. A great parade is held in Honolulu, the outstanding features of which are brightly garbed *pa-u*-riders astride lively horses, *hula* girls in grass skirts on floats, and *lei*-sellers dressed in flowing *holokus*. The parade is followed by commemorative exercises in the capitol grounds. The celebration is concluded with a musical program in the evening, when Hawaiian choruses vie with one another in an art which they love.

The Hawaiians, as a rule a most lovable and hospitable people, have as yet a restricted appreciation of money values; they have not the individual acquisitiveness or the ability of commercial self-protection needed to cope successfully with a rising competition. By 1870 much of their land had passed into other hands. Even now they have not become adjusted to the competitive economic order of modern America with its steady effort and rugged individualism. Some of their more sacred traditions are opposed to the practices needed for commercial success. They have markedly different habits of work and count success in terms other than commercial achievement. At present they hold less than 6 per cent of the real estate in the territory.

The majority of persons of Hawaiian ancestry are urban dwellers gaining a living as government employees, teachers, clerks, stevedores, longshoremen, laborers, and *lei*-sellers, and in other occupations. Several thousand living on small farms, homesteads, and native *kuleanas* on the various islands engage in subsistence agriculture[2] and fishing. In remote valleys and coasts some conservative Hawaiian folk live much as did their ancestors a century or more ago. Typical Hawaiian communities are situated on the coast among pandanus and coconut trees, where the natural conditions are ideal for them. They get fresh water from rivers, springs, or wells. Taro, their most important food plant, grows best on terraced flood plains and delta lands. Sea food is plentiful, and the art of obtaining it has been handed down for centuries.

Stone walls line the roadway and the ancient land holdings, or *kuleanas*, on which the homes stand. Some of the house sites have been abandoned and are overgrown with guava and lantana. Fishing nets hang carelessly over walls and porch railings, and bamboo fishing poles lean against frame homes. Outrigger canoes are drawn up on the beach, and a framework beside them is used for drying and repairing nets.

[2] These are not included in the commercial small farmers mentioned earlier.

At each home there is a sort of garden in which a few vegetables are being crowded out by flowers, native *ti*, and weeds. Somewhere about the yard is a board for making *poi* from boiled or steamed taro, and several stone *poi*-pounders. On some *lanais* (verandas) are gourds, *lauhala* baskets and mats woven from the *hala* or screw pine, and drying strips of *hala* used in weaving. Conspicuous in the community is a church, commonly of New England architecture.

Because the drift of Hawaiians from the country to the city has not been in the best interests of many, attempts have been made from time to time to check it. Rehabilitation projects are being carried on now under the auspices of the Hawaiian Homes Commission, established by act of Congress in 1920; provision is made for leasing land to Hawaiians on a ninety-nine-year lease which may not be transferred to people of other races. There is also a Territorial Land Commissioner, operating since before the islands were annexed by the United States, through whom Hawaiians, as well as those of other races, may get possession of government lands in fee simple.

The "Other Caucasians" who are permanent residents have brought to, and maintained in, the islands a new and alien culture. About half of them are from continental United States. Most of the remainder are of English, Scottish, or German extraction. Their language, English, is the medium of conversation among the different racial groups, although it has been modified by the introduction of a few useful words and expressions from Hawaiian and other languages spoken in the territory. A local form of "pidgin English" has wide currency, especially in the contacts between racial groups on the plantations.

The great expanses of sugar cane and pineapple fields betoken the "Other Caucasian" occupancy. As already suggested, it was very largely through their enterprise and industry that the great agricultural development of the islands has been achieved. They have turned large areas formerly unused or used for grazing to the carrying-on of the two great commercial enterprises.

Few of the "Other Caucasians" have ever been unskilled laborers in Hawaii. On the plantations and in other industries most of them have been owners, managers, administrators, or skilled laborers. They also occupy the main business and professional positions in the urban areas. Since the demand for immigrants has been one for cheap labor, the number of *haoles* who came to settle permanently on the land has been small. Altogether they are the ones who are largely responsible for developing the industrial, commercial, and social structure of the territory. They have made the most profitable economic adjustments to the natural environment. "Big business" is largely controlled by *haoles*, who constitute only about 9 per cent of the population (not counting the army and the navy). They also help the other groups to fit into the American mold of citizenship and government. Although much in the minority on the islands, they are most evident in the city of Honolulu.

Opportunities presented to the Portuguese have favorably affected their establishment in the islands, and they early acquired better positions and pay than the Chinese. They had the advantage of naturalization and of acquiring homesteads. They now occupy a position in the islands like that of other Latins on the mainland of the United States. A few have been successful small farmers; some are dairymen; and a good many have remained on the plantations, where they have risen to skilled positions. They are found also in many other kinds of business.

In homesteaded areas the Portuguese live in neatly painted cottages set back from the government roads. Wire fences keep trespassers out of the gaudy flower gardens which border the homes on three sides, and behind the homes are vegetable gardens. Near some back doors are stone ovens for baking bread.

The most significant exotic cultures in the islands are those of the Orient, since Japanese, Chinese, Koreans, and Filipinos make up nearly two-thirds of the total population. Buddhist temples, Shinto shrines, and Chinese joss houses are much in evidence. Gaily colored Japanese kimonos, Chinese jackets and trousers, and Filipino headdresses, worn on special holidays, add color to the local scene.

The Chinese, thrifty and hard working, arrived early enough to take advantage of special opportunities afforded in the economic development of the islands. They gradually moved away from sugar-cane plantations and found other lines of work. Many of them became wealthy through rice-growing, an industry which they were well accustomed to carry on. Some of them who came without wives sooner or later married Hawaiian women, and their children now hold important places in government and business. The Chinese are importers, managers of many small stores, market gardeners, and practitioners of medicine, dentistry, law, and other professions. In 1930 about 75 per cent of the Chinese in the territory lived in the cities of Honolulu and Hilo; the proportion is much the same today.

The few small rural Chinese colonies are nearly all on deltas or river flood plains where rice and taro are raised. Water buffaloes lie lazily at the borders of the rice fields or taro patches or wallow in muddy holes. Close by the homes are old, concrete threshing-floors, most of them now unused. There are usually duck houses and chicken coops about. Near the time of rice harvest, lines of tin cans, rattled to scare rice-birds, hang above the waving green; and grotesque scarecrows stand ominously in the paddies.

The Chinese in Hawaii, considerably fewer in numbers than the Japanese and for a longer period exposed to Hawaiian and American civilizations, have become more completely readjusted than the Japanese to the new environment, culturally as well as economically. Their native culture is much less evident than that of the Japanese, mainly because their numbers are fewer. However, they still retain some of their oriental economic and social institutions and celebrate various holidays on their old calendar.

One bank in the territory is owned and operated entirely by Chinese, and another is largely in their hands. There are also Chinese societies whose memberships are made up of people from the same village or district in southeast China or of families with the same surname. Buch Toy village has a flourishing society in Honolulu; so has Chan Inn. The Lum families have a society; also the Wongs. The Laus, Chongs, Quons, and Chus have combined to form one organization because of historical family associations. Such associations are, for the most part, social.

The old Chinese New Year, depending on the lunar calendar, is celebrated late in January or early in February. It is an immigrant institution which has persisted in spite of a change in China, where the Western calendar, based on the solar system, is now used. In the Chinese calendar the first day of the year is also the first day of spring. To the Chinese the new year, therefore, means new life, rebirth, regeneration.

The number of Chinese language schools in the territory is relatively smaller than that of the Japanese. Many Chinese children have fathers and mothers who were born and brought up in the islands and who speak English fluently. There is, therefore, not the same need for such schools as among the more recently arrived Japanese. Some children of Chinese ancestry, however, attend language schools for reasons similar to those of children of Japanese ancestry.

There are now 12 Chinese language schools in the islands, with 78 teachers and 3,255 students. Most of the teachers are Hawaiian-born Chinese, graduates of the schools in which they teach. These schools form for parents and children a sentimental tie to China. Recent troubles in the Far East have engendered a patriotic feeling among Chinese abroad. Many young Chinese in Hawaii know almost nothing about the Chinese language and culture, and the parents would like them to be informed. Because business positions in Hawaii other than in agriculture are becoming increasingly difficult to obtain, there is renewed interest in China as a place for Hawaiian-born Chinese to earn a living.

Old customs and traditions of the Chinese are fast disappearing in the Hawaiian Islands, and those that remain are being changed or modified. In families where there are old people who grew up in China, the oriental customs tend to remain longer; but even the old people are not so strict in their observances now as they were some ten years ago.

The traditional Chinese attitude toward girls has changed in Hawaii, for they have become an economic asset. Through contacts with other civilizations the Chinese in the islands have gradually lost their repugnance to the idea of women going outside the home to work for remuneration. One of the first occupations to attract Chinese women was teaching. The Chinese revere learning and have a great respect for teachers. Education, provided for only a few in China, is the most important stepping-stone there to positions of wealth and honor. And so it is not surprising that early successful attempts of women of Chinese ancestry in Hawaii to secure work outside their homes were in the field of education. As public-school teachers they have shown the way for their sisters in other lines: stenography, bookkeeping, clerking, hair-dressing, and, recently, ushering in local theaters.

The immigration of Japanese was so great before the exclusion act of 1924 that they and their children now comprise more than one-third of the population of the territory. Coming in such large numbers, they have been able to maintain more of their native culture and traditions than have the smaller groups of earlier arrivals. Their assimilation, as distinguished from that of their Hawaiian-born children, has been correspondingly retarded. They are found in considerable numbers on sugar and pineapple plantations and in every job from field labor to engineering and scientific agriculture; they are also represented in nearly every kind of trade, business, and profession in the territory. They are the most numerous small farmers in the islands; coffee farming is carried on largely through their energy; large numbers of them engaged in truck farming, market gardening, and flower gardening supply local markets with fresh fruits, vegetables, poultry, and flowers. Another business actively conducted by the Japanese is hog-raising, about 90 per cent of this being in their hands. Many Japanese have taken up rice farming, supplanting Chinese, who have moved into more profitable occupations in Honolulu and elsewhere or have gone to live in that city with their children.

Two thousand stores in the territory are owned and operated by Japanese. Some of the establishments opened by the older generation of Japanese have been taken over by the younger people born and educated in the islands. About 2,500 Japanese are engaged in the building trades as architects, contractors, carpenters, painters, electricians, and plumbers.

A distinctive Japanese landscape is best found in a truck-farming district. Farms of from ½ to 5 acres consist of geometric patches of green onions, *daikon* (oriental radish), *gobo* (great burdock), cucumbers, and unwavering rows of carrots and cabbages. There are small groves of bamboo near some of the houses; and about most of them a medley of potted plants: chrysanthemums, azaleas, zinnias, and dwarf pines. Rainbow-colored garments on clotheslines, soya tubs for making soybean sauce, yellow raincoats, and a collection of sandals are conspicuous features of the picturesque scene.

Without much effort the Japanese in Hawaii have maintained in considerable degree their cultural, as well as social and religious, institutions chiefly because of their large number and the many business and social organizations within that group. The New Year's festival is celebrated much as it is in their homeland, and Boys' Day and Girls' Day are observed in Hawaii even more ceremoniously.

The Japanese Chamber of Commerce of Honolulu represents the interests of the Japanese business community in that city, especially the wholesale and retail merchants. The Japanese Merchants Association represents retail merchants only. There are three large Japanese banks in the territory, two of which are branches of banks in Japan. The last is owned and operated entirely by local businessmen with local capital.

In every district, camp, town, and city in the islands, the Japanese have formed *kumiai*, or clubs. Some are small, with a membership of only a dozen or so heads of families. Others represent as many as a hundred families. The Japanese Benevolent Society of Hawaii is one of the older Japanese organizations in the territory. It was instrumental in founding, among other welfare work, a Japanese hospital and a home for the aged Japanese.

The Japanese Educational Association represents 167 Japanese language schools throughout the territory. They have 643 teachers, of whom 286 are Americans of Japanese ancestry; the remainder are Japanese subjects. There are 39,123 pupils. Japanese language schools were built by parents, who also contribute funds for the salaries of teachers and for keeping the school buildings in repair. Reading and writing the Japanese language are the principal studies. The ability to speak, read, and write the Japanese language gives the children a medium of communication with their parents without which social intercourse would be very difficult. A knowledge of Japanese is especially important when children grow up and leave home. Otherwise, communication with their parents lapses, and family ties are easily broken. Very few of the older parents speak English, for they have had neither the opportunity nor the time to study it.

Ten Japanese journals furnish information to the Japanese communities and, to some extent, mold public opinion. The *Nippu Jiji* and the *Hawaii Hochi*, both dailies, have the largest circulation and are the most influential.

The United Japanese Society of Honolulu, composed of

PUPILS AT A JAPANESE-LANGUAGE SCHOOL IN HAWAII

representatives of fifty-eight Japanese organizations, is the central Japanese organization in that city. It takes a leading part in all activities in which the Japanese community is asked to participate. Not only does it work in the immediate interest of the Japanese people, but it also endeavors to bring about more and more cordial relations between the Japanese and other racial groups. The Japanese Civic Association is a nonpolitical and nonsectarian organization co-operating with organizations engaged in public welfare. One of its recent accomplishments was an expatriation drive during which 382 dual citizens were assisted in severing their ties from the Japanese government.

In many Japanese homes where the children are young, the style of living is more nearly Japanese than American. Rooms are furnished with Japanese mats and also with pieces of occidental furniture. On the walls are a few cabinet-size pictures of members of the Japanese imperial family. In a room not open to casual visitors is a Buddhist or a Shinto shrine before which the parents bow in homage and prayer daily. Outside the door is a stand where members of the household replace their street shoes or sandals by *zori*, or slippers, before crossing the threshold. In the evening, after the day's work, members of the family dress in comfortable kimonos. Food is typical of that in Japan: rice, fish, vegetables, and tea. As the children grow older, they demand occidental food about which they have learned and for which they have developed a taste in the home-economics classes and cafeterias in the public schools. They also become accustomed to occidental furniture at school and consequently like to have chairs and tables at home.

A peep into many Japanese homes reveals simple furnishings and utensils similar to those found in American homes.

English, as well as Japanese, periodicals and newspapers are in evidence. As one goes by the houses, bars of popular western airs and snatches of Japanese songs are heard on victrolas and radios. On the porches and in the yards are children of all ages—little tots mothering dolls in broken Japanese and English, older ones playing marbles or chuckling over "funny papers" with occasional outbursts in pidgin-English, others trying to work out picture puzzles or to color pictures according to models and directions, and the oldest reading or, if girls, sewing.

Many young people insist on fruit and cereals for breakfast. In some Japanese homes from which all the children go to school, rice is not served at the morning meal. The evening meal consists of Japanese and American dishes. Chopsticks are generally used by all the members of the family. While very young, both boys and girls wear kimonos more often than when they are old enough to choose their own clothes. For public wear young men and women have adopted American styles of dress almost entirely. Fashionable young women have permanent waves and evening gowns. The styles of both sexes are influenced by "movies," magazines, books, and school friends.

In a good many homes the children are Christians although the parents are Buddhists. There are 137 Japanese Buddhist and Shinto priests in the Hawaiian Islands, and 37 Japanese Christian pastors. Nearly all the Buddhist and Shinto priests teach in the Japanese language schools and earn much of their living in that way. Buddhism has approximately 128,000 adherents and 67 Buddhist temples; there are 259 Shinto shrines. At most of the temples are branches of the Young Men's Buddhist Association, which has headquarters in Honolulu.

In 1934 the Y.M.B.A. sent a delegation of 120 members to the second Pan-Pacific Y.M.B.A. conference in Tokyo.

At Buddhist Sunday schools, a Christian take-over, children are given pictures with Buddhist principles printed at the bottom. Hymns like those at Christian Sunday schools are sung, some of them the same tunes but with appropriate word changes. Songs like "Buddha loves me this I know," set to the air of the well-known Christian hymn, are common.

Japanese New Year festivities are similar to those in Japan. Homes are decorated with emblems of happiness and prosperity: bamboo indicating health and strength, orange, or *dai-dai*, expressive of hope that the family pedigree may flourish, and pine signifying long life. A feast is enjoyed with special foods—black beans for health, herring roe for posterity, and seaweed for happiness. Exchange of New Year's greetings begins as soon as the New Year is rung in, the head of the family going from house to house, beginning at the homes of the highest in social station among his acquaintances. During the day a table of special delicacies is set, at which all visitors sit, sip the *omiki*, or liquor blessed by the gods, and partake of the foods.

Many Japanese weddings in Hawaii are carried out in oriental style—colorful events which Americans delight to attend. Match-making has been done by go-betweens, and elaborate wedding arrangements have been made by the parents, guardians, relatives, or friends. The bride's parents have purchased a Japanese chest filled with new clothes, a Japanese bureau, a sewing-box, and other feminine paraphernalia. Just before the bride leaves her home, her parents prepare a farewell party, inviting relatives, neighbors, and friends, who present gifts on their arrival. On the eve of the wedding the bride, in *montsuki*, or Japanese wedding gown, her hair dressed in Japanese fashion, goes to the neighborhood Shinto shrine, where she meets the groom and the wedding ceremony is performed. Following the ceremony a banquet, prepared by the groom's parents, is held. Not infrequently the parents of both bride and groom go into debt to make the affair as pretentious as possible, and the onus of payment may descend to the young people.

Two Japanese holidays that belong especially to the children are celebrated in a colorful way in Hawaii: May fifth for the boys, and March third for the girls. For the boys' festival, on *Tango* day, a tall bamboo flagstaff is erected in the garden and from it a giant carp of paper or more frequently of cloth is flown for every son in the family. The carp, like the salmon, is able to cross strong tides, swim against swift currents, and leap waterfalls. So the son shall press on against life's temptations and overcome all difficulties. The girls' day, *Hina Matsuri*, or Feast of the Dolls, honors the daughters of a family. Rows of little dolls decorate a series of steps built in the best room in the home. The day is generally celebrated by a special dinner to which relatives and other friends are invited.

Each year Japanese residents of the territory celebrate in a colorful way their *bon odori*, or Buddhist ceremonial dances. Ceremonies are held outdoors in various parts of the islands between the middle of July and the middle of August. *Bon* drums are gotten ready, and *hachimakis* and other accessories are prepared for use at the big occasion, at which hundreds of boys and girls, dressed in gaily colored kimonos, move arms and legs in rhythmic gesture to the accompaniment of the music.

The traditional respect of the Japanese for law and authority is in evidence in Hawaii in that less than 10 per cent of the total criminal offenders are Japanese although the Japanese constitute 37 per cent of the population. Many Japanese disputes are settled out of court. Prominent or older men act as judges before whom the disputed points are arbitrated and settlement is reached.

The courtesy and patience of the Japanese, other outstanding traits, are especially displayed by proprietors and clerks in stores as occidental patrons "rummage" through their merchandise. There is always a smile and always a willingness to show another bolt of silk or to bring forth another kimono.

Members of the second generation take on occidental culture slowly because of the influence of their parents. However, most of the parents, especially those who have gone back to their home country for a visit, prefer to live in Hawaii rather than in Japan. The second generation knows little about Japan and does not understand or appreciate the significance of many of the customs carried on there. Festivals revered and celebrated by the older group are enjoyed merely as social occasions by the young people.

It seems especially difficult to change the ideas of Japanese-born parents about wedding celebrations and the bride's trousseau. Brides insist that less be spent on traditional costumes and more on useful articles. And so sewing machines, pots and pans, and suitcases are appearing among wedding presents. In the summer of 1935 the United Young Men's Buddhist Association of the island of Hawaii met to discuss the wedding situation and formulated a set of rules and observances which they hoped to carry out.

The younger married generation prefer to give their children Caucasian names. The grandparents prefer Japanese names. So there is generally a compromise, and two names are given—one Caucasian and one Japanese; William Ysugio Hiraoka, the name of a student of the author, is typical. In a few families where parents are Buddhists and children are Christians, funeral services have been performed in both Buddhist temples and Christian churches.

Japanese parents, citizens of Japan, measure the conduct of their children by Japanese standards, the only ones they know. At home they complain that their sons and daughters do not speak polite Japanese and that they do not strive to improve their knowledge of that language. Caucasian Americans complain that the second-generation Japanese speak pidgin-English at school and that, therefore, their influence is detrimental to the best education of Caucasian children. The adjustment of the second-generation Japanese is more difficult than that of any other group in the islands. Their families are more recently established than the Chinese and consequently less affected by American culture; their larger numbers make them more conspicuous than other races; and they feel the effect of relations between Japan and the United States.

The older of 116,000 American citizens of Japanese ancestry in Hawaii are now passing thirty years of age. The majority, however, are still in their teens or younger. A few hundred have completed collegiate studies and are beginning to establish themselves in the islands as physicians, dentists, lawyers, agriculturists, teachers, engineers, and the like. They are still in the process of feeling their way, trying to make necessary adjustments in order more profitably to become a part of the social, economic, and political life of their community. Some of them feel that they have a unique international obligation which their racial brothers and sisters in Japan are not in a position to assume. In the present interdependent world, especially when the affairs of the Pacific are gaining world-wide significance, the "new Americans," by virtue of their being the citizens of America, Japan's friendly and powerful rival, feel obliged to undertake a pioneer mission to promote better and more amicable relations between the two countries. Association with the older Japanese people in Hawaii for fifty years has brought out their valuable qualities of character. There is reason to believe that during the next fifty years the descendants of those early comers will make even greater contributions to the progress of the territory than their ancestors.

The Koreans, small in number and widely scattered, are also represented in various trades and professions in the territory. A great many in Wahiawa, on Oahu, are tailors and laundrymen, doing business with the large military contingent at Schofield. Among the oriental groups, the young Koreans are rapidly leaving their national characteristics behind. The older people, especially the women, still wear the white national costume, live on a Korean diet, and have the old outlook; but this is not so of the young. The number of Koreans in a community in general is small, and their neighbors very probably belong to some other racial group or groups. Outside forces making for a new outlook, therefore, are greater than those within the group itself. This new outlook for the young brings about many perplexing problems and conflicts, especially those of filial piety and respect for old age. The young people resent not being allowed by their parents to take advantage of American privileges and opportunities and especially dislike being stigmatized as "old fashioned." The situation is aptly put in a recent editorial in the *American Korean News:*

> Another reason for the apparent conflict of taste between the two generations is the fact that they have little in common save racial affinity. The old want the young to live in a conservative atmosphere under rigid discipline and at all times to practice filial piety, so dear to their hearts, but the young revolt against such restrictions. They want to live a "free life" because, as they reason, this is a "free country."

Another major point of conflict is social freedom. The social code of Korea is very strict and inflexible. It demands that women and girls lead secluded, stay-at-home lives and never mingle openly and freely with the opposite sex. In Hawaii the American social code allows the free intermingling of young men and women. And so the change from Korean to American culture is causing conflict; but, as the years pass, the trend toward the manners and customs of the West becomes more and more marked, and it will not be long until the vestiges of old Korean culture have entirely disappeared in Hawaii.

The Filipinos, the last of major groups to come to the Hawaiian Islands, are still found in general as common laborers on sugar-cane, pineapple, and coffee lands. Factors tending to retard their assimilation are their comparatively short period of residence and their maintenance of native cultural traditions, principally because they are concentrated in plantation settlements. Thrifty, intelligent, and hard working, they seize any opportunities that arise for bettering their economic status. Many save money to take back with them to the Philippines. In 1933 they were distributed as follows: 37,233 working as sugar-cane laborers; 2,334 in pineapple fields; 731 raising coffee; 278 growing rice, taro, and vegetables; 112 in cattle industries; 221 in gardening; 350 in stores; and 1,370 in miscellaneous occupations. The proportion is somewhat similar today.

Filipinos in Hawaii can best be understood and appreciated

by knowing their cultural and historical background in the Philippines. Their colorful folk dancing, quaint marriage customs, gaudy clothes, forms of recreation, and methods of self-defense are largely carried over from their homeland. In his native islands the life of the Filipino was governed largely by unwritten laws, social practices of ancient derivation, and customs some of which can be traced far back into the history of his Malayan ancestors, and there were also intricate kinship relationships and duties. In Hawaii some of these customs and traditions run counter to the modern manners.

About 80 per cent of the Filipinos in Hawaii are Ilocanos, from northwestern Luzon; the rest are Visayans and Tagalogs. The Hawaiian sugar-planters in general find the Ilocanos more satisfactory workers in the cane fields than the other groups, perhaps because of their economic and social background. They lived in an isolated part of the Philippines, where there was and still is a considerable pressure of population on the means of subsistence. They are the latest of the recruited laborers, their immigration beginning in the early 1920's. Many of the Filipinos are young men, few of whom brought wives; and the very small number of Filipino women in the territory has led to keen competition for them on the part of the men.

Filipino communities have fewer marks of identification than districts inhabited largely by other racial groups. Washings of brightly colored shirts and white trousers hang on sagging clotheslines. In sheltered parts of verandas stand 5-gallon gasoline cans with the lower half of one side cut so that it hinges horizontally—improvised Filipino bachelor stoves. A good clue to a Filipino neighborhood is a much used volleyball court.

Old Filipino social customs are still followed in plantation camps or villages. Some marriages are brought about by parental arrangement. Surrounded by a circle of relatives and friends of both families, the prospective bride and groom hold a public conversation. If those interested think the couple congenial and that the marriage will be a success, the wedding takes place. The newlyweds, the bride in a full, gathered skirt, a blouse with puffed sleeves, and an elaborately decorated neckerchief, and the groom in a gaudy silk shirt and natty suit, march formally through the camp, accompanied by a band and a procession of wedding guests. The bride's position in the family is different from that of the Japanese or Chinese housewife. She holds the right to the purse and latchkey; she is always consulted by her husband about important business dealings.

Among the Ilocanos, deaths are occasions for general and prolonged festivities. An orchestra is hired to play throughout the day of the funeral, and the burial procession to the cemetery is headed by a musician. A banquet is spread, and relatives, friends, and acquaintances are invited to partake of the feast. Among the Visayans, funerals are solemn affairs without music; they wear black bands on the left arms as signs of mourning; their women wear black for a year.

In Hawaii the possession of a knife or dagger is a carry-over from rural districts in the Philippines, where policemen are few and protection and justice, to a large degree, are dependent upon personal action. Although in general it serves simply as a useful appurtenance like a pocketknife, in time of need it may be a convenient weapon for another purpose.

Cock fighting in Hawaii is enjoyed by some clandestinely, as it is an unlawful pleasure. The Filipinos are accustomed to the sport in the homeland, and they find it difficult to conform to the territorial law.

Filipinos in Hawaii are especially careful about their personal appearance. They spend much of their earnings on good clothes, wear stylish shoes, and have their hair cut and trimmed so as to show to advantage their raven-black locks. A common sight in the late afternoon or evening is a group on a *lanai* (veranda) waiting turns at the barber's "chair," an improvised wooden box. On Sunday afternoon one sees many groups of five or six in automobiles, each Filipino sharing the ownership of a car.

The rate at which Filipinos adjust themselves to the new cultural environment depends largely on the extent of their contacts with non-Filipinos, particularly Americans or Americanized groups of other cultural descent. Those who live in isolated plantation camps naturally are slower in becoming familiar with new standards of social conduct.

Because free Filipino immigration was terminated in 1934, there will be a tendency toward the stabilization of the present Filipino population of Hawaii. There will be less drifting back and forth than hitherto. Older members with families in their native land presumably will return; but the great majority of the young, unmarried laborers, as well as those with families in Hawaii, will probably remain. The children, knowing little of their ancestral language and cultural heritage, will grow up as American citizens with a new outlook.

The Americanization of Filipino families in Hawaii is shown in part by the work of the Home Economics Division of the Agricultural Extension Service of the University of Hawaii. In a typical Filipino home on a sugar-cane plantation on the island of Hawaii, the writer noted such work in progress. The living-room was simply fitted with reed furniture; above a harmonium hung a calendar of the Manila Assurance Company; on the table lay a Christian hymnbook with verses written in Ilocano and Tagalog dialects; underneath it a copy of *True Detective*, featuring, according to the title of the leading article, the "low-down" on Dillinger. A home-cooking demonstration was held in the kitchen with the aid of a kerosene stove; that room had neatly whitewashed walls on one of which were pinned pictorial advertisements for men's "model clothes"; on the opposite wall were pasted four colored pictures of pretty Caucasian women and children in comfortable homes; the most attractive picture in the kitchen, looked at perhaps more often and longer than the others, since it was pinned above the sink, was one of George and Martha Washington.

Nine Filipino women and four children, on benches or standing, grouped themselves near the demonstrator. The women were clothed in print dresses; and their long, dark hair and brown faces contrasted with the lighter hues of the cloth. Some of them conspicuously wore earrings, bangles, and other jewelry. The demonstrator explained how the ingredients for raisin cookies were mixed, the instructions being interpreted to the group in Ilocano. While the cookies were in the oven, the subject of a club baby, fed on a standard American diet, was discussed. Finally the roll was called, and the demonstration for the next meeting announced—one on sewing and dressmaking, at which new patterns were to be practiced. Thus are Filipino mothers in Hawaii taught the art of Caucasian housekeeping and homemaking, and thus are our brown Filipino nationals Americanized.

Other groups of immigrants have come to the islands in

small numbers but are not conspicuous among the population. The Spanish have largely amalgamated with the Portuguese. Norwegians, Germans, and others have almost entirely lost their identity in the *haole* population of the territory. Puerto Ricans, also small in number and widely scattered, have experienced difficulties in adjusting themselves economically and socially. About one-third of the male wage-earners in this group still work as plantation laborers; the rest have drifted into other occupations or are supported by charity.

STRATEGIC VALUE OF HAWAII

The thousands of soldiers and sailors of the army and navy stationed in the Hawaiian Islands betoken the importance of the territory as one of the great defense outposts of the United States. For more than a century the islands have been of interest to the navy. The first commercial treaty between the kingdom of Hawaii and a foreign power was negotiated on behalf of the United States by Captain Jones of the U.S.S. "Peacock" in 1826. From then on to 1860 American naval vessels visited the islands at intervals. In the latter year an area at the port of Honolulu was leased to the navy as a coal depot. In 1887 the United States government secured the exclusive right to enter Pearl Harbor, on the island of Oahu, and there to establish and maintain a coaling and repair station for the use of its vessels.

In 1900, two years after the annexation of the islands, a presidential proclamation raised the coal depot in Honolulu to the dignity of a naval station. In 1908 Congress appropriated $3,000,000 to straighten the Pearl Harbor Channel and to establish a naval station there. In addition to the shore establishment, certain portions of the United States fleet are now permanently based at Pearl Harbor. For the operation and upkeep of all installations, ashore and afloat, in the Hawaiian Islands, the navy maintains about 350 officers, 4,000 enlisted men, and 1,200 civilian employees.

The occupation of Hawaii by the United States Army dates back to the admission of the islands into the Union as a territory in 1898. In 1910 various independent army posts in the islands were consolidated into a military district, included in the Department of California. The forces now compose the Hawaiian Department. Eight military posts and forts are located on the island of Oahu. At Schofield Barracks, 25 miles from Honolulu, about 12,000 officers and men and 2,500 civilians are stationed regularly. The army forces are largely for the defense of Pearl Harbor.

Pearl Harbor is an excellent naval base. Commodious and naturally protected, it is situated in the Pacific some 2,000 miles off the coast of North America. From it a fleet can readily defend the trans-Pacific routes from, say, Hongkong, Nagasaki, and Vladivostok to the western mainland of the United States.

It was the war with Spain and the acquisition of the Philippine Islands which brought home to the American people the necessity of having Hawaii as an integral part of the United States. Since then, the construction of the Panama Canal has multiplied the value of the territory many times. The island of Oahu bears the same relation to the defense of the canal that it does to the Pacific Coast.

The fortifications of Hawaii, the most powerful naval, air, and military base in the world, with corresponding defenses at Panama and comparable facilities in Alaska or the Aleutian Islands, form a mid-Pacific line across which neither hostile ships nor airplanes can risk passage. This line offers the first powerful resistence to an enemy trying to raid or assail the west coast of the mainland; it is the best defense of the United States and perhaps the only practicable one.

THE FUTURE

It is not expected that land utilization in the territory in the future will be much different from that at present. The production of sugar will continue to be the major industry. While factors beyond the control of the producers will continue to affect the value of the marketed product, the science and skill exercised in the production of this crop will enable it, in the long run, to hold its own. The area used for pineapples has decreased during the last ten years, and it is not anticipated that there will be any significant change in the future. The competition of other canned fruits and fruit juices with pineapples is keen, and extensive advertising is necessary to maintain the market for this typical Hawaiian product.

Areas used for coffee farming and rice production will probably be smaller in the future. Coffee farmers find it increasingly difficult to compete successfully with those in South American countries, where labor is cheap. Rice farmers cannot hope to compete with the large-scale production of rice by machinery in California. The future of the taro industry depends in large part upon the marketability of canned *poi*.

It is hoped that the acreage used for vegetables, fruits, and nuts will increase, especially that for vegetables. As already pointed out, the development of truck farming is dependent largely on bringing into cultivation lands where irrigation can be practiced. The development of small farming of that kind bears an important relationship to the strategic value of the

Territory of Hawaii to the United States. If steamer service between the islands and the mainland were cut off or seriously curtailed by a war in the Pacific, the importance of a local food supply would be paramount. During 1938 the island-produced foodstuffs used by the army alone reached a value of more than $500,000.

The number of tourists who come to the islands will not increase very much until more transportation facilities are available. Efforts are being directed to appeal to visitors during the spring and autumn seasons, the times of lesser travel to the territory.

Certain aspects of the future of the Territory of Hawaii are closely related to the future of the Pacific. That ocean is destined to increase greatly in importance as a medium of trade and commerce. Honolulu may become a point of concentration and distribution for cargo to and from all points on the greatest body of water in the world. Besides being some 2,000 miles nearer to the Orient than ports on the west coast of the United States, Honolulu offers more sailings of large freight and passenger vessels to the Orient than does any other American port. Honolulu may, indeed, become the entrepôt of the Pacific, especially should an incentive be given by the establishment of a free port. The importance of Honolulu as a port in trans-Pacific air service is already established. Pan-American Airways has achieved the extraordinary feat of overnight service from San Francisco to Honolulu. From Honolulu the flight to Manila is made in the following stages: to Midway Island; to Wake Island; to Guam; and to Manila, a total distance from San Francisco of 7,996 statute miles.

The future trade relations between the territory and mainland United States and between it and other ports of the world will increase with any increased development of the agricultural products of the islands and with growth in population. The value of that trade for 1938 is summed up in the accompanying table. The growth in freight and passenger traffic between the islands and the west coast of the mainland is shown by the addition, during the last ten years, of half a dozen new steamers to fleets of the lines in that service.

	Imports from—	Exports to—
Mainland United States..	$ 95,074,599	$123,706,502
Foreign countries........	8,640,868	2,039,369
Total..............	$103,715,467	$125,745,871

The degree of intermarriage in the islands furnishes evidences that the races of Hawaii are in the process of becoming one people. In earlier periods such marriages were largely between Hawaiians and Caucasians, and Hawaiians and Chinese, and more recently between all groups. After some decades the terms now commonly used to designate the various groups according to the country of birth may be forgotten. Even now there is a growing sensitiveness among the Hawaiian-born and educated when they are classified according to the land of their parents' nativity. They would enter fully into the inheritance of America and would be called "Americans."

The future political relations of the territory with the mainland are of special importance to the people of the islands. To its disadvantage, Hawaii has at times been treated differently from the states in the Union. Recently there has been a restriction of its sugar output in connection with which a foreign country was given preference over an integral part of the

United States. Some appropriations for public improvements for the benefit of all states have been denied to Hawaii, although Hawaii was taxed with the states to pay the expenses of the improvements.

It was through mutual agreement that the Hawaiian Islands became a part of the United States in 1898. As outlined in the Organic Act, the president of the United States, with the consent of the Senate, appoints the governor. Hawaii elects its own senate and house of representatives. One delegate, accredited at Washington, has the right of debate but not of vote, nor have the people of Hawaii any part in the election of the president. Political relationships thus far have been, for the most part, very amicable and profitable to both sides. The annual territorial budget is about $12,000,000, and with the various county budgets some $24,000,000. The federal government expenses are annually $100,000; the federal income tax from Hawaii amounts to $5,000,000 a year. In the vast development which has taken place since the union, it is interesting to note that the major part of the capital has come from within the islands and that the income therefrom remains there.

Many people in the territory think that the conduct of its inhabitants has earned for it the privileges of a commonwealth in the Union. In October, 1935, a subcommittee of five members of the Committee on Territories of the House of Representatives held hearings in the Territory of Hawaii upon the question of admitting it as the forty-ninth state of the Union. Statements were made by Hawaiians, Caucasian-Hawaiians, and Asiatic-Hawaiians, by full-blooded white Americans, by citizens of Chinese and Portuguese ancestries, by citizens of Japanese descent, and by distinguished members of the territorial house of representatives and senate. The great majority of the civil, educational, and legislative leaders of various racial extractions, creeds, and colors who appeared before the commission favored the entrance of the territory into the union of states which compose the great American republic. More recently a joint committee of the Senate and House of Representatives of the Congress of the United States visited the islands "to conduct a comprehensive investigation and study of the subject of statehood and other subjects relating to the welfare of the Territory of Hawaii." Among other things, this committee called attention to the fact

> That the present disturbed condition of international affairs, while not a permanent deterrent to the aspiration of the people of Hawaii, suggests the wisdom of further study and consideration of this question, and possibly the holding of a plebiscite at some future time. . . . . That while great progress has been made by the people of Hawaii in every phase of activity, no hardships will be incurred by such delay, during which the Territory can continue its development along traditional American lines.

OTHER MID-PACIFIC ISLANDS OF THE UNITED STATES

The other mid-Pacific islands of the United States may be divided into two groups: those west of the Territory of Hawaii and valuable mainly as airplane bases on commercial flying routes to Asia; those south of Hawaii and similarly valuable on routes to New Zealand and Australia. The islands of Guam and American Samoa are also important naval bases.

The Leeward Islands of the Hawaiian Archipelago stretch away in a long line for 1,300 miles northwest of the inhabited islands; they are part of the Territory of Hawaii. All of them are very small, some merely reefs. The ocean in their vicinity is notorious for uncertain and dangerous currents and for abrupt changes in the depth of the water. They were set aside as a bird reservation in 1909 and are now the haunts of many thousands of sea birds. They are seldom visited and, with the exception of Midway, are uninhabited.

Midway consists of a circular atoll and two islands which it incloses. It is a United States reservation governed by a naval officer and is the site of only a cable station, a flying field, and a lighthouse. It is properly not a part of the Territory of Hawaii, although under United States jurisdiction, as it was discovered and claimed for the United States in 1859, when Hawaii was still an independent country. It is planned to fortify Midway and to make it into a naval base as a defense outpost west of Hawaii. Kure (Ocean Island), just over the horizon from Midway, is the most northwestern point in the Leeward chain.

Wake Island (19°18′ N., 166°35′ E.) is an atoll occupying an area about 4½ by 2 miles. Its three islets, separated by shallow waters, have a maximum altitude of about 20 feet. They are waterless but have a scrubby growth of vegetation, with an occasional small umbrella tree or similar type of tree. Wake Island was uninhabited until 1935, when the Pan-American Airways Company established a sufficient number of people there to take care of flight needs. The company now has hangars, storehouses, homes for the staff, a hotel for passengers, and other necessary equipment.

Guam Island (13°27′ N., 144°45′ E.) is the southernmost, largest, and most populous of the Mariana group; the others, fourteen in number, are under a Japanese mandate. The island is about 30 miles long, varies in width from 4 to 8 miles, and has a total area of 225 square miles. The northern portion is a great limestone reef tilted to the south and exposing a seafacing cliff 400–600 feet high; most of the other shores are

Courtesy of T. L. Kirkpatrick

DRYING OF COPRA

In American Samoa copra is dried on mats to facilitate carrying it under cover when rain threatens.

cliffed also. The southern half consists dominantly of low volcanic hills, deeply weathered and dissected by numerous valleys. Port Apra, on the west coast, is well protected and has anchorage at all seasons for all classes of ships. Agana, the capital, with a population of 13,000, is 5 miles from Apra Harbor. The Island is the top of a great volcanic cone built up from the deep Pacific bottom. The highest point is Mount Lamlin, 1,334 feet.

The climate of Guam is tropical with moderately high, uniform temperatures and a seasonal rainfall, most of the 90 inches falling between June and November. This, in general, is also the season of the most destructive typhoons. From December to June the northeast trades prevail, bringing little rain except to the windward slopes of the higher elevations. In spite of the heavy rainfall, the limestone area has weathered into a deep, good soil, covered with a forest growth except where cleared for cultivation. In the dry season the clear skies and refreshing trade-wind breezes represent the tropical climate at its best. In spite of the more or less monotonous, though not disagreeable climate, some Americans find the island most attractive and are satisfied to make their permanent homes there.

The native inhabitants, about 21,000 out of a total population of 22,000, are of Indonesian stock and call themselves "Chamorros." They are a mixture of Philippine Tagals and Spaniards dominantly; but, as their social and commercial contacts have been with the Philippines and other islands of the East Indies, there have been many other blood additions. Their language now is a dialectic combination chiefly of Tagal, Spanish, and Malay. They grow some crops; but, although the surrounding waters teem with fish, the sea foods used are very few. Corn, taro, rice, yams, and sweet potatoes are common crops, and coffee is produced for export. The coconut tree, as in so many tropical isles, plays a most important role, for, in addition to food, it also furnishes material for homes and cooking utensils. Oxen and water buffaloes are the draft animals. Since the American occupation of the island, sanitation and health, as well as the economic situation, have been greatly improved both by education and by assistance in agricultural methods.

Much debate has taken place in Congress as to whether or not Guam should be fortified. Mention of fortifications on Guam evoked voluble protests from Tokyo, since this island is within the Japanese sphere of influence in the Pacific, nestling within a shoal of Japanese-mandated islands. The sum of $5,-000,000 has recently been granted for improving Apra Harbor and naval and military equipment there.

The island is an important link in the east-west chain of islands belonging to the United States. On the present airplane route to the Orient the distance from Honolulu to Midway is 1,304 statute miles; Midway to Wake, 1,185 miles; Wake to Guam, 1,508 miles; Guam to Manila in the Philippines, 1,589 miles; and to measure the value of these small island stepping-stones is largely a matter of evaluating, for the future especially, the importance of trans-Pacific air service.

South of the Hawaiian Islands lies the isolated Johnston Island; and farther south, in a linear arrangement, stretch the Line Islands. The latter include Kingman Reef, Palmyra, and Jarvis, belonging to the United States. Fanning and Christmas Islands in this group are claimed by the United States and Great Britain. West of Jarvis and nearly on the Equator lie Howland and Baker Islands. Great Britain occupied Jarvis,

Howland, and Baker many years ago but abandoned them after their guano deposits had been worked out. Jarvis, "taken" by the United States as a result of occupancy under authority of an act of Congress approved in August, 1856, was exploited by Americans also for guano and was later left unpeopled. Colonists from Hawaii went to these three islands in 1935, and at present each island has a population of 4 inhabitants.

West of the Line Islands lies the Phoenix group, which includes Canton Island and Enderbury Island, both jointly governed by the United States and Great Britain. These two islands are located nearly 2,000 miles south-southwest of Honolulu and about 700 miles north of American Samoa. At one time Canton furnished a safe landing place and anchorage for whalers, and Enderbury was important for its guano deposits. Their value now lies in their strategic position on projected air routes to Australia and New Zealand.

It is likely that islands in the Pacific belonging to other countries will be used by American air lines by agreement with the governments concerned. It is reported that Pan-American Airways will launch a regular service to Australia and New Zealand soon. The big planes en route to Australia are to call regularly at Noumea in New Caledonia, a French possession. An alternative route is Hawaii, Canton Island, Suva (British), and Auckland.

Eastern or American Samoa is the most southerly possession of the United States in the Pacific. It comprises the island of Tutuila and all other islands of the Samoan group east of 171° W. From west to east the islands are Tutuila, Aunu'u, Ofu, Olosega, Ta'u, and Rose. Ofu, Olosega, and Ta'u, generally known as the Manua group, lie some 60 miles from

Tutuila. Aunu'u is part of the eastern district of the island of Tutuila. Rose Island is a coral atoll, uninhabited. In 1925 the sovereignty of the United States was extended to Swains Island, 200 miles north of Tutuila.

Tutuila is irregular in shape, about 18 miles long and between 5 and 6 miles wide in its widest part and has a total area of about 40 square miles. Extending nearly the whole length of the island is a mountain ridge, with many spurs separated by deep valleys. The island is very rugged in the east and bold and precipitous in the north but has a broad, fertile plain in the southwest. Matafao Peak, near the center, reaches an elevation of 2,141 feet; and Mount Pioa, on the opposite side of Pago Pago Harbor, is 1,717 feet high. Higher lands are heavily forested with trees remarkable for their size and variety, and there is a luxuriant undergrowth. The greatest indentation in the coastline is Pago Pago Bay on the southern side of the island, formed, it is asserted, from the crater of an extinct volcano.

Ofu and Olosega Islands, small and mountainous, are near together. Ta'u Island is cone shaped, with its center 3,056 feet high. Swains is a small, circular, coral island, only 20 feet above sea-level, inclosing a brackish lagoon. The islands of American Samoa are of volcanic origin, except Rose and Swains Islands, which are coral atolls.

American Samoa, about 14° south of the Equator, has a climate similar to that of scores of islands in the southern half of the Pacific. The range of temperature is very small—only 2°—from 82° in February, the warmest month, to 80° in July, the coolest month. The normal annual rainfall at Pago Pago is nearly 200 inches. The larger portion of this falls during the season from November to March, which is also the warmer season; but there is also considerable precipitation from April to October. The relative humidity ranges from 70 to 90 per cent during the wet season and from 40 to 60 per cent during the dry season. In such a climate people from the temperate zones have to adapt themselves by not engaging in strenuous mental or physical activities during the middle of the day. The natives rise before daylight and do the harder work of the day in the morning.

Tropical hurricanes cause serious damage in Samoa from time to time. In 1915 the destruction of crops and other property was so great that the United States Congress felt it necessary to come to the aid of the American Red Cross in an attempt to relieve some of the distress.

The hot climate necessitates wearing little clothing. The dress of Samoans consists of a *lava lava*, or loin cloth, formerly of tapa, made by women from the bark of the paper mulberry tree, but now of cotton; the women wear, in addition, a waist or upper garment; small children run about naked. Airiness in buildings is also essential. Samoan houses, the outstanding feature of Samoan landscapes, are adapted to the environment with simplicity and beauty; their high, steeply pitched roofs thatched with sugar-cane leaves slope to within 4 or 5 feet of the ground on all sides and are supported all the way around by posts, the spaces between which are open, save for coconut-leaf screens, which are lowered only in time of high wind and rain. The native house and dress give the islands an atmosphere of remoteness from Western civilization.

The population of American Samoa, 5,679 when the islands were taken over by the United States, has now increased to about 12,000. The people are Polynesians, living in approximately seventy villages on the plain of Tutuila and on narrow strips of land along the coast of that island and on similar strips on the other inhabited islands in the group. They own nearly all the land on the islands communally in groups; American laws, promulgated by the naval authorities, provide that there shall be no alienation of land held by the Samoans to nonnatives.

Bananas, the main food of the Samoans, are obtained abundantly with little effort on the part of the natives; when the fruit is fully formed but still green, it is peeled and baked in the oven, or *umu;* a little fruit, allowed to ripen, is eaten raw. Taro, eaten at feasts and served to visitors, is planted on dry land in many very small plots, some of them no larger than six-hundredths of an acre. To plant a patch, the ground is cleared of weeds, and a pointed stick, or *oso*, is pushed into it about 6 inches and rotated to make an opening into which a taro top is inserted; the soil is then tamped down a little with the bare foot. The root or corm of the plant is, like bananas, prepared for food by baking it in the native oven rather than being made into *poi*, as in Hawaii. The leaves, baked with coconut "cream," are a great delicacy and almost the only flavoring that Samoans use. The Samoans like breadfruit and eat a large amount of it when the trees are in fruit, usually in March to November; in seasons of plenty a little is preserved in pits for use at any time of year, but particularly after hurricanes, which, by their destruction of crops, cause famines. Some bananas are also similarly preserved. Yams, kava, and sugar cane are other crops in the native agriculture. The last is more important for the leaves used to thatch native homes than for the juice.

The livestock in American Samoa consists of scrub breeds of hogs, cattle, chickens, and even horses. Pork is always part of a native feast; a visitor to a native village is invariably treated to baked chicken. Here and there a few horses are used to bring breadfruit, taro, and especially bananas in baskets to the villages; they are also used to carry copra.

The coconut tree is very valuable to the native Samoan not only for its food product but also for the shelter it provides. The timber is used in building houses; the leaves, plaited by women, for trays; the "milk" for drinking; the meat of the nut for food; the oil for cooking and native puddings; the shell for drinking cups; and the husk of the nut for sennit for tying the framework of houses. The dried meat of the coconut, or copra, is important to the Samoan as an export crop for which he receives money to buy things which he has begun to consider necessary. Canned beef and fish, wheat flour, and cotton clothes now play a role in native life. In 1935, a representative year, 1,554 tons of copra were exported from American Samoa and brought a price of $70,108.

There is a growing export trade from American Samoa in curios and mats, fostered by the government under the Department of Native Industry. The leaves of the pandanus, used for mats, are almost exhausted in the American islands, and some are now brought in from British Samoa. This export trade of native artifacts may eventually equal in value the trade in copra.

Samoans are good fishermen and procure large supplies with lines from native outrigger canoes and with nets and lines along the shore of their islands.

Samoan institutions consist of an interesting mixture of Western Christian religion, inculcated for more than a hundred years mostly by the London Missionary Society, and of native Polynesian customs. All the people are Christians and belong to native mission churches; they attend services regularly and give freely to the support of native pastors. The most impressive part of their church service is the singing. Villages vie with one another in building and keeping up churches to such an extent that the architectural beauty of a church building is taken as the stamp of general achievement of the natives.

Samoan villages are governed by *matai*, or chiefs, who meet at intervals to discuss matters dealing with the village welfare. They look after the interests of their families in the village *fono*, or gathering of the chiefs; they oversee the division of lands, the production and division of food, the care of the sick, and matters relating to income and expenditure. The *aumaga*, or male commoners, work co-operatively for the village welfare under the direction of *matai*.

Social customs play a large part in Samoan life, and nothing may interfere with their proper observance. The attention given to dignity and gracefulness in serving the *kava* drink emphasizes the fact that Samoan society is based on prestige and titles. Every important stage in the erection of a Samoan house is marked by a feast. Long and slow preparation is made for the feasts which accompany the celebration of births, marriages, and deaths. At such times agriculture is neglected. The increase in population during the last three decades has begun to press on the means of subsistence; but, as yet, the Samoan has interested himself but little in providing bigger crops for the larger number of people. His wants have been abundantly supplied in the past, and he sees no cause for concern about the future.

Pago Pago, on Tutuila, the chief port of American Samoa, is the headquarters of the naval government. In addition to the regular naval officers and sailors, there is a *Fita Fita* guard of native Samoans who have enlisted in the navy for duty in Samoa only. Pago Pago is a regular port-of-call for American steamers on the way to New Zealand, which stop for only a few hours, as there are no hotels for tourists. Pago Pago is the best harbor in all the Samoan Islands and may some day form an important outlying defense of the Panama Canal. The harbor was formerly a stopping place on the airways route to New Zealand.

As already indicated, the future of all these small islands is closely related to future activities of the United States in the Pacific. Their value as bases on air routes or as naval stations has already been established; that value will increase with the further development of trade and traffic through the world's largest ocean.

THE COMMONWEALTH OF THE PHILIPPINES

By CORNELIO C. CRUZ, LUIS J. BORJA and WILLIAM H. HAAS

PRESIDENT ROOSEVELT'S SIGNATURE IN March, 1934, to the Tydings-McDuffie bill ended American rule over 7,000 or more islands in the western Pacific and created a new political unit, the commonwealth of the Philippines. To those present at the signing the president remarked: "This is a great day for the Philippines. It means the beginning of the Philippine republic." He neglected to add that to the United States the signing had even greater significance, for it pointed to a great change in the traditional American attitude toward expansion.

The situation was probably unparalleled in history. The American nation had grown great in pushing out its boundaries; and now, instead of annexing more territory, it was giving up one of its richest possessions to satisfy Philippine leaders and some American business interests. The signing had an additional meaning to the Philippine people, for they had traded certain economic advantages for political ambitions. They had given up the richest tariff-free market in the world for the full right to manage their own affairs. Nominally they already had been politically independent, for Uncle Sam had been a most indulgent godfather against whom they had had no real grievances. It need not seem strange, therefore, that when the new independent status was announced in the Philippines, there was little public rejoicing, and many people even expressed regret. In his inaugural as first president of the islands

THE INAUGURATION OF THE PHILIPPINE COMMONWEALTH
MANILA, NOVEMBER 15, 1935

Manuel Quezon summarized the nation's feeling thus: "The Philippines look back with gratitude to the day when destiny placed the land under the beneficent guidance of the United States."

There was good reason for a feeling of regret at losing such an unselfish tutor. At all times the American policy had held more or less tacitly to the McKinley view that the American mission in the Philippines was one of assistance and not of exploitation, to be ended as soon as the need for control had passed. From the time of the Provincial Government Code in 1901 until the enactment of the Second Organic Act in 1916, the foundations for self-government were assiduously being laid. From then on, the Filipinos had the major voice in the government of the islands. William Howard Taft, as first civil governor, initiated and fostered many of the policies followed, and later supported them while Secretary of War and finally as president of the United States. His policy was one of the "Philippines for the Filipinos," and during his incumbency as governor the Philippine government was changed from a government of Americans assisted by Filipinos to a government of Filipinos assisted by Americans. Although he took a conservative point of view as to the time of American withdrawal, he felt convinced that the United States some day should and would grant complete independence.

The Philippine Islands have constituted not only the most unusual but also the most distant domain under the American flag. Their distance from the mainland unquestionably has had no small part in the evolution of the policy of control. Although a part of the Union, the Philippines were neither state, territory, colony, nor naval base but, according to the Division of Insular Affairs of the War Department, a "non-incorporated territory." The people were not citizens of the United States, therefore, but citizens of the Philippine Islands of the United States, and held most of the rights and privileges of American citizens but paid no federal or income taxes. They made their own laws and had their own currency, postage stamps, and even their own schedule of tariffs. In all cases in which American laws did not specifically include the islands, the local laws prevailed. Thus the islands did not have woman suffrage until locally adopted, nor was the Prohibition Amendment ever in effect.

HISTORICAL SETTING

Philippine history may be said to have had its beginning in April, 1521, with the death of Ferdinand Magellan, who was slain in battle while trying to help a native chief who had accepted the faith and had pledged loyalty to the Spanish king. This occurred during his famous attempt to circumnavigate the globe with his fleet of five ships and 268 men. Although a part of his crew under his subcommander, one Juan Sebastian del Cano, reached Spain, they did so in only one ship with 18 men—a pathetic ending of an epoch-making, first circumnavigation of the globe. From now on, however, Spain laid claim to the islands and named them *Islas Filipinas*, in honor of King Philip II.

But long before Magellan had set eyes on the island of Samos and had entered into a blood compact with the chief of Cebu, the islands were well known to other countries. From archeological evidence it is reasonably certain that for centuries before the coming of the Spaniards the islands were in regular trade communication with China. There is some evidence, also, that they were dependencies of successive Hindu-

Malayan empires from about A.D. 200 until 1325. Later they were successively under the Javanese Empire, the Ming Dynasty, and Japan, and some of the islands are believed to have been under Borneo for a brief period. It is possible also that Portuguese adventurers visited the islands before their "discovery" by Magellan. Whatever the facts, the early history is more or less closely tied up with the various oriental civilizations, of which little is known. The people of the islands during this early period had developed some form of writing, but nearly all written records were destroyed by the early church as coming from the devil, and the little left has not been very helpful.

Some time elapsed after the naming of the islands before Spain attempted to make her claim on them good. A certain Don Miguel de Legaspi very wisely was chosen for the purpose of claiming them; and in February, 1565, with his fleet of four vessels and 378 men, including 5 priests, he anchored off Cebu. At that time the natives were hostile to all invaders, but fair treatment and a salutary restraint on the excesses of the soldiery soon gained for the Spanish newcomers a place in their affections. For this, Legaspi, a keen student of native psychology, was mainly responsible. Having established a settlement on Cebu, he baptized the chief and his followers and made them loyal to Spain. After his arrival he heard of an important trading-point to the north on the island of Luzon. With a recruited force of 300 men, he set out for Manila in 1571, and in May of that year laid out a Spanish settlement there. He rebuilt the native fort, erected a government house, a church, and one hundred and fifty houses, and designated the city as the capital of the archipelago.

The Philippines, however, were not held by Spain without

a struggle. The bitter rivalry in trade between Spain and Portugal, except for the years 1581–1640, extended also to the Orient. The Dutch likewise began to take an active interest in the Far East, but after a series of reverses in conflict with Spanish warships they were willing to concede the archipelago to Spain. The first clashes with the British began about 1578 and lasted for a full one hundred years. In 1762 the British attacked, and they held control of Manila until the close of the Seven Years' War, in 1763. In the meantime they also overran southern Luzon and the Visayas. Elsewhere they were successful in inciting the Filipinos in rebellion against the Spaniards and at the same time in cementing their own friendly relations with the people. The defeat by the British was a severe blow to Spanish prestige and influence over the natives, but after the return of the islands Spain again had complete mastery. Although the British made the world conscious of Philippine trade possibilities, it was not until 1837 that Manila was opened to foreign commerce. In spite of its restrictive colonial policy, Spain, nevertheless, did much for the islands. The warring tribes were welded into a more or less homogeneous people, and there were improvements in commerce and general culture.

During all the years of Spanish domination, the soldier and the priest were supreme, at one time the one and at another time the other. The governors-general represented the Spanish crown; the bishops, with scarcely less power and sometimes with more authority, carried out the missionary plans of Rome. The conflict between the church and the state occupied so much attention that in the friction the people were forgotten. Ever uppermost with those in authority were the interests of the mother-country, of securing the maximum for the home treasury. Corrupt officials also made the most of their opportunities. It is reported that General Weyler, later of Cuban fame, after three years as governor-general accumulated a fortune between $2,500,000 and $3,000,000. In the reaction following the restoration of the monarchy at Madrid in 1871, the struggle between the church and state flared up anew. The clergy was at a very low moral ebb at the time, and the first great popular demonstration against the church occurred in 1888. This rising discontent against the church, together with other subversive movements against the state, culminated in a revolutionary pronouncement with the slogan "Long Live the Philippine Republic." Armed resistance naturally brought forth imprisonments, deportations, and executions, and the revolutionary movement was on. During the early part of this period there appeared on the scene Emilio Aguinaldo, who later clashed with the United States and still later was a defeated candidate for the first presidency.

At this juncture events elsewhere were leading up to the American entry through the Spanish-American War. On April 25, 1898, the day of declaration of war on Spain, Commodore Dewey, in Chinese waters, received orders from Washington to "proceed at once to the Philippines," and by the first of May of that year he had destroyed the Spanish Philippine squadron. The protocol of August 12 (August 13, Manila time) suspended hostilities. The *de jure* sovereignty of Spain continued until the Treaty of Paris, signed December 10, 1898, had been ratified by both governments. Although the Spanish government still tried to maintain order in the parts nominally Spanish, the pressure of revolt and the lack of supplies forced General Rios to withdraw outlying garrisons. As no American troops were available to take their place, the insurgents occupied the evacuated territory, including the rich city of Iloilo. In discussing what was to be done with the Philippines the United States Senate on February 14, 1899, passed a resolution, part of which read:

> . . . . but it is the intention of the United States to establish on said islands a government suitable to the wants and conditions of the inhabitants of said islands, to prepare them for self-government and in due time to make such disposition of said islands as will best promote the interests of the citizens of the United States and the inhabitants of said islands.

The pacification of the islands now became the major objective of the American government. The end came with the capture of General Aguinaldo, who on April 19, 1901, took the oath of allegiance to the United States and, by proclamation, advised the people to stop fighting. Since that time he has cooperated in the further pacification of his country and has given his full adherence to the United States. The Philippine legislature in 1920 granted him a life-pension of $6,000 per annum. In his report of 1902 the Secretary of War stressed "that the insurrection has been brought to an end both by making a war distressing and hopeless on the one hand and by making peace attractive . . . . on the other." The pacification, however, was not without its toll. The American losses were: killed, 245; wounded, 490; captured, 518; missing, 20. The insurgent losses were fully ten times as great.

For their rehabilitation the islands were placed under a governor-general, appointed by the president of the United States. Of governors there has been a most notable array—eleven in all—including such men as Taft, Smith, Forbes, General Wood, Stimson, all acting under the War Department. The last of the governors, Frank Murphy, now a member of the Supreme Court, automatically became the first

United States high commissioner under the new independence order. As early as 1916 the Congress of the United States abolished the old Philippine Commission by substituting the Jones Act, which granted the islands an elective senate of 24 members and a house of representatives of 91 members. This virtually gave the islands their independence except for a few appointive offices. What ultimately emerged was a Malay state demanding officially from the American government its own sovereignty as a natural right.

Even without full independence the government had developed into a state clothed with dignities, rights, and privileges, with another state responsible for its behavior, territorial integrity, and defense, for its credit and its prosperity, and for its citizens abroad. Under normal procedure the American government could not enact a new law for the islands. The governor-general could suggest one; but if the Philippine legislature refused, there was no recourse except force. The American government could have abolished the Philippine legislature; but to have done so would have been an exercise of power with an implication of force behind it, an act contrary to accepted American principles. Under the situation prevailing, the granting of a tentative independence, in the light of so much Filipino agitation, seemed entirely logical.

THE PEOPLE OF THE ISLANDS

The inhabitants of the Philippines are known collectively, irrespective of physical characteristics, as "Filipinos," although the name applies more specifically to the Christianized and more active and progressive peoples. Racially, the people have been divided into at least three groups—Negritos, Indonesians, and Malays—with an indeterminable degree of admixture. Much, however, is still to be learned about the racial origins, and authorities are not always in agreement. Very early, it is believed, these people came in successive waves probably from eastern Tibet, over southern China, Siam, and Burma, and crossed the southern seas to Borneo, to the Philippines, and to the neighboring islands. In substantiation of this belief there is a fairly close resemblance of the Philippine people to the Javanese, Siamese, and the people throughout the Malay Peninsula. Within the Philippine Islands, with some exceptions, the people are much alike physically, the recognized difference being chiefly one of dialect. As a whole, they are of medium size, about 3 inches shorter and 30 pounds lighter than the average Caucasian.

Classification, for useful purposes, is exceedingly difficult. Color designations have no significance. For want of a better way the Census Bureau has classified the people as Christians and non-Christians. The Christian Filipinos are a fairly homogeneous people, although they may be locally designated as Ilocanos, Tagalogs, Visayans, or Bicolanos, according to the dialect spoken. As a rule, natives born in the northern part of the island of Luzon are called Ilocanos; those born in the central and southern parts of this island are known as Tagalogs and Bicolanos, respectively. The central islands to the south of Luzon are inhabited by the Visayans. Unfortunately, some writers speak of these groups as "tribes," a designation greatly resented by them. They insist they are Filipinos and that the various names signify nothing and are useful only in making a linguistic classification of the Christian Filipinos.

The Christian Filipinos make up fully nine-tenths of the entire population. They are the representative people of the islands and most commonly are the ones referred to by the term "Filipinos." They are the natives that came under the influence of the early missionaries, who succeeded in molding them into a new type. In its influence on these Filipinos the church made remarkable, almost unbelievable, progress; but there were groups also that, for some reason or other, the church could not touch. Even at this late date, in the less accessible parts of the islands some of these selfsame groups, non-Christians, are still living in a semi-wild state. Although the term "non-Christian" is an extremely unsatisfactory one, the people cannot be called pagan because most of them are Mohammedans; nor can they be called wild or savage, for some are quite as gentle and cultured as their Christian neighbors.

Although the Christian Filipinos are the dominant group, being the leaders in politics, professions, agriculture, and business, and in general endowed with high aptitudes, the non-Christian groups need special consideration. Of these, the woolly-headed Negritos, probably the aborigines of the archipelago, are among the smallest people on earth. Although suggestively Negroid in their color and mops of kinky, black hair, they have neither the projecting jaw nor the long skull of the African Negro. Numbering about 60,000, they roam the more inaccessible mountain and forest regions and depend on native plants and animals for their food. They are widely distributed from Mindanao and Palawan to Luzon. As a group they are pagans of low mentality with an inordinate craving for alcoholic drinks. They are preyed upon by the other groups, and many of them are kept in abject peonage and slavery. Because they are seemingly incapable of defending themselves, their extinction is only a matter of time. More and more, also, they are being absorbed in blood mixtures.

The Igorots, another pagan group with many local differences, are probably the descendants of the first Malay immigrants who settled in, or were later driven into, the mountainous interior of the island of Luzon. They appear to be related to the tall races of southeastern Asia. Numbering about 200,000, they are the most numerous of the truly pagan people of the islands and unquestionably also the most promising. Their ability in constructing and maintaining the stupendous rice terraces in the northern highlands of Luzon has placed them in the forefront of important backward peoples of the world. Until rather recently they were as barbarous as the primitive Malay tribes, with whom they share the same savage practices of head-hunting and family feuds. Their chief food is rice, but the most delectable dish is roast dog. The progress made by this fierce group during the American occupation has been little short of phenomenal. They now feel free to come from their homes in the hills to Baguio, the summer capital of the Philippine government, carrying on head or back their wares for the public market. Both men and women are well developed physically, are tall, and have yellowish, copper-brown skin, oblique black eyes, and straight black hair.

The Moros, numbering about half a million, are the largest of the non-Christian groups. They have become characterized chiefly by their fanatical adherence to the Mohammedan faith and by their hatred for the Christian Filipinos. Moro is the Spanish term for "Moor" and was applied indiscriminately by the early mission workers to all Filipinos embracing the Mohammedan religion. Even today the term "Moro," therefore, is a religious designation and not a racial or linguistic classification. Originally of Malay origin and probably pagan as immigrants, the Moros came under the influence of Mohammedanism sometime during the fourteenth century. When the Spanish came, two centuries later, they found the Moros in general control of the southern islands and actively and forcefully engaged in Mohammedanizing their pagan neighbors. Their militant attitude made the Spanish missionary, as a proselytizer, a potential enemy; and soon attacks on the Spanish outposts and on the Christianized neighbors became common. In these attacks they not only killed but also enslaved their captives. They were much feared; and the flocking of the pagan natives, under order of their chiefs, to join the Spanish outposts as the lesser of two evils may account in a measure for the remarkable accomplishments of the early missionary.

The Christianization of the natives was made much easier by existing conditions. By the time of the Spanish advent, the natives had become a fairly homogeneous people, well organized into groups under local chieftains. In many respects their organization was very similar to that of the feudal states in Europe during the Middle Ages. To make the resemblance still more complete, jealousies, feuds, and internecine wars between chiefs were common. The Spaniards put an end to this type of violence by organizing the people into larger units under the control of the church. As a result, many chieftains, with their people, came to the church voluntarily, not uncommonly with a greater desire for protection than for the salvation offered. The so-called "Spanish conquest" of the islands involved, therefore, little bloodshed; conversion of the natives was the fundamental aim. The dominant element in the control was not to exploit the resources but to save the souls of the inhabitants. To those who came under the wings of the church for one reason or another, the Spanish influence was truly great. The people not only received a new religion of hope but also a new system of government, new social usages and practices, and a new outlook. Those who resisted the influence of this more advanced culture, like the pagans of the north and the Mohammedans of the south, remained more or less stagnant during the succeeding centuries.

The animosity of the non-Christian groups to civilizing influences continued well into the period of American occupation and, to a degree, is still present. At first, force seemed to be the only way to put these recalcitrant groups under law and order. The Moros were especially troublesome, and the feeling arose in the American army that "the only good Moro is a dead one." Expeditions were sent against them but with little permanent effect. In later years the cardinal and most effective policy became one of conciliation, one which did not interfere, if possible, with religious beliefs and prejudices. As a result, life-activities and religious practices like polygamy and even slavery have been condoned. This conciliatory attitude has even granted them partial self-government. They have not taken kindly to the schools established in their territory, as the things taught have a tendency to undermine well-established customs. Unless their hostility to outside influences can be broken, they will continue to be a very serious problem.

Before coming to the islands the native groups already had a distinct culture of their own, to which they added elements in the island environment. Much has been written on the various cultures represented; but, in summary, fundamentally all were oriental and, in the main, showed a strong Hindu influence. Upon this cultural mixture the conquering Spanish engrafted a Latin civilization, with much success in some parts and with none in others. With American domination came new elements calling for many readjustments. This period must have seemed revolutionary to the masses of the people. At present, therefore, the culture is still a mixture of native, Hindu, Mohammedan, Spanish, and American in all stages of amalgamation, still to be fused into one unit. It is this evolutionary background that must be considered in the future of the Philippines. Cultural developments and customs with their centuries of fixations cannot be changed in a day. The Christian Filipinos, for all their past, are a surprisingly well-integrated unit.

The cultural progress made by the Filipinos during the American regime has been most remarkable, even revolutionary. A new people with an occidental outlook has arisen out of a medieval past. Oriental inheritances still linger and in many sections still dominate; but American educational, economic, and political lessons have been too well learned by the great majority to be forgotten. It is difficult to appreciate fully the problem of readjustments that faced every progressive Filipino when he tried to fit himself into the new order. The accelerated tempo of life brought in by the Americans and their ability to do things at once and on time are not yet wholly his; but neither is he unaware of their value nor unappreciative of their presence. His is the only Christian nation in the Orient, an element not to be overlooked in considering spiritual growth.

The rapid increase in the population of the islands during American control is perhaps the most outstanding fact. There has been more than a doubling of the number of people since Spanish control. An increase from 7,635,426 in 1903 to 10,314,310 in 1918 (the second census), to 12,588,066 in 1930, and to 16,000,313 in 1940 is not readily explained. On this basis the average density of population per square mile was 61 in 1903, 91 in 1918, 110 in 1930, and 139 in 1940. The population, however, is very unevenly distributed, from an estimated density for 1935 of 628 persons per square mile in Cebu and 576 in Iloilo to 15 in the province of Agusan in Mindanao and 13.5 in the province of Nueva Viscaya in Luzon. The entire island of Mindanao has a density of only 34 per square mile, but the provinces of Pampanga and Pangasinan in the central plain of Luzon have a density of 361 per square mile. Even in view of the dense population in parts, the islands can scarcely be considered overpopulated. Estimates based on present conditions have placed the maximum population the islands can maintain at 50,000,000.

LOCATION AND CLIMATE

The climate of the Philippines is determined to such a degree by the location that the one can scarcely be considered without the other. Located between 4°40′ and 21°10′ N., the archipelago lies very specifically within the northern tropics. The all too common belief that tropical regions are unbearably hot is not supported by the facts in the Philippines. The high temperatures of the middle latitudes are never approached in any part of the islands. Temperatures may rise to 100° F., but such records are so exceptional as to be of special scientific interest. In Manila rarely does the temperature go below 60° F. and just as rarely does it reach 100° F. Invariably the nights, especially the very early morning hours, are sufficiently cool for refreshing sleep. Freezing temperatures occur in the highest mountains. By and large, the mean annual temperatures throughout the Philippines lie between 75° and 85° F. Temperatures, therefore, may be designated as moder-

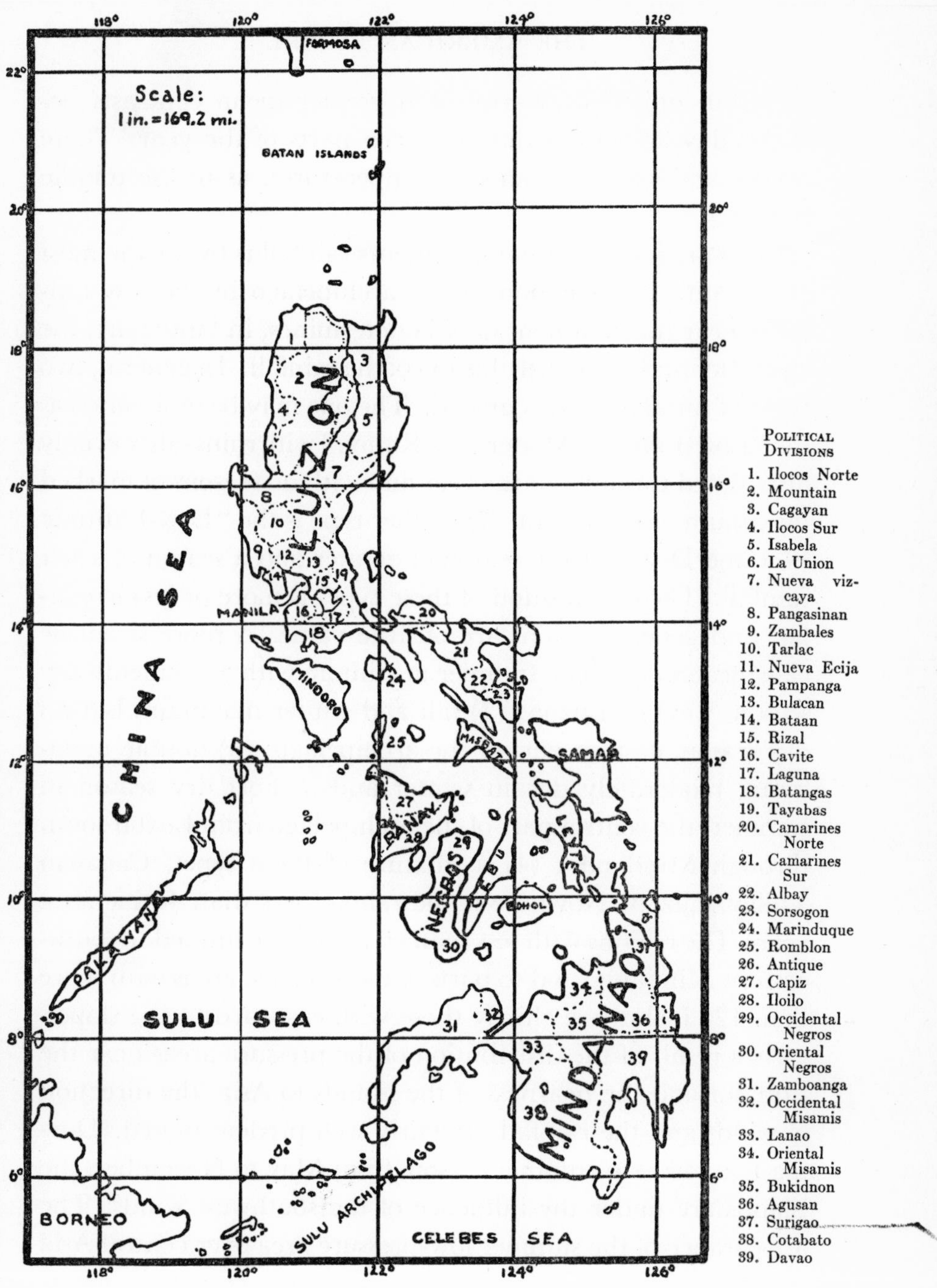

MAP OF THE PHILIPPINES WITH THE NAMES OF THE MAJOR ISLANDS AND THE LEADING PROVINCES INDICATED

ately but uniformly warm, with greater mean contrasts between day and night than between parts of the year. There are no seasonal variations in temperatures, as in the middle latitudes.

In an analysis of climatic elements rainfall is by far the most important. The location of the archipelago in the low latitudes near the continent of Asia determines, in large part, the character and areal distribution of the rainfall. In general, two types of rainfall are recognized. The one may be designated as the "Low-Latitude Moderately Rainy," with rains fairly evenly distributed throughout the year and with no seasons of marked maximum or minimum. The other type is the "Low-Latitude Wet and Dry," with a season of greater and a season of lesser rainfall. The distribution of these types is more or less irregular, and generalizations are of little value. A more scientific classification is: (1) a summer maximum with a decidedly dry season, western Luzon; (2) fall and winter maximum but no dry season, eastern part of the archipelago; (3) double maximum, moderately dry in winter and a short dry season in summer, the central part of the archipelago from Luzon south through Mindanao; (4) a mixture of these types, Cagayan Valley, Luzon. Nowhere is the rainfall less than 40 inches a year. The regions with less than 60 inches are limited to southeastern Mindanao and to parts of the Visayas; areas with more than 120 inches are chiefly those with eastward-facing slopes.

As a result of the distribution of the pressure areas near the Equator and the nearness of the islands to Asia, the direction of winds and the rainfall are fairly well predetermined. During the northern summer season, from May to November, the islands are under the influence of the southwest winds. The appearance of the summer low-pressure area over central Asia accentuates these southwesterlies, which, in the main, bring the rainier season to many parts of the archipelago, especially to the western slopes of the mountains. As the season changes and a high-pressure area is formed over the Gobi Desert, winds blowing out of this area combine with the trades to form fairly strong north and northeast winds. During this season the north and northeastern parts of the Philippines and the windward slopes of elevations receive rain. The western parts and slopes are then dry or nearly so. The rainfall conditions, however, are by no means simple. Besides the location near the Equator and Asia, there are many other local factors, chief of which is altitude, the effect of which is especially marked in the Philippines, as the mountain ranges stand athwart the dominant winds.

Unfortunately, their location on the western periphery of the North Pacific places the islands in the path of the typhoon, locally known as the *baguio*, of the same order as the tropical hurricane of the West Indies. The *baguios*, which commonly originate to the northeast or east of the Philippines, travel in a west-northwest direction across, or to the north of, the archipelago. *Baguios* are rare over the islands of Mindanao and Palawan in the south but do occur there. Not all of these tropical disturbances are of equal intensity; some are more destructive than others. They have been divided into two major groups, the "severe" and the "ordinary," the latter being the more numerous. During 1908–18 the Weather Bureau recorded 45 of the severe and 61 of the less destructive type. Like the tropical hurricanes of the West Indies, they occur most frequently during the autumn months of September, October, and November, although they may occur during any month of the year, most rarely in February. Their destructiveness is a matter of record and is a distinct handicap to the islands in which they are of frequent occurrence.

Not all the destruction of the *baguio* is caused by the wind; the accompanying downpour of rain is responsible for some of it. Much of the very heavy precipitation of the summer months in the northern half of the islands is traceable directly to this tropical hurricane. This is especially true when the typhoon pulls in the warm, moisture-laden winds from the west and southwest over the much cooler mountain areas. In the direct path of the *baguio* in July, 1911, the station at Baguio in western Luzon recorded the extraordinary rainfall of 34.6 inches in a single day and 46.0 inches from noon of the fourteenth to noon of the fifteenth. In one single hour the amazing total of 8.4 inches was recorded. At this same station, located about 160 miles north of Manila, 259 inches are recorded for 1935, of which 92 inches fell in August. During four successive days the rainfall gauge recorded 98 inches of rain. When such or a somewhat lesser downpour occurs in a region with a season dry enough for the ground to have no cover of growing vegetation, the erosive effects and the resultant drainage changes are beyond the comprehension of most people who have not witnessed such conditions.

A major advantage in this tropical location is that the islands are able to produce any type of tropical product desired. In addition, subtropical and even middle-latitude products may be and are grown at the higher altitudes. Vegetables from American-grown seeds are now being marketed in the larger centers where there is a demand. With the possible exception of sugar, crops may be planted and harvested at any season, and there is no off season for growth except in the areas with prolonged dry seasons. Nor are there any serious climatic hindrances to outdoor work. The rural workman commonly continues his labor no matter what change has occurred. Some activities become somewhat seasonal, falling to that part of the year best suited. Provincial fairs, outdoor exhibits, salt-making, the drying of fish, and the like are dry-season activities, but they are not necessarily limited to that one season. Where the dry season is severe and long enough, trees shed their leaves, and the plumage of birds becomes dull. The advent, then, of the wet season is similar to spring in higher latitudes.

Located near Asia, the islands enjoy a frontage on some of the world's important highways of commerce. The Philippines not only offer an open frontage to the main steamer tracks of eastern Asia but also serve as termini for the North Pacific and Hawaiian routes and as important ports-of-call for round-the-world ships coming from Europe via Suez. The islands are also on the main shipping routes from Australia and the East Indies to China and Japan. The relation of the archipelago to eastern Asia is somewhat similar to that of the West Indies to the United States. Both regions are the nearest tropical areas to densely populated middle-latitude lands; but, strangely enough, the trade between the Philippines and eastern Asia is, in general, less than 10 per cent of that between the West Indies and the United States. In a measure this may indicate the possible future trade relationships with eastern Asia.

REGIONAL CHARACTERISTICS

Of the 7,083 islands listed, with a total area of 114,400 square miles, nearly equal to that of New England and New York State combined, the larger number by far have no present economic significance. Many of the smaller ones are merely projecting rock masses, at times awash by a high sea. The steep, rocky shores of others make landing by boat extremely hazardous, if not absolutely impossible. Of the larger islands, about 1,000 have some significance; and, of them, about 460 are as much as a square mile or more in area. Only 11 are sufficiently large and well known to be considered in any survey. They are: Luzon, 40,814 square miles; Mindanao, 36,906; Samar, 5,124; Negros, 4,983; Palawan, 4,500; Panay, 4,448; Mindoro, 3,794; Leyte, 2,799; Cebu, 1,695; Bohol, 1,534; Masbate, 1,255. The total acreage is 73,216,000 of which, according to estimates, 63 per cent, or nearly 46,000,000 acres, are suitable as some type of crop land. However, at present less than 10,000,000 acres are devoted to crops.

To appreciate even partially the general character of the group as a whole, a survey in some detail for a few of the larger islands is advisable. Luzon, in the north, is not only the largest but also the best known and most important in the archipelago. As is so common in nearly all the major islands, some parts are very highly developed, other parts almost untouched. The northeastern section of Luzon, represented by the eastern slopes of the eastern range, has shown little development and is one of the most isolated sections in all the islands. The only access is by boat; and the regularity of the coastline, with its paucity of indentations, makes even this approach difficult and at certain periods of the year hazardous. Outside of a small number of Negrito communities, there are few resident people. The exploitation of the timber resources by outside lumber companies is the chief activity; but the steepness of slopes, heavy rainfall, and lack of harbors have not been conducive to regular and assured profits. The chief claim of the region to fame is that in the small town of Baler was born Manuel Quezon, the first president of the commonwealth.

COCONUT PALMS ALONG A PROVINCIAL HIGHWAY IN THE ISLAND OF LUZON

These waving palms are familiar sights along almost all of the archipelago

The Zambales region in the southwest of Luzon is a rugged highland section inclosing, in part, Manila Bay. This elevated region receives the drenching rains of the southwest winds from May to October and in consequence is most deeply dissected. The extremely heavy rains, as already noted for Baguio on the border of this province, are the more effective from an erosional standpoint because they follow the long dry season, when all vegetation is dead or dormant.

The region is sparsely populated, with little development even for food production. Rice, the leading crop, is grown for local consumption only, although an occasional surplus is marketed. Sugar cane, bananas, corn, tobacco, vegetables, mangoes, and some native plant foods represent the plant products of the area and in a measure indicate the potential cash crops should the area ever attain greater development. Along the coast and on the foothill slopes, the coconut is becoming more important in spite of the long rainless season. In higher grassland areas livestock is slowly coming to the fore as local demands increase. Local isolation is the chief handicap. No region can develop very much without reasonably fair transportation facilities. With better transportation there are strong possibilities that more progressive groups, such as the Ilocanos and Tagalogs, will enter the region.

The Cagayan Valley, the longest in the Philippines, lies between the eastern and central cordillera of northern Luzon. The river is about 220 miles long and is navigable for ocean-going vessels of shallow draft for about 70 miles. Its rich alluvial soils have made the valley the great tobacco district not only of Luzon but of the whole archipelago. The region has become famous for its filler, binder, and wrapper tobaccos, especially the wrappers designated as the "Cagayan" and the

"Isabella." Rice is the important food crop and in time may displace tobacco as a cash crop. In addition to these two major crops the normal supply of other products for local use is common throughout the valley. The agricultural part of the valley is somewhat handicapped by a drought period of three months or more, although the less rainy part of the wet period does aid in the harvesting of crops. The steep upper slopes of the valley are heavily forested and are less affected by droughts. Even on the upper slopes, however, under the influence of local topographic features, there are fairly dry areas covered with a short, scrubby growth. During the dry season fires may overrun these hillsides, exposing them to the severest type of erosion. Unfortunately, the valley opens up to the north and is shut off from Manila by a terrain so rough that it has become known as "No Man's Land." However, a good automobile road with bus and truck service now connects this valley with Manila.

Mountain Province, lying west and southwest of Cagayan Valley, includes the thoroughly dissected portion of the Cordillera Central, the backbone of Luzon. Being a mountainous region, with an average elevation of about 4,000 feet above sea-level, it possesses for its latitude a moderately cool climate throughout the year. Indoors and in the shade a wrap is necessary for comfort, and in the evening some artificial heat is needed. The upper reaches of the hills, rising to 9,400 feet (the elevation of Mount Pulog, the highest peak in Luzon), are covered with pine forests and, in the north, even with oak, giving a character to the region which its latitude belies. The contrasts between it and the near-by lowlands are so marked as to be almost incredible—papayas, bananas, and other tropical fruits are grown almost side by side with carrots, cabbages, and other mid-latitude vegetables. The region as a whole is necessarily sparsely populated. Although the natives speak different dialects and are known by different names, there exists a general uniformity in methods of tilling the soil and in customs of ancestor-worship and other customs and superstitions.

Although many parts of Mountain Province are very much isolated, even from one another, one section is easily accessible from Manila. Because of its marvelous scenery and delightful climate, the town of Baguio, on the southwest margin of the province, has become the "summer capital." Located in a troughlike depression in the tableland, this "City of Pines" has an individuality all its own. It is unquestionably the premier mountain resort in all the Philippines. Every year at the advent of the warm season in Manila about the middle of March, which is also the end of the school year, the hegira begins. Government officials and others of means make their homes there, with a new round of social events, until about the end of May, the beginning of the rainy season. Baguio, however, is so accessible to Manila, either by train or automobile, that it serves as a rendezvous the year round for many of Manila's "four hundred." Aside from scenery and climate, a home there offers much, especially to American and English families, in the way of fresh vegetables, fruits, chickens, eggs, and the like, produced in the justly famous Trinidad Valley, 3½ miles northwest of the city.

In other parts of Mountain Province, however, the isolation has made the inhabitants depend on their own ability to wrest a living from the soil. Even with the utmost frugality and ingenuity the natives produce barely enough for a hand-to-mouth existence, and no effort is too great or labor too arduous to assure a bountiful harvest. Even the little children have their appointed tasks of keeping the birds from the fields. Ingenious mechanical devices are also installed for the same purpose. Crisscrossing over fields are bark strings to which are fastened objects to disturb and frighten the birds. Not only are the fields zealously watched at all times, but unusual frightening devices and traps are set out for rats, wild pigs, and other animals. After harvest the utmost precautions are again taken against any intrusion upon the private food supply. Granaries are very carefully closed, and the secret manner of locking against theft by man is known only to the head of the family. The food supply in these regions is the treasure to be guarded above all else, for it sustains life.

In the Bontoc region are the famous rice terraces of the Igorots, created to increase the food supply. These terraces are so unique for primitive peoples that some have come to believe that early Chinese immigrants must have taught the people the art of building them. Perhaps the skill shown in building is the accumulation of experience in the many re-buildings during the centuries past. Whatever the origin, the terraces were already admired by the Spanish missionary in the early sixteenth century. Beginning at the base of the mountain and continuing nearly to the top, they follow natural contours rather closely in a series of steps of varying width and length. The rocks which serve as a dam, and even the soil behind the dam, may have been brought in from near-by regions. The construction is by man power alone, with the crudest of tools and guided only by native ingenuity. The terraces are built on the windward, or rainy, side of mountains below the flow of springs. Placed end to end, it is said, they would go halfway around the world at the Equator. In times of great

RICE GRANARIES OF THE IFUGAOS

An ingenious device is used on the uprights to keep rats from getting into the granaries.

downpour, to which this region is subject, the terraces may be swept away wholly or in part, and the weary task of rebuilding, requiring months, starts all over again. With the loss of a terrace, some of the food supply is gone also—a real catastrophe, as a crop for the year is lost.

On the terraces the rice is planted by hand from seed beds when the stalks are 5 or 6 inches high. The practice is similar to that used in the lowland sections of the Philippines and throughout the Orient generally. The building of the terraces and the preparation for planting are the work of all, because the time is limited, but the transplanting is very specifically the work of women. In the subprovince of Kalinga the general practice of a second planting as soon as the first crop is harvested makes this the "rice-granary" and the most densely populated part of Mountain Province. Two plantings are possible because sufficient water is available throughout the year for irrigation. In other sections, where the drought period is not too severe, millet may occupy the terraces when free of rice, generally from May or June to January or February. In other places during the off-season, cabbages, onions, beans, lettuce, mustard, and even cotton may provide the second crop of the year.

Other crops are grown in places without the aid of terraces. Chief among these are corn, mountain rice which needs no irrigation, yams, sugar cane, tobacco, coffee, cacao, bananas, and a host of other products native to the region. These crops are for home consumption, and it is only when there is a surplus that anything is sold or bartered in the markets. The cane is used principally in the manufacture of *basi*, a fermented beverage made from its juice. Another alcoholic beverage is *tupuy*, made from fermented rice. A common house brew is *sabeng*, made from a mixture of *gabe*, *camote*, and general refuse, especially the leftovers after the celebration of the *canao*. The *canao* is a feast fitted to almost any occasion; but the most important *canao* is at the end of the year, when the agricultural gods are invoked to ward off calamities and evil spirits. During this feast chickens, pigs, and even cattle are sacrificed to propitiate the gods. Records seem to indicate that even human beings were needed at times to satisfy hostile divinities. During the weeks of celebrating the *canao* there must always be a bountiful supply of *basi*, *tupuy*, or *sabeng*, or all three. The *canao* with all its barbaric customs is an indication of the general uncertainty of the food supply of the region.

The people of Mountain Province, although superstitious and primitive in their general outlook, are very promising. They show great skill and ingenuity. This is especially well expressed in their industries and handiwork, perhaps relics of early Spanish missionary teachings. The work of the loom, laces and other needlework, basket-weaving, and the like are most commonly looked upon as work for women and girls. The men are equally adept in making the primitive tools needed especially for their wood and wicker work. Were it possible to market more of their wares, these diligent and serious-minded people might soon be placed into another cultural stage.

Mindanao, next to Luzon in size and within 10° of the Equator, lies at the southern end of the archipelago. The contrast in development between Luzon and Mindanao is most marked, the one with parts very highly developed, the other with large areas little known or even unexplored. Its backwardness and its lack of development except along the coast may be traced more or less to its dense vegetative cover. The vast extent of its virgin forest is a distinct handicap to agricultural development. Settlement in such areas of heavy forest cover necessarily must start along coasts, especially in embayments, and also along stream courses; and such areas in tropical regions are not uncommonly the least desirable. To clear such land where rains continue throughout the year is next to an impossibility. Few lands are worth the effort. A dry season with dormant vegetation and fire gives man a distinct advantage. Even after a clearing has been effected by girdling and fire, there is a constant struggle between man's efforts to keep clear the land and nature's efforts to repossess it. Given the least opportunity, new forests spring up like magic, and cleared land never lies fallow for very long. Settlement in such tropical lands is more than the clearing of the land of trees and stumps; it is a never ending struggle with new forest growth.

Although Mindanao may be thought of as fairly densely populated with its million and a quarter people, or 34 persons per square mile, yet many extensive areas are devoid of people except for forest wanderers. The population is distinctly a coastal one. Most of the people live along the east and north coast, perhaps because that area is near the more densely populated Visayan group to the north and also because of the exhilarating effects of the trade winds, sometimes spoken of as "the doctor." Another center of settlement is the Agusan Valley, corresponding geologically to the Cagayan Valley in Luzon, each being between the eastern and central cordillera. Other settlements on the north coast are in the province of Misamis; those in the southwest are centered around Zamboanga, the only important rubber port, and the ports of Cotabato and Kiamba. Agricultural development is dependent upon topography and soils as well as upon climate. Much leaching has made the soils of the island highly lateritic; they are very poor except where the land is underlain by limestone or young volcanics. Much of the agricultural development has been possible by plantation agriculture with labor-saving machinery. The Japanese have been especially active in this type of agriculture, and they practically control the province of Davao.

The forest cover is the chief latent resource of Mindanao, although gold, iron, and other minerals may ultimately rank high after a more thorough scientific exploration of the island has been made. Fairly reliable estimates place the area of high-grade commercial forests at about 65 per cent of the total area. As is characteristic of tropical forests elsewhere, there is an unusually large number of species; but there are no stands of a single species comparable to the fir, spruce, or pine forests of middle latitudes. A comprehensive plan for preparing and marketing such a diverse variety of timber has never been developed. The woods are roughly divided into four groups: (1) Extremely hard and heavy woods, too heavy to float on water even when dry. These are strong, durable, and well fitted for use in the tropics, where insect pests are a menace. Their hardness and heaviness, however, are a distinct handicap in their preparation and handling, especially for export. (2) Less hard and less heavy woods, most used locally where durability is the major requirement. Unfortunately, the most preferred types are more or less restricted to areas not readily accessible. (3) Many species which are lighter, softer, and less durable than the first two groups, including the tanguiles and red lauans, known commercially as "Philippine mahogany." (4) The lightest and least durable woods, which find the greater market because of the ease in handling and working them. Mindanao may be a rich storehouse when tropical woods shall have come into widespread use.

Palawan, an isolated island in the southwestern part of the archipelago, is narrow and long, being the exposed part of a mountain ridge. The roughness of its topography adds to its internal isolation, which is expressed even in its unique native fauna, such as the scaly anteater, the mouse deer, and other bizarre forms. The chief reasons for its isolation are (1) the presence of dangerous shoals and coral reefs along its border; (2) the distance necessary for interisland traffic; (3) the extreme ruggedness with its tropical jungle; and (4) the fact that the island has become, unfortunately, a favorite rendezvous for smugglers and pirates and a hiding place for criminals. As a result, the island, relative to others, is sparsely populated, having only about 18 persons per square mile. Because of this isolation the government has established on its shores the leprosarium for lepers and the Iwahig penal colony for the worst criminals.

Among the most important products coming from the diverse natural resources of Palawan are timbers and other forest products, such as rattan, dyewoods, tanbarks, resins, gums, beeswax, and honey. Small quantities of rice, corn, vegetables, fruits, and dairy and poultry products reach Manila. Forest products will remain the leading export for a long time to come, inasmuch as more than 70 per cent of the area of the island is forest land. The open pastures and brush lands offer considerable opportunity for the livestock industry. The shallow coastal waters are rich in marine life, but at present only trepang and sea shells are exported, the former to China and the latter to Manila for the button industry. From the limestone cliffs in the north edible birds' nests are gathered for export to China. It is hoped that the many caves rich in bird guano will become the basis for a fertilizer industry.

Not only in Luzon, Mindanao, and Palawan but in all the islands mountains are the dominant physical features and give direction to all economic development. In fact, for the Philippines as a whole, four anticlinal ridges form the complex relief of the entire group. They are the basic structures of a great mountain system extending roughly north and south and almost wholly submerged. As in most mountain systems, there are also extensive lava flows, now in the main covered with soil formed through disintegration. There also have been explosive volcanoes which have spread their ejecta widely throughout the archipelago; a few of them are still active. The most prominent chain of all, the Cordillera Central, forms the backbone of the island of Luzon and extends south through Mindanao. There are other ranges also, with lowlands between them like the Agusan and Cagayan plains. In the Visayan group, greater submergence has left only one ridge within each island. In Mindanao, as in Luzon, there are several north-south ridges; the main one of these, in the central portion of the island, includes Mount Matutum, 9,610 feet, the highest peak in the archipelago. As a result of its geologic history, the archipelago has very few extensive flat-land areas.

The many minor differences from island to island in land form, climate, soil, and the like indicate also a great variety in types, stages, and degrees of development. The island of Leyte has fully 50 per cent of its area in crops. Fertile and densely populated Panay is, with the exception of Luzon, the leading rice-producer. Cebu, with nearly half of its acreage in crops, has, next to Luzon, the largest acreage in coconuts and grows corn almost to the exclusion of rice as a food crop. The cane fields of northwestern Negros vie with those of Luzon as sugar-producers. Samar, like southern Mindanao and eastern Luzon, has more than 40 per cent of its area still in forest. In spite of their outer superficial likenesses, there is a great variety of life-conditions and responses between and within the islands. In the broad homogeneity of conditions in the archipelago there is also a heterogeneity of people, products, and possibilities.

MINERAL RESOURCES AND THEIR DEVELOPMENT

During the past decade the interest in gold-mining has increased enormously. From a production in 1928 valued at less than $2,000,000 the output increased so that ten years later its value was over $20,000,000. In 1935 the Philippines produced more gold than Alaska and were second only to California in American territory. In practically every province gold-mining claims have been filed with the government bureau, and mining has been carried on. Active production has been confined to five general regions, however: (1) Mountain Province, Luzon, the oldest and most important gold region in the Philippines; (2) the island of Masbati; (3) the province of Camarines Norte, southeastern Luzon; (4) the province of Bulacan, east of Manila; and (5) the provinces of Surigao and Zamboanga, Mindanao. The gold is mined from both placers and lodes, and the discovery of new ore bodies is by no means simple. A heavy overburden of mantle rock, jungle vegetation of almost impenetrable density, and inadequate transportation facilities make prospecting most difficult. Some ore bodies are only potentially valuable now but might, with improved transportation facilities, become rich producers.

In recent years the industry has shown a most healthy growth. Although gold was mined by the natives long before the arrival of the Spaniards and continued to be produced under their rule, the industry scarcely held its own until the arrival of the Americans with modern machinery and skill. Since then the profits have started many "booms." Of the many companies organized before 1930, only three, however, have survived to the present. Since 1930, technological advances and the raising of the price of gold per ounce from $20.67 in 1933 to $35.00 in 1934 have given much impetus to gold-mining in the Philippines. Prospecting was stimulated throughout the islands, new companies were organized, and old ones enlarged their plant capacities. Of the eighty-eight companies licensed in 1935 to sell stock, six were paying dividends, and during five years or less three paid their stockholders, in the form of dividends, an aggregate sum in excess of the total capital invested. Any further technological advances or improvement in transportation may make rich ore-producing bodies out of present worthless rock masses.

The most important iron ores known are in the provinces of Bulacan and Camarines Norte in Luzon, Surigao in Mindanao, and on the island of Samar. Only the deposits at Mambulao, Camarines Norte, are being exploited commercially. Their annual production is about 500,000 tons, shipped almost exclusively to Japan and furnishing employment to about 2,000 people. The ferrous content of the ore is high, roughly 61 per cent; and the estimated high-grade ore reserves are some 5,000,000 tons. The Bulacan deposits are worked by Filipinos in primitive fashion and made into cast-iron implements for local use. Their reserves may be as much as 1,000,000 tons. The largest of all known deposits are in Surigao, where the workable reserves of 54 per cent ferrous content or higher have been estimated at 500,000,000 tons. These lateritic ores are distributed over an area of some 40 square miles, and fully half of them are in beds more than 9 feet thick. The ore beds are not continuous but are on slopes and hilltops within an altitude range of from 1,500 to 2,000 feet. Although this reserve has been known for nearly thirty years, no attempt thus far has been made to exploit it commercially. Because there is a lack of coking-coal, none of the deposits can ever be of much value to the Philippines except locally and as an exportable commodity.

Since chromium is one of the rarer alloy metals, the deposits of chromite have considerable significance. The world's known supply is limited, and nations eagerly seek political control of important deposits for industrial and military needs. The ore chromite is now being mined in Camarines Sur and in Zambales, two widely separated regions in Luzon. The deposits in Camarines Sur contain at least 100,000 tons of ore of more than 55 per cent chromic oxide content. Exports began in 1936, and shipments of 25,000 tons annually to the United States are now made. The Zambales deposits, believed to be among the largest in the world, contain about 10,000,000 tons of ore. Lesser bodies are known in other parts of Zambales, in the island of Samar, and in Surigao, Mindanao.

There are many other minerals in the islands, some of which in time may be of considerable importance. Very definitely there are deposits of silver, copper, and manganese. Although silver is now produced chiefly as a by-product in the extraction of gold, there are silver mines of considerable promise. Copper ores of low grade are abundant in Mountain Province, Luzon, in the island of Panay, and in the Sulu Archipelago. The development of these deposits is still in initial stages. Manganese deposits are reported from various parts of the archipelago; but only in Ilocos, Luzon, has there been any activity, and the ore has been shipped to Japan. The reserve is estimated at 100,000 tons. Deposits of coal have been located in Cebu and in Camarines Sur, Luzon, but Australian and Japanese coals have amply supplied the limited needs. Wildcat ventures for petroleum have not yet brought in any producing wells; and geologic conditions are, for the most part, unfavorable. Unquestionably, the mining industry is still in its infancy, and any estimates for the future, in the very nature of the case, must be considered unreliable.

FOREST RESOURCES

The commonwealth is rich in tropical woods. The estimated forest cover is placed at 41,886,000 square miles, or 57 per cent of the total area of the islands, of which about four-fifths is sufficiently high grade to be counted as commercial timber, with 5,464,740,000 board feet. Such estimates, however, although based on scientific data, may be far from the mark, since many parts of the islands are still unknown to the scientific investigator. The stands of commercial timber have a wide distribution, with the greater acreage by far on the island of Mindanao. The Philippine government owns most of the forests and administers them through its Bureau of Forestry as forest reserves and national parks, for local usage, and by leasing certain areas to lumbering companies, who pay as much as $1.25 per cubic meter of lumber cut. In recent years such leases have paid the government more than $500,000 annually.

At present the value of these extensive forest areas to the Philippines lies chiefly in the protection they afford against excessive erosion, which is such a terrific menace. Without forests the major part of the islands would soon become uninhabitable. The extremely heavy short-period downpours bring destruction to exposed slopes undreamed of by those who have not had practical experience with such floods of water. The damage done lies not only in the gullying and even canyon-making in the mountain areas, but more particularly in the deposition of debris upon agricultural lands at the bases of ruined slopes, making them also worthless for crop purposes. The Bureau of Forestry is most keenly aware of the danger and, where possible, does not permit lumbering on such critical slopes. Although the actual wealth within the forest lies dominantly in the lumbering possibilities, there is a host of other products which add immensely to the forest wealth, such as rattan, cutch, resins, gums, rubber, dyewoods, spices, gutta-percha, palm nuts, and the like. In fact, the Philippines can supply practically all the tropical products called for in the world-markets.

The lumbering industry in the Philippines has been slow to develop. During most of the Spanish regime there was practically no lumbering, as the occasional mill near Manila found it difficult to meet the competition of cheap Asiatic lumber. That which existed was most primitive; carabaos, or water buffaloes, moved the logs slowly and laboriously to the coast, where, after being squared to reduce weight, they were loaded into vessels for transportation to market. To the incoming Americans, some of whom had had experience in lumbering regions at home, the excellent stands at or near tidewater suggested splendid possibilities. Sawmills were soon established, but logging was still continued in the native fashion with carabaos. With time, however, new equipment was imported, companies were enlarged, and the steam engine replaced the carabao and, to a degree, the native workers. The development in recent years has been remarkably rapid, and there is probably no tropical area anywhere with a more effective system of logging and marketing than is now found in certain parts of the Philippines.

Although much pioneer work in harvesting and marketing these mixed stands of heavy tropical hardwoods is still ahead, the problem of the most effective use of the cutover lands should perhaps receive even more attention. The natural tendency to cut the more valuable types and to permit the forest to replace itself is sure to result in degeneration. Strangely enough, reforestation is now being undertaken in areas of former unwise clearing. In many places agriculture and industry have followed the lumber mill. In some of the more desirable agricultural areas under wise supervision, the natives have used the money earned at the mills to buy and clear the land and then have sold the produce grown to the lumber camp. In the wake of the mill prosperous communities soon started. In some of the more fortunate areas much of the forest wealth was transformed into local development projects. Unfortunately, in other sections the land passed into the hands of speculators, and with it have gone also many of the possibilities of an orderly development.

As a potential supply of tropical hardwoods for American needs, the Philippine forests are of the first order. The great number of species, each with its special characteristics, make possible the fulfilment of practically every need. Although most of the names of the various woods are meaningless when first heard, certain groups already have become fairly familiar. The great bulk of the lumber comes from the lauan group, known in trade as "Philippine mahogany." The major use for the red lauan is for interior finish, furniture, and musical and scientific instruments and cases. The white lauan and the almond are second choice, being close grained and taking stains readily. The apitong is much harder, making very serviceable floor-covering, as well as interior boat and auto trim. For paneling and trim, price is commonly the most important consideration in the American market; but for furniture, radio cabinets, and the like, current style is the principal factor in the selection of a particular wood. The demand for certain woods is, therefore, most variable and uncertain. From the general standpoint of price, Philippine mahogany occupies a median ground; it is neither the cheapest nor the most expensive cabinet wood sold in the American market.

In spite of the natural richness of the Philippine forests, certain areas are already feeling the effect of man's attack; Mountain Province, Luzon, is an example. Less than half a century ago this was a thickly forested mountain area, mostly in virgin timber. At present in various sections the forests are unable to meet the legitimate demands of the gold-mining industry, and mine timbers must be brought in from neighboring provinces. Many of the open, parklike areas covered with cogon, a tough reedy grass, are a product of forest fires during the dry season. The pernicious system of *caingin*-making by the natives in the more remote parts for the purpose of getting crop land is a serious threat. In this system the native girdles the larger trees in order to kill them and then, during the dry season, sets the area on fire. The ashes neutralize the soil and add potash as a fertilizer, but with the coming of the rains the soil is leached again, and after the second or third crop such lands will produce little. A new area is then burned over, and the same processes are repeated. In this and in various other ways a rich heritage is gradually disappearing, and the land is made useless through erosion.

PHILIPPINE CASH AND EXPORT CROPS

The introduction of sugar cane into the Philippines antedates any historical record, and probably early Chinese traders from Taiwan were responsible for it. In spite of the early introduction of cane, however, the making of sugar was slow to develop. In early Spanish days the cane was ground in homemade wooden mills, and the juice reduced in open kettles to a coarse muscovado. Not until 1795 is there a record of any export, and not until 1860 did the first steam mill produce sugar. Even during the first decade of American control the old order continued, with the first up-to-date mill built in Mindanao in 1910. The progress, only moderate for another decade, has since made sugar the leading product of the islands. From 1920 to 1934, the peak year, the sugar-cane acreage increased 55 per cent; total production, 253.9 per cent; and the yield from 0.957 to 2.186 short tons per acre. The total production for this period rose from 465,000 to 1,650,000 tons. In 1935 the sugar went under the quota system, with a marked reduction from the peak year.

The growing of sugar cane is an important item in the life of the people, and there are few places in the Philippines where, for one purpose or another, it is not grown. As an industry, however, sugar production is very specifically centered in relatively few regions. Normally more than half comes from the island of Negros, Occidental Province accounting for approximately 50 per cent of the total Philippine production. Luzon ranks second, producing in the central plain north of

Manila and in the provinces of Batangas and Laguna south of Manila Bay about one-third of the total for all the islands. The rest of the sugar comes from the islands of Panay and Cebu. The number of people wholly or partly dependent on the industry has been estimated recently at 1,900,000. In the districts named, when the industry was at its best, in 1934, it supported approximately four-fifths of the people. In addition to those directly engaged in producing sugar, others are partly dependent, being engaged in transportation, merchandizing, and the like.

The sugar industry of the Philippines is organized on a basis favorable to the increase of local capital. The industry consists of individual planters who grow the cane on their own or rented land for the "central," a center for processing the cane into marketable products. A few of the centrals also grow some cane, but the amount thus produced is a negligible part of the total. Individual planters operate on a long-time milling contract with the central, which usually provides an equal division of the sugar produced or is on a 60–40 basis in favor of the planter. Some planters prefer to work without a contract, selling their cane outright or on the best terms offered by any central. The production of sugar is very specifically a home industry, as fully half of the capital invested in the centrals is controlled by the Filipinos, the remaining half being about equally divided between Spanish and American investors.

The importance of sugar as a cash crop is reflected in Philippine trade statistics. This commodity alone accounts for nearly 50 per cent of the total value of all exports, shipped chiefly from the ports of Manila and Iloilo. At the peak, in 1934, sugar exports reached 1,275,000 tons, valued at $65,-450,000. In the three years 1932–34, inclusive, sugar accounted for 63, 61, and 59 per cent, respectively, of the total Philippine exports. The quota limitations of the United States caused the export for 1935 to drop to 573,500 tons. Since then production and export have varied with the regulations and restrictions imposed. Since 1930 more than 99 per cent of the sugar marketed has entered the free American market, about four-fifths entering Atlantic ports via the Panama Canal. Because practically all exports enter the American market, any adverse condition or legislation in the United States will necessarily affect adversely the industry in the islands.

The waving coconut palm is a familiar feature along almost all coasts of the archipelago and is the basis of a very important industry. The tree grows wherever warm temperatures, plenty of moisture, and moderate breezes prevail. The typhoon, however, is a serious enemy. The industry is centered chiefly in Luzon, which contains nearly one-half of the total acreage planted. Mindanao is second, with about one-sixth of the total acreage; and none of the other islands accounts for as much as one-twentieth of the total. However, in many sections other than those enumerated, the coconut and its products are the leading revenue-producer. The province of Tayabas in Luzon obtains about 75 per cent of its revenue from this source; six other provinces, from 50 to 75 per cent; and ten others, from 25 to 50 per cent. These figures, however, by no means portray the full importance of the coconut to the Filipinos. Outside of being a cash crop, the tree supplies most of the fundamental needs of food, clothing, and shelter for thousands of people who know little of the export demand.

The vicissitudes of the industry have been many. As early as the time of Magellan, Siamese junks were at the islands trading for copra, the dried meat of the coconut. Under Spanish control copra, with other island products, was included in the general ban on trade; and the exports, except from smuggling, were almost nil. With the lifting of this ban about sixty years before American occupation the industry again began to develop slowly, supplying in part the needs of European manufacturers in the making of soaps and oleomargarines. With American occupation and the opening-up of American markets, the industry grew rapidly, expanding five times during the years 1899–1908; and by the beginning of the World War the Philippines furnished one-fourth of the copra in world-trade. The oil, being very rich in glycerin, a product needed in certain high explosives, found a ready market in Europe during the World War, and trade increased proportionately. As prices rose, production increased; but both dropped as precipitously with the cessation of hostilities, and to an over-expanded industry came grief. By 1920 every coconut-oil mill with one exception was forced into liquidation. The survival of the copra-crushing industry in the Philippines on an export basis has since been made possible by American legislation favorable to the Philippine industry, which imposed a duty of 2 cents per pound on coconut oil from other countries. This duty is sufficiently high to exclude the processed oils from other countries.

The coconut-growing industry in the islands consists, in the main, of small enterprises. Large plantations of 1,000 acres or more are rare, and most groves are less than 10 acres in extent. In general the coconuts are grown on the share-tenancy basis, in which the tenant clears the land, plants and cultivates the grove, and harvests the nuts. At the same time he can raise subsistence crops on the *cococal*, if he has the ambition, for his own needs. When the coconuts are ready to be picked, the tenant prepares the copra, of which he gets one-third for his efforts. When he has the means, he may prefer to pay a cash rental for the land and harvest the whole crop as his own. There is however, almost an infinite variety of arrangements between the landed proprietor and the tenant. At its worst, tenancy is like share cropping, with the tenant so deeply in debt as to be in practical slavery, from which he cannot or does not care to escape. By and large, however, this part of the industry is in the hands of the common people, who, under favorable conditions, have an opportunity to acquire sufficient capital ultimately to own a small *cococal* of their own.

By far the larger part of the coconut crop is prepared for export. Estimates place the total local consumption from 10 to 20 per cent of the total. The remainder is exported primarily as copra, coconut oil, desiccated coconut, meal, and cake. Mainly because of inferior drying, Philippine copra usually commands next to the lowest prices paid in the world-market. In recent years over 85 per cent of the total export was shipped to the United States, the chief market, where the inferior grade has been found suitable for soap-making. Fully 90 per cent of the processed oil is exported as coconut oil, the rest being consumed locally or exported in the form of margarine, cooking-fats, soaps, or other manufactured products. The residue, copra cake and meal, remaining after the oil is pressed from the copra, is exported as cattle food principally. The only important market for copra cake is in northern Europe, whereas that for meal has been in the United States. The meal also has been used locally as fertilizer; but sugar-growers, the chief fertilizer-users, have found it unsatisfactory.

Abacá, whose trade-name is manila, or manila hemp, is a member of the banana family. It is an excellent cordage-producer, and the Philippines have a practical monopoly in its production. Abacá must compete with sisal, especially in binder twine and rope, but the characteristics of each are so distinctive that their specific uses rarely overlap. At present it is grown on about 10 per cent of the crop land, and the acreage of about 1,100,000 has varied little from year to year. Although the acreage may remain much the same, the production of fiber varies considerably from year to year because of trade conditions. The average annual production is approximately 200,000 tons. About 2,000,000 people are more or less directly dependent on it for their livelihood. Of these, about 600,000 heads of families are directly engaged in growing manila hemp as their chief crop. The principal regions of production are in the island of Mindanao, in southern Luzon, and in the islands of Leyte, Masbate, and Samar.

Of the four leading export crops—sugar, coconuts, abacá, and tobacco—the last is the least important. For the decade 1926–35, its value varied between only 4.7 and 7.1 per cent of the total value of all exports. As the plant is very sensitive to its environment, the growing of quality tobacco is restricted specifically to certain areas. The Cagayan Valley in northern Luzon is the major center; Isabella Province in this valley is the largest producer of high-grade leaf tobacco in the islands, has the largest yield per acre, and sells its tobacco at a higher price than does any other section. Tobacco is also a major crop along the northwest coast of Luzon and in parts of the islands of Cebu, Negros, and Panay. Although tobacco is never widely grown for local consumption, the industry is in the hands of about 75,000 small farms and 15 large plantations. The tobacco is purchased from the growers, and from the assorting warehouses it is either exported or shipped to a factory, where it enters the manufacturing process. In general the industry is in the hands of Filipino landowners, although Spanish capital controls several large plantations.

In addition to the four cash and export crops, there are other crops, designated as "sustenance" and "cash," or "barter," crops. Of these, rice, occupying about 50 per cent of the total crop acreage, is by far the most important. In acreage of the food group, corn is next, and bananas are third. In a certain measure, corn is a substitute for rice. In the uplands, where elevation, relief, water, or some other element is unfavorable to the growing of rice, corn partly or wholly takes its place as a food. Corn may be the chief food in these areas, or some may be sold or bartered in the rice areas for the much more desirable rice. Corn will always remain important to certain groups of people, but, compared to rice, its significance is not very great. Although the crop area is only a little less than one-fourth that of rice, the local value of the rice is nearly ten times that of corn. In comparison with rice and corn, bananas are a poor third as a major item in the diet of any one group. However, they are widely grown throughout the islands, and their value as an added item in the general diet can scarcely be overestimated. In some coastal regions fish is also an important item of diet.

TREND AND CHARACTER OF PHILIPPINE–UNITED STATES TRADE

After Spanish restrictions were removed in 1898, the commerce of the islands expanded greatly, although rather slowly at first. The great increase came with an expanding American trade. Of the total value for both imports and exports, the American portion was 11 per cent in 1900, 41 per cent in

1910, 65 per cent in 1920, and 72 per cent in 1935. During this period the trade with other nations more than held its own and for certain years was more than three times that at the beginning of American occupation. Sales from the Philippines to the United States, except for two brief periods under special conditions, have been greater in value than their purchases from the United States; but this situation prevailed even prior to American occupation. Under normal conditions the Philippines have consistently maintained a credit trade balance with the United States. The commercial relations, therefore, have been more profitable to the Philippines. The growth in imports from the United States was an average of 9 per cent of the total for 1899–1901, 42 per cent for 1909–14, and 64 per cent for 1930–33. The average export values to the United States increased from 18 per cent for the period 1899–1901 to 35 per cent for 1905–9, 73 per cent for 1923–28, 82 per cent for 1930–32, and 83 per cent for 1933–35. This trade balance against the United States was highest in 1933, when the Philippine side of the ledger showed $47,723,000. The quota system and other regulations have reduced this balance markedly.

The future outlet for the leading export commodities of the islands is a matter of serious concern to the Philippine people. Commercial relations are so preponderately with the United States that the gradual recession and ultimate elimination of the tariff-free American market will be a serious blow to local economic conditions. During 1939, Philippine exports to the United States were valued at over $92,000,000, or about 75 per cent of the total to all countries. Of all the exports, sugar is far in the lead, with a value of almost $50,000,000, or about 53 per cent of all shipments to the United States for 1939. With the exception of small amounts of molasses, syrup, and alcohol, nearly all of the cane products exported during the last decade have come to the United States. The export of sugar to the United States has increased both absolutely and relatively. As late as 1928 it constituted only 40 per cent of the total exports to the United States, whereas it accounted for 71 per cent in 1934, the highest for any year. What a severance with the greatest sugar market of the world may mean for a country dominated by a sugar economy is beyond human intelligence to foretell.

In view of complete independence there are various possibilities in the Philippines for the sugar industry. The most desirable arrangement for the islands is the maximum extension of time before the full tariff rate goes into effect. This, if special considerations were granted, might mean tremendous losses for the United States. Under existing regulations it has been estimated that for the year 1935 the "premiums" which the United States paid for Philippine sugar entering under the duty-free quota, in comparison with the cost of an equivalent amount at world-prices, amounted to $43,456,000. Or, on the basis of existing duties, the annual loss of revenues on Philippine sugar may be calculated as varying from $17,000,000 to $37,000,000. The United States can scarcely be expected to sustain such annual losses through an open agreement with any foreign state no matter what the relationships have been. Another possibility is to find other open markets, but sugar is the "outlaw of commerce," and its imports are controlled by high protective tariffs. There is the possibility that sugar might be replaced in the islands by another export crop. Such an eventuality, however, is not in the offing, nor is it possible, if the experience of other tropical countries has any significance. Another possibility is to forego exports and make the country a self-sustaining nation. Whatever the changes, it is difficult to see a situation comparable to what has been.

For the Philippines the export of coconut products is second in value only to that of sugar. The value of this export, $27,000,000, is derived from three major products—oil, copra and desiccated coconut. In world-trade this is second only to that of the Netherlands India. During the decade 1925–34, the world-trade in coconut oil and copra increased more than 63 per cent, but for the same period the Philippine increase was 88 per cent. In other words, in 1923 the islands supplied 33 per cent of the world-trade in these two commodities, but by 1934 this percentage had risen to 38. In respect to world-trade, the Philippine export increased not only in absolute but also in relative amounts. More than half of the Philippine export was oil, whereas most of the world-shipments were copra. The Philippines have had the advantage of a tariff-free market for oil and were able to keep the refining industry at home. The advantage of a tariff-free market unquestionably has made the remarkable advance in the Philippines possible.

Because of the variety of their uses, many coconut products are exported in new forms. It is estimated that only about 90 per cent of the coconut oil is exported, the rest being consumed at home or exported in further processed forms, such as vegetable butter and lard, soaps, fatty acids, glycerin, and the like. At present, domestic plants supply most of the needs of the islands in cooking-oils and vegetable fats. These are rapidly replacing imported Chinese lard, peanut oil, cottonseed oil, and various greases. Relatively only small amounts of these exported coconut products enter the United States. The foreign markets which import the largest amounts of the edible oils are the Straits Settlements and Netherlands India. Other coco-tree products which enter the export field are coconut shell as charcoal for gas masks; coir, the fiber of the coconut husk going mostly to India for the manufacture of brushes, brooms, and the like; palm sap and coconut milk, made into various types of beverages and vinegar; coconut flour, paper, and plastics. The great variety of uses to which the products may be put will aid the islands materially in readjustments when the American market is cut off. However, when the Philippines are forced to compete with other nations for this market, an entire readjustment of the industry will be necessary.

As an export commodity, abacá and its manufactured product, cordage, ranks third, with a total export value of nearly $13,000,000. Since 1903, when abacá and cordage made up 68 per cent of the total exports, they have declined, relatively, until in 1932 they represented only 6 per cent of the total. The proportion has increased since then to nearly 10 per cent. The low point, reached in 1932, was the result of a severe decline in price, and consequently in quantity also. The rise in the value of other exports, especially sugar and coconut oil, also helped to depress the percentage rank of the abacá exports. Most of the export is in the form of the fiber, and the principal markets are the United States, the United Kingdom, and Japan. Interestingly, each country imports a different grade and therefore does not compete in the buying market. The United States buys the high grade, the United Kingdom the medium grade, and Japan the poorest grade, mostly for the paper industry.

The competitive position of abacá is different from that of

sugar and coconut. In each of these the competition is keen, but the Philippines have a practical monopoly in abacá. However, in the United States this fiber, for binder twine, has strong competitors in several other fibers, especially sisal. For binder twine the choice generally is on a basis of price, with a slight advantage in favor of sisal that has been insect-proofed. The provisions of the Independence Act limited the free importation of Philippine cordage to 3,000,000 pounds per annum, since raised to 6,000,000. The United States imports of manila cordage from the Philippines have become increasingly important, amounting to approximately 12 per cent of the total production of hard fiber cordage and 90 per cent of the total cordage imports. Unlimited independence will not materially affect the situation with reference to abacá. At least, the future for this product holds a less gloomy picture than for the other commodities mentioned.

Philippine exports of tobacco and tobacco manufactures are of three types: leaf tobaccos; cigars; and minor products, such as cigarettes, stripped filler, scrap tobacco, and smoking and chewing tobacco. During the past decade export of leaf tobacco has been the most important, comprising from 27 to 50 per cent of the total tobacco exports. Spain has been the principal importer of leaf tobacco, taking from 50 to 80 per cent in value of leaf exports. Leaf also goes to Japan, France, Belgium, and China. Of the cigars produced, approximately 72 per cent are exported, of which about 65 per cent goes to the United States. These exports have constituted from 45 to 70 per cent of the total value of all tobacco exports. Exports of cigarettes are small, accounting for less than 1 per cent of the Philippine production. During the past decade there has been an enormous increase in the consumption of American cigarettes—from 400,000,000 to 2,000,000,000—an increase from 8 to 41 per cent of the cigarettes consumed on the islands. Normally over 90 per cent of the stripped filler and scrap tobacco goes to the United States.

There is a sharp competition in the tobacco trade between the Philippines and the United States. Cigars retailing in the United States for 5 cents or less are the major item in the Philippine export. During the past decade this item has increased from slightly more than three billion cigars to more than four billion, the increase being due, it is believed, to a demand for cheaper cigars during the depression years. The cigars imported from the Philippines have represented from 4 to 6 per cent of American cigar consumption. The tide seems to be turning, as in more recent years Philippine cigars have found a serious competitor in the American machine-made cigar so lavishly advertised by the manufacturers. It is evident that any new tariff discrimination against the Philippine product would be a material handicap to the island producer, which might, however, be compensated by an elimination of American cigarettes in the islands. Since 65 per cent of the Philippine cigar production is exported and 60 per cent of the total manufacture goes to the United States, and since only 1.5 per cent of the American cigarette production is sold in the Philippine market, it is very evident that any disruption of sales between the two countries would be more serious to the Philippines than to the United States.

In addition to the exports already noted, there are others of a somewhat different order but in themselves of considerable importance. Of these, embroideries rank high, not necessarily in value but in the additional money income they represent to the family. During the ten-year period 1926–35, exports of embroideries were highest in 1929, with a value of more than $6,000,000. From this high mark they declined to less than $2,000,000 in 1933 and then rose again to $5,000,000 in recent years. The industry is chiefly a household one, with centers at Manila where American cottons are cut and stamped before distribution for buttonholing, hemstitching, and the like. The completed articles are collected by the contractor and delivered to plants where they are inspected, assorted, laundered, and packed for export to the United States. American cotton cloth is used in order to avoid the tariff which is assessed on goods containing more than 20 per cent foreign material. As it takes about nine months from the time the order for the cotton goods is given until the finished product can be delivered, the output necessarily is limited to those articles in which there is little style change.

At present Philippine embroidery meets no serious competition in the United States. Its relative place is fairly well assured as long as present prices are maintained. Competition from American machine-made goods is not very serious, as the Philippine product is definitely of higher grade. The embroideries from Texas, New Mexico, and Arizona, with their large Mexican population, are also not of the uniform high standard set by the inspectors in the Philippines. With Puerto Rico, where goods are similarly prepared by native women and sold in the same class with Philippine products, the competition has been more keen. The Philippines seem to have the advantage, however, in spite of the longer hauls, and the Puerto Rican industry is disappearing largely because of the operation of recent minimum-wage legislation. Since about half the cost of producing embroidered garments lies in the material imported, there is every reason to suppose that, when full tariff is applied to Philippine embroideries, the industry will be most seriously affected. The income of 30,000–50,000 families will then be affected, perhaps cut off completely.

Forest products depend less upon exports than do any other commodities. Fully 80 per cent of the logs and lumber produced enter domestic commerce, and less than 20 per cent are exported. The forests, therefore, have never figured very high in trade statistics. During the decade 1926–35, their export never exceeded 3 per cent of the total Philippine exports. In 1929 exports of logs and lumber reached their peak of $3,600,000 but declined to a low of $835,000 in 1935, when they represented 2.5 per cent of the total exports. The quantity of logs and lumber exported in 1935, however, was greater than in 1929. Most of the export goes to the United States and Japan. In more recent years Japan has been expanding her needs, with increasing imports from the Philippines. In 1935 about 62 per cent of the volume of logs and 31 per cent of the total value of exports of logs and lumber went to Japan. The large domestic consumption gives the industry a distinct advantage over others. The dominant home demand is for mining timber, which fortunately uses the lower-priced lumber. With the rapid development of the home industry the import of lumber has gradually declined, until in recent years the amount was less than 0.05 per cent of insular production.

Next to logs and lumber, cutch, the dyeing and tanning extract from the mangrove tree, is the most important export. The mangrove has a wide distribution throughout the island group; but only in Mindanao, Palawan, the Sulu Archipelago, and Luzon are the stands sufficiently extensive to make the establishment of plants for the extraction of cutch profitable. Cutch was not produced on the islands before 1928, and the total number of people now engaged in the industry is between 7,000 and 8,000. The export now approximates 13,000,000 pounds, practically all of which goes to the United States. The value of the extract is between 2 and 3 cents per pound, and its relative importance to the total exports has never been over one-half of 1 per cent. Although no product similar to cutch is produced in the United States, the extract nevertheless competes with chemical products more or less similar in their effects. Because of its minor position, a duty of 15 per cent at the time of independence will not materially affect its marketability in the United States.

Although rubber is still a minor product, it is growing in importance and may become much more important in the future. The necessary restrictions of temperature, a minimum of 70° F., and abundant moisture, about 100 inches with no less than 2 inches per month, prevail in a large part throughout the islands. The islands, especially Mindanao, lie close to, although outside, the great plantation areas of Malaysia and of Netherlands India. Conditions in Mindanao have thus far proved most favorable, and several projects have been developed in its southwest sections with more or less success. Exports are increasing; and were it not for the well-established plantations near by and the general world-depression in rubber, the showing would be much better still. The development centers in southwest Mindanao around Zamboanga, where all the exported rubber comes from. Unquestionably, large parts of the archipelago are unsuited because of the dry season. The typhoon in the north, even were other conditions favorable, would also be a severe handicap.

Of the many minor exports, Philippine hats have limited possibilities. The industry is centered around the small towns of Baliuag and Lukban, in Luzon. It is dominantly in the hands of individual native workers, although machine-made products for domestic consumption are becoming increasingly important. The machine-made hat uses a lower-grade material like bamboo, straw, abacá, or similar fiber. The handmade hat, comparable to the so-called "Panama hat," is made from the buntal fiber obtained from the leaf of the buri palm and is the one that enters the American market. The largest export was in 1928, with 1,426,000 hats averaging, in the uncompleted state, less than $1.00 apiece to the Philippine exporter. After its edges are completed and the hat is bleached and blocked, the retail price for the better grade may reach $15.00. Small buntal hats are designed primarily for women. The demand is a changeable one, dependent on styles. Not more than from 40,000 to 60,000 weavers would be affected should the tariff regulations, after independence, cut off the American market altogether.

Ocean-pearl buttons, another minor export, seems to be losing out. The button industry is centered around Manila and uses mother-of-pearl, the *Trochus*, and snail shells, gathered chiefly in the shore waters of Palawan and the Visayan Islands. During the past decade the export has been gradually but regularly decreasing, from an approximate value of $450,000 to $250,000. The Philippine product in the American market must compete with an American industry with an annual output of from $8,000,000 to $14,000,000 built up on native mussel shells and imported marine shells. The buttons from imported ocean shells, chiefly from Australia, make up about 25 per cent of the total American industry. The competition is not only with the American machine-made product but also increasingly so with buttons made from plastic materials.

Although now a very minor industry, pineapple-canning is believed to offer a fair future. Pineapple-planting was begun in 1928, and the crop area has been increased to about 2,000 acres. The first export of canned pineapples was made in 1930 and increased rapidly until 1933, when the product was placed on the restricted basis adopted by the Hawaiian producers. The Hawaiian Islands supply approximately 98 per cent of the American market, the rest coming from the Philippines and Cuba. Competition with the Hawaiian product should not be serious, as production costs in the Philippines are lower because of lower wage rates, lower land values, richer soils, and a more extended harvest season. Ocean distance is not an item, as freight rates to the mainland are, in the main, the same for both places. The specific advantages for the Philippines may, in the future, counterbalance any differential in tariff rates. In this, as in nearly every other export commodity entering the United States, the outlook for the future is dependent on future tariff agreements. Without a Philippine-American agreement controlling tariff regulations the Philippine export trade to the United States is not very hopeful.

THE PHILIPPINES OF TOMORROW

Much uncertainty has attended American-Philippine relations in the past, and a still greater uncertainty lies ahead under independence. Scarcely had Spain given up her claims on the islands when Filipino leaders began their agitation for "complete and unqualified" independence. The United States has persistently rejected such plans as being not consistent with Philippine interests. Three presidents since the World War—Harding, Coolidge, and Hoover—very specifically opposed independence. President Hoover, moreover, vetoed the Hare-Hawes-Cutting independence bill. Even as late as 1932, out of 246 American journals polled, only 21 favored independence. President Roosevelt has since reversed this policy, granting independence as outlined by the Tydings-McDuffie bill. This sudden change of attitude at a time when international morality seems at its lowest ebb is not easy to explain. To inquire into the reasons for it, however, is less productive than to ask what the meaning of it is to the Philippines. The effect on the United States is so insignificant in comparison as to be negligible. For the Philippines, however, the necessary readjustments are revolutionary. The progress in the islands during the last third of a century has equaled that for any three preceding centuries. Will the new commonwealth of the Philippines be able to maintain this pace in its development; will it, as an independent nation, be able to maintain even its present status? Unfortunately, there are too many uncertainties involved to make conclusions more than mere possibilities. However, it is possible to outline, with some assurance, certain probabilities.

The progress made in the Philippines under American rule has been little short of phenomenal. Under the Spanish order, general lawlessness and even brigandage flourished throughout the islands. In their places now is a well-ordered government with an efficient constabulary of native soldiers, who, through their devotion to duty, have made the islands as law-abiding as is any other progressive nation. Where formerly individual rights were suppressed and the standard of justice was largely a mockery, today under native judges the supreme court of the Philippines carries out constitutional guaranties in a manner leaving little to be desired. Aside from the stupendous changes in trade and industry, there are now roads, schools, the control of epidemics through sanitation, and a marked advance in a more intelligent outlook on life by even the less fortunate of Filipinos. In one generation a medieval despotism has been transformed into a genuine approach to a true democracy. No such progress, however, could have been possible without the co-operation of a people competent and proud of their achievements.

The principle underlying the Independence Act is that responsibility must go hand in hand with authority. For an extended time the one without the other is impossible. When, therefore, the Philippine republic is launched on July 4, 1946, American responsibilities of all kinds will cease. Until then the United States will remain responsible for internal stability and external security. Of political stability, there is little question, except as difficulties may arise in carrying out the principles of the new economic order. The success of the home government will depend upon the patriotism and wisdom of the upper class now in control. Externally the situation is less assuring. The Philippines are in no way prepared to resist aggression alone. The nation most feared by Filipinos is Japan, in spite of that nation's denial that it has any interest in the islands. More serious than actual aggression is an economic penetration, which is already functioning on a large scale and which may result in the control of commerce and industry and ultimately lead to military intervention and political sovereignty. However, what will happen will, to a very large degree, depend upon future American-Philippine relationships.

A complete separation from the United States will mean a tremendous readjustment for almost every phase of life. All products now receiving preferential treatment in the American market (fully 80 per cent of the total value) will, to a greater or lesser degree, be adversely affected. The exports most seriously affected, perhaps curtailed or even prohibited altogether, are sugar, coconut oil, tobacco and its products, embroideries, and pearl buttons. The other products, such as straw hats, canned pineapples, cutch, and cordage, will be less seriously affected. It is possible that with the reduction of exports in the leading items, sales of these secondary commodities may even be increased. Without a free American market the losses sustained from reduced profits will necessarily have their repercussions at home in other lines. The necessary readjustments will be most severe on the most highly developed and most prosperous sections of the islands, and much of the accumulated wealth is directly traceable to the tariff-free American market. The commonwealth, however, is fully aware of these problems, and the National Economics Council has several programs under consideration to meet the contingencies.

Any program which aims at a reduction of costs of production to counterbalance American tariff requirements is beset with difficulties as well as dangers. To reduce production costs, a new areal distribution of crops must be made, eliminating all marginal and submarginal lands. At present the cost of production for most crops is higher in the islands than in most tropical regions, chiefly because of the higher wages paid. The islands will not be able to compete in sugar in the American market largely because of this differential. There are possibilities in improvement of seed, in cultivation, harvesting, grading, and marketing; but these are slow processes at best, and, besides, other countries are on the lookout to the same end. Furthermore, any real improvements are commonly preceded by the employment of workers of greater intelligence; this demands higher wage scales and higher standards of living. Production costs are not infrequently cut by business corporations, but this implies dictatorial power over people who are interested only in the maintenance of the wage scale. In the agriculture of the Philippines, however, the large number of producers may not be willing or may be unable to make the necessary cost reductions. Even should costs of production be reduced sufficiently to meet the differential, the uncertainties of new legislation are always on the horizon. The assurance of a free, protected market for all exportable surpluses has been a blessing for the Philippines that not many nations are permitted to enjoy.

If, after independence, there is no market in which the country can dispose of its surplus products without loss, then such surplus must be reduced and imports must be reduced correspondingly. This will mean a program of self-sufficiency and a great readjustment in reducing the acreage of some crops and increasing production in others at costs perhaps greater than import values. Many such ventures might require subsidies and may be losing ones. A reduced export of agricultural products would bring about an industrial expansion with minor manufactures. There seems little reason, however, why certain imported products should not be domestically produced to meet some of the demands. In order of values the major products imported are cottons, tobacco manufactures, breadstuffs, and dairy products. In a planned economy the imports of these could be markedly reduced without a great material loss to the country, probably even with some gain.

This would mean a wider distribution of kinds of crops.

The most likely to succeed is a greater production of cotton and the manufacture therefrom of cotton goods. For a period of years this has been, by far, the leading import item, although not the greatest item in the import trade from the United States. Cotton has been grown for many years, but the average yield for the 3,000 acres or more in cotton is only about 200 pounds per acre, which is less than that of the lower-yielding states. The work of the Department of Agriculture in the Philippines may in time produce higher-yielding varieties adapted to Philippine conditions. The quantity of tobacco could be greatly increased, but only a very high tariff rate might induce the Filipinos to buy Philippine-made, in preference to American-made, cigarettes. Wheat is now grown in the Cagayan Valley, and the crop unquestionably could be greatly extended. Other imported commodities, such as potatoes, onions, cacao, coffee, citrus fruits, and the like, are already being produced to meet limited demands.

An increased industrialization is also possible. The lack of capital need not necessarily be a great handicap, as many industries, such as soap, shoe, perfumery, cosmetics, confectionery, and the like, need small initial outlay of capital. The manufacture of paper from rice straw and from abacá or similar material, as in Japan holds possibilities, although the success of any program of increased industrialization rests, in large part, on the existence of an adequate supply of relatively cheap motive power. The amounts needed for some industries are not great. Not much can be hoped for from the small deposits of low-grade domestic coal, but imported coal from Australia or Japan is relatively cheap. A goodly number of hydroelectric power sites are also available, for the potential water resources are large, but the initial expenditures for dam construction and installation of machinery are great. The problem of obtaining adequate capital for entering an industrial period rather abruptly is a most serious one.

In addition to the economic factors, the future political outlook is of most vital consideration. The transfer of sovereignty of the Philippines from Spain to the United States was not of their choosing but was the result of one of those unexplainable fates of history. The islands had been in revolt for some time and, in a measure, welcomed the Americans as an aid in driving out Spain, expecting, at the same time, that the Americans would withdraw when that was accomplished. The Filipinos had already succeeded in some of the outlying regions in displacing Spanish rule wholly or in part. With the fall of Manila, Filipino leaders were not willing to concede control of all the islands to the United States. As there were not enough American soldiers in the islands to make the victory complete, the revolt continued for some time against the United States instead of against Spain. Scarcely were the islands under American control, when Filipino leaders began to agitate for "immediate and unqualified" independence. Although no promise of independence was made at the time of the peace treaty, it was definitely stated that the acquisition was not the result of a war of aggression but in the interest of the Philippine and American people. At no time did the insurgent force co-operate with the United States.

The unparalleled development in the Philippines under American control must be ascribed to the free-trade relationship with the United States. As early as 1907 Mr. Taft, as chairman of the Philippine Commission, secured this free-trade agreement, which subsequently was never changed. With rich undeveloped resources ready to be placed into the world's greatest market, tariff-free, American capital flowed into the Philippines, and the transformation began on a gigantic scale. To have brought this trade agreement to a close with the passage of the Independence Act would have been too revolutionary for the island government to survive. Generously enough, the act provides that the tariff agreement shall remain in force during the first five years of the commonwealth. In the sixth year and in each year following, a 5 per cent export tax is to be levied until the period of probation is complete. Thereafter, on July 4, 1946, the Philippines are to pay the full import duty on commodities entering the American market, and to all intents and purposes they are to be treated as any other foreign power. The amount to be collected by the Philippines as export tax is to be used as an island sinking-fund for the liquidation of the foreign debt and to meet the necessary readjustments in seeking foreign markets.

That the time limit set by the Independence Act is far too short to make the necessary readjustments is becoming increasingly evident. Were the provisions to be carried out to the full, the collapse of the Philippine economic system would seem to be inevitable. In view of present trade restrictions and handicaps it may even be questioned whether the Philippines can maintain present standards by "going it alone" after any extended period of readjustment. The domestic development has not been one of mushroom growth brought about by an exploitative system which leaves a desert behind. On the contrary, it has meant millions invested in roads, schools, and other public improvements. It has meant also the introduction of the most up-to-date machinery, equipment, and technical skill, placing the commonwealth in the fore of progressive nations, with a higher standard of living than that of any

Official photograph—U.S. Army Air Corps

AIRPLANE VIEW OF THE PORT OF MANILA WITH ITS SMALL BUT IMPORTANT PASIC RIVER

The several periods of architecture may be recognized

other of the major nations of the Orient. Much of this advance may be attributed to Philippine co-operation, and perhaps the loss in economic advantages is counterbalanced by the pride in nationhood.

Internal situations may be controlled much more easily than external ones. Set adrift, the Philippines will be helpless in a world where international honor is at such a low ebb. The greatest danger is not necessarily from an outside attack and subjugation but from an economic penetration which ultimately may lead to the same end. Of such possibilities, Japanese aggression seems to offer the most serious threat. There are no exclusive regulations at present affecting Japanese immigration, and about 20,000 trade emissaries are already in the islands. There is no intent on the part of the Japanese of becoming citizens; and when they are grouped, as in the province of Davao in Mindanao—18,000 out of a total of 29,000—Japanese is the exclusive language learned in Japanese schools and used in stores, banks, and newspapers. To all intents and purposes such a settlement is a Japanese colony, not a part of the Philippine commonwealth. A regular Japanese steamship line connects Davao with Yokohama and carries Japanese products. Because of a coastline many times that of the United States, the physical defense of the Philippines is practically impossible, but a direct attack on any of the islands is not likely, since the individual islands may be alienated much more readily by economic means. Unquestionably there will be a politico-economic migration of the islands toward Japan.

Whatever the ultimate results, it is incumbent on the United States to launch the Philippines on their career as an independent state under the most favorable auspices. On the other hand, there can be no responsibility without authority. Although the American people in general realize that the occupation of the Philippines was in the nature of a "sacred trust," it must be evident that this trust cannot continue without occupation. To break that trust now in the face of the many problems would be un-American; and quite surely, also, the new republic will not be launched under conditions that will mean certain failure and dissolution. Without the spirit of co-operation which has characterized the past, there is little hope of success for either Philippine or American control. The future of the Philippines hinges on such co-operation.

"MANIFEST DESTINY" IN GREATER AMERICA

By ISAAC J. COX and
WILLIAM H. HAAS

IN THE EVOLUTION OF THE AMERICAN commonwealth certain tendencies or forces seem to have been dominant in giving form and individuality to the national structure. In this the history of the nation is more or less comparable to the evolution of well-known animal forms, in which certain inherent tendencies seemingly come to the fore at critical times to give direction to the general trend. Strikingly enough, in the course of this development the nation has never suffered great adversities, as is so common in animal forms, which might have dwarfed the physical outlook or curbed the visions of an energetic people.

Prominent among these tendencies has been the unbounded faith of the people in the future of their country. This unquestioned confidence in ultimate success for both the individual and the nation has been the dominant element in the molding of American attitudes on national policies. Fundamentally, it is an individual trait based on the general assumption that any person may rise above the station to which he is born. It likewise has become a national characteristic, sometimes arousing unfavorable criticism but proving, in the main, a never failing incentive to effective co-operation in our political, social, and economic development.

Inspired by such a faith and facing a virgin continent, our forebears readily became territorial expansionists. The first half of the nineteenth century witnessed the purchase of

Louisiana and the Floridas, the annexation of Texas, and the acquisition of California and the Far Northwest. The readiness with which the successive territorial acquisitions became a part of the union of states was convincing proof to those responsible that "Manifest Destiny" was truly directing the course of the nation and that the whole Western world was America's possible limit. This conviction survived even the untenable proposals of the mid-century to absorb all of Mexico and the Canadas and was a major factor in gaining reluctant approval for the purchase of Alaska. Not even the abortive filibustering expeditions of the fifties into Mexico, Cuba, and Nicaragua, or the failure of premature efforts to acquire Santo Domingo and the Danish Islands, had a dampening effect on this acquisitive spirit. Its latest manifestations came at the turn of the century, when Puerto Rico, the Canal Zone, and the Philippines passed under the American flag, and Cuba narrowly missed its folds.

The tendency to invoke "Manifest Destiny" did not necessarily mean an excuse for expansion or an insincere attitude. The practice had its origin, no doubt, in the numerous instances in early American history, when opportune events seemingly pointed the way out of a given crisis. These timely leads were unsought, and some of them were even embarrassing. Of many such cases, the purchase of Louisiana and of Alaska and the annexation of Texas are typical. Although this recognition of an obscure guidance has been a strong element in American life, in no period of American history did it lead to serious abuses. In our early Indian policy, it is true, there is little to commend and much to condemn; yet, even here, the steps taken merely continued policies that were believed to be born of necessity. Aside from the Indians, only a few Spanish and French Creoles and Mexican pioneers were affected by territorial acquisitions of the nineteenth century, and unquestionably their status was improved. Even modern Mexico is much more of a unit than it would have been had there been no defection of Texas or loss of California. California, like Texas, would not long have remained under the control of Mexico City; and the population of each area, including subsequent additions from Mexico, not to mention contingents from other parts of the world, is infinitely better off because of its incorporation in the American union. A less blustering attitude on our part would, it is true, have avoided much mid-century unpleasantness.

Not always, it must be acknowledged, have our foreign diplomats lived up to the best traditions of American life; yet such is hardly to be expected in a democracy where the spoils system is in vogue. Therefore, it is with considerable justice that some publicists below the Rio Grande have referred bitterly to "dollar diplomacy" and have not hesitated to attribute "hypocritical pretensions" to the "Colossus of the North." The ulterior motives impugned may or may not have been in the minds of those responsible, but the fact remains that the policies carried out and resented by those spokesmen as tending to make the whole Western world subservient to the North American order have not materialized; in fact, the nations they represent are on a stronger economic footing because of such policies. The universal tendency for a large and wealthy nation to draw weaker neighbors into its economic and cultural orbit is well recognized, but it does not necessarily imply an ulterior motive that looks forward to establishing political control as well. If such an underlying motive had always been in the minds of the American people, many sections now continuing their old political order would at present be flying the American flag.

Too often critics of American capitalistic imperialism assume that "investments" and "intervention" are synonymous terms. They are all too ready to assert that the effects of any large corporate investment necessarily must be bad. This thesis, however, can scarcely be supported, since many nations are not in a position financially or experientially to develop their own resources. The United States, for instance, bore such a relationship to Great Britain even after it became independent. The general educational effect resulting from imported capital, technical skill, and equipment may far outweigh any harm done by economic penetration. Furthermore, in the case of the Caribbean up to the time of the World War, European investments surpassed in amount those of the United States, and at the same time Europe dominated the trade. Some Spanish-American countries have advanced relatively little, in comparison to others, largely because foreign capital had little chance there for profitable investment. Argentina has attracted little outside financial help in developing its petroleum resources, while Venezuela, with such help, has the distinction of being the only South American country without an external debt.

The turbulent political history of some Latin-American countries will account for certain instances of intervention. Indeed, had such nations been located elsewhere, with other world-powers as neighbors, they might not have survived to the present as independent units. Mostly from the Old World have come the claims for indemnities after each recurrent period of unrest. In recent times, however, such claims have rarely been collected because of the attitude of the United

States. After a revolution, whether successful or not, the country affected has often become involved in loans at most onerous terms, some of them at rates that could never be paid in full. Foreign bankers who drew heavy commissions were fully aware of the situation and inevitably, when such loans went into default, were pressed by unfortunate bondholders to demand punitive measures for collection. These demands not infrequently were backed up by battleships. To such a visitation was Venezuela subjected in 1903, and threats of similar action had already been made on Haiti and later were to occur in other Caribbean countries. In such cases the burden of settlement fell upon the shoulders of the United States.

In these situations came the later resort to the Monroe Doctrine, even when there was no threat at permanent occupation. Holding to the larger interpretation of the doctrine, the United States in some cases, whether rightly or wrongly, made itself partly responsible for the solution of these financial tangles. Likewise, foreign nations, being more or less helpless, looked to the United States to bring the defaulting nations to terms. To protect itself in such an unhappy situation, brought about by an accumulating foreign pressure, the Roosevelt administration in 1904 resorted to an economic supervision of the Dominican customs. Subsequently this fiscal policy was applied to various Central American countries as well and gave rise to caustic criticisms not only in other Latin-American countries but also at home. Nevertheless, during the decades when this type of supervision prevailed, the Caribbean fared far better than during the earlier period of European dominance. The surprising feature of this type of guardianship has been that, despite the opportunities offered to expansionists, such nations after a period of enforced supervision are again conducting their own affairs and are free to repeat old mistakes. Quite manifestly those responsible for these interventions have proved to be opportunists and have modified their own views to meet public opinion at home and to avoid suspicion abroad.

The fear and distrust aroused at the turn of the century by America's underlying program of expansion developed a real terror in the minds of some New World publicists. An ill-defined inter-American policy meant to them that the acts of one administration in the United States might be reversed by the next. Yet a general tendency to deal justly with each question on its merits has aroused the respect of other world-powers and has led many smaller nations to place their trust in the innate honesty and sense of justice of the American people. Even in the Old World, mineral concessions have been granted American corporations in preference to those of other nations because of faith in American fair dealing. From these and other cases the impartial historian must credit the United States with a determination not to use its great power to bully weaker nations into line with its own so-called "imperialistic policies."

Yet, whether analysts of our national policy approve or condemn, the fact remains that the United States has grown great and powerful under the aegis of a real or fancied "Manifest Destiny" without inflicting serious injustice upon any other nation. In its growth it has added contiguous, as well as noncontiguous, territory to the original domain. In the main this occurred when undeveloped continental land masses in the New World were less highly prized than they are now. As a result, America's moral reputation is seldom challenged, and its attitude is respected throughout the world. Its rise in prestige has, in considerable measure, been due to its adherence to the principles of the Monroe Doctrine without using that policy merely to further its own selfish ends. Although this practice has tended to isolate the New World from the Old, and to give the United States precedence in the former, it has also recently given rise to considerable apprehension at home, in the other Americas, and abroad. Will the United States, in view of dwindling world-resources and the possible concerted action of totalitarian states, be able to maintain a leadership based largely on isolation and good will?

Have the American people too freely assumed the existence of both factors? Have they been equally ready and willing to give up certain powers and rights when conditions seemed to justify such action? The recent act to grant the Philippines independence is a case in point. Such legislation is so foreign to the thinking of some nations that they attribute it to fear and inherent weaknesses. Nearer home the Platt Amendment, regulating Cuban affairs, has been dropped, and the unilateral Monroe Doctrine has given way to a policy of sharing the responsibility with our Latin-American neighbors. The traditional "big-brother" attitude assumed toward some of the weaker nations south of the Rio Grande is gradually disappearing as those nations rise in prestige and power. For the peace of the Western world this healthier development of multilateral unity has far-reaching possibilities. The spirit of co-operation in Pan-American affairs has been greatly furthered by the great concentration of wealth and power in the hands of one nation—the result, it is to be recognized, of earlier opportunities for expansion. Moreover, genuine co-operation, rather than control, has put the United States in a more favorable position to aid its neighbors in time of need and to receive help from them in return. Such a policy is not grounded on fear or aggression but on a recognition of mutual rights and opportunities, exercised in a spirit of helpful co-operation.

OVERSEAS ACQUISITIONS

The wisdom of our overseas expansion, which includes Alaska and the Canal Zone, may in one or two cases, at least, be open to question. To evaluate the results, however, an acquaintance with the geographic facts presented in previous chapters must be assumed. There is need to consider not only what these acquired territories mean to the United States but also what the change in status means to those who are now asked to be loyal to the American flag. Ideally, of course, this political change should have improved their economic and social well-being, or else the acquisition has been of questionable value to them. However, it must not be assumed that one unfavorable development vitiates all other considerations. It is difficult to apportion the benefits of annexation, for many of the factors involved have never been weighed in the balance. Most certainly, however, the occasional subordinate status of a weaker state in the New World has in no way proved detrimental to other independent American states.

It is difficult to estimate the value of the Virgin Islands. Economically they are and will continue to be a distinct handicap to the United States. Possibly they justify the expression "effective poorhouse" attributed to former President Hoover. They have no undeveloped riches that are ready to be exploited, nor do geographic conditions arouse faith in a more intensive development of known resources. Even specialties like bay rum have a very limited future. The change in flag has not benefited the people materially except in so far as they have been aided by direct relief measures. The future does not hold out much promise of a tourist trade of sufficient volume to supply the present population with an adequate income. The islands are too far from the mainland, and, although attractive to the casual visitor, they suffer when their advantages are compared with other areas. They were not purchased, however, for their scenery or resources but for the magnificent harbor of St. Thomas, which otherwise was in danger of falling into foreign hands. As it is, the islands now constitute an American possession; and, although their prospects for the present may prove disappointing, we have the assurance that no other nation can readily avail itself of their strategic features.

Recent developments in Puerto Rico also point to its increasing military importance to the United States. For the present at least, this outweighs all other considerations. In the hands of a hostile power, this island would threaten the safety not only of the Caribbean but of both continents. For the good of the Western Hemisphere the United States must, at all costs, maintain its supremacy in the Caribbean. As the gateway to this strategic area, Puerto Rico has an even greater value than the Virgin Islands. Independence, so clamorously demanded by a minority group of its people, will not solve Puerto Rico's local problems. Greater autonomy and less political juggling will not in themselves reduce the number of people on the island. Its population is so out of proportion to the possibilities of decent living that political unrest may be expected to continue indefinitely. There are few openings for the many earnest young men and women graduating from the high schools and the university. As a result, a goodly number of them develop radical and anti-American views. In a sense, the situation for the poor has become more serious with the taking-over of much of the best food-crop land for the production of sugar. However, it is extremely doubtful if Puerto Rico can solve its problems alone. Our need of the island is manifest, and equally apparent is its need of continued connection with the United States The real problem is the kind of relationship the island should bear to its rich sponsor.

The Panama Canal Zone is the innermost defensive sanctuary of the Caribbean, and, as long as the canal is untouched and under American control, the United States may feel fairly secure. It is our greatest single military reservation, and at the same time it doubles the efficiency of our fleet. So important is it that plans are now under way for greatly increasing its defensive value. Through it military and naval forces may move quickly from ocean to ocean; without the canal our fleet would be hopelessly divided. In case of war the future status of the whole country might well become dependent on a single emergency transfer. The canal represents the foremost of man's engineering feats. The sanitary measures associated with its construction form an outstanding social accomplishment. It may never return in tolls the capital expended in building it, but the prestige thus gained gave the United States a new international status. The Republic of Panama likewise owes everything to the building of the canal. Not all its consequences, however, have proved so beneficial. The opening of the canal had an adverse effect on other transcontinental routes in Canada and the United States, and especially in Mexico. The measures that attended its inception and our later relations with Panama have given rise to considerable ill feeling in all Latin America, and a number of delicate problems connected with its administration still remain unsolved.

Alaska stands in a class by itself. Bought at a time when the nation could ill afford the purchase, its worth as a profitable investment has been proved again and again. It is the only one of the outlying acquisitions of virgin territory with rich and varied resources ready to be garnered and without a population sufficiently large to absorb all the exploited products. As a result of its purchase, enormous wealth has been and still is pouring into the United States. From a military standpoint, it has greatly increased the problem of national defense, and its security makes necessary a larger Pacific fleet. Its proximity to eastern Asia and its distance from American centers of control are distinct weaknesses. The conflict of interests in the seal fisheries of the Pribilof Islands and, more recently, the salmon controversy—also with the Japanese—are indicative of what may be expected in the future. With the rising importance of the airplane in war, the region becomes more than ever a strategic outpost for the United States and for Canada as well. Although not necessarily an invitation to aggression, Alaska nevertheless constitutes, at present, a weak point in our national security. On the other hand, its facilities may be so developed as to make it one of the strongest links in a first-line defense.

In the same line of western defense lie the Hawaiian Islands. Practically in the same longitude as parts of Alaska, they may well be considered as belonging to the Western world. This mid-Pacific group is as favorably located with respect to the United States as to any other nation. No hostile power would be likely to derive any permanent profit from attaching or attempting to control them. Even if the Philippines are cast adrift, Hawaii will always be an important link in all airplane routes to the Orient. The same considerations will apply also to Midway Island, to Guam, and to the Samoan group south of the Equator. As a producer of tropical products, the Hawaiian Islands form a distinct asset even though they contain few unexploited resources. The United States likewise is the natural commercial outlet for Hawaii. It is, therefore, difficult to imagine a situation in which the Hawaiian Islands would be happier or more prosperous, whether independent or subject to another world-power.

A short-range forecast even for the Philippines is beset with unusual problems which a brief treatment cannot cover. Interrelationships are so complex and political aspects are so abnormal that any analysis on a practical basis may be wide of the mark. The United States has attempted to make of these islands a training-school in self-government for the Filipinos. The result has proved costly, with little prospect of relief from continued liability. What is more, the islands project our line of defense into a land-hungry area some 7,000 miles from our shores and therefore add immeasurably to our strategic problems. There are no adequate returns for such a risk. A continuation of our stewardship, therefore, becomes a thankless job, resulting in little except further misunderstandings and prospective international friction. Especially is this made evident by an address in which President Quezon told the Filipino youth, according to the press, that he prefers "a government run like hell by the Filipinos to a government run like heaven by the Americans." On the whole, complete independence by 1946 or sooner would prove an economic blessing to the United States, although a disaster to the islands.

The military problem of the Philippines is complicated further by the changed conditions in the Far East since the passage of the Independence Act in May, 1934. Comparative peace ruled the world then. Japan had already set out on its present course, but few realized the ambitions that underlay it. Economically, the situation is not very different except that world-markets are lately more restricted through the growth of barter. Cut loose from the United States, it is extremely doubtful that the Philippines will be able to maintain the present living standards to which they have been raised by American support. To continue the present economic structure under independence is impossible, a fact well recognized by thinking Filipino leaders. The United States has already paid, many times over, all of its moral obligations to the Philippines.

In the general picture of American expansion the overseas areas that still remain under the American flag present few of the economic advantages that they seemed to offer forty years ago. The cost in general is too great except as they afford some additional security. The attempt to impose upon them something approaching American standards of living has been costly to ourselves and of doubtful advantage to them. Yet the necessity for adequate defense renders the continued possession of Alaska, Hawaii, and the Samoan Islands unquestionable. They constitute important naval outposts to the west. Puerto Rico and the Virgin Islands perform the same service to the east. Between them lies the Panama Canal, affording speedy access to both series of outposts. Viewed in this light, these areas seem to constitute the *sine qua non* of American defense.

"MANIFEST DESTINY" AND THE FUTURE

Whatever the future may hold in store for it, the United States has not made and is not now making the most of its opportunities if its policy is to be influenced by the ideals of totalitarian states. Canada offers a case in point. There was a period in the late forties of the last century when a union with the Dominion might have been possible. Agitation for annexation centered in Montreal, where in 1849 the Annexation Manifesto was issued. This document contrasted conditions in Canada with those in the United States and drew the conclusion that the "true solution [to the ills suffered by the former] could be found only in a friendly and peaceful separation from the British connection and in a union upon equable terms with the great North American Confederacy of Sovereign States." Although the manifesto may have represented only a minority of the people in British North America, in the light of more recent events one must feel some regret that two peoples so alike in language, religion, government, ideals, and economic standards were not then more closely united. Many American leaders were lukewarm or even hostile to the proposal, on the ground that such a union would affect American prosperity adversely. The Reciprocity Treaty of 1854 represented a compromise, but even this did not survive the bitterness engendered by the Civil War. Recurrent proposals for union since the formation of the dominion in 1867 have aroused hostile responses in both countries. Frequent controversies over fisheries, the seal trade, and the Alaskan boundary have tended to drive the two nations farther apart.

These incidents, minor though they have proved to be, are regrettable from the standpoint of a continental and racial solidarity, but they confirm the view that a political union of Canada and the United States on a basis of equality is impossible. Canada's connection with the British Empire, as the present war shows, draws her outside the orbit of any possible exclusive New World policy. Yet our unfortified frontier emphasizes the many common ties that bind the two peoples in spite of occasional differences. During the Taft Administration a major attempt to eliminate the growing tariff wall between the two countries failed. Yet its whole object, according to its sponsors—to give "free play to productive forces as far as possible regardless of political boundaries"—was most laudable. Greater success has attended more recent limited trade agreements and proposals to develop common power facilities and to give greater unity to existing railway systems, to waterways and highways, and to a co-ordination of defense measures. Thus, while a political union with Canada is still with the future, some form of economic reciprocity and mutual security is not only desirable but mandatory, and the European war has brought such a possibility nearer.

Recent world-events have brought new elements into the foreground. Canada has always felt secure with American good will along her southern border and the Royal Navy on the high seas. Such a security, however, seems to be fading. With the strained relations in the Far East, involving the mother-country, the dominion became defense-conscious, and in 1935 initiated on the western coast a program of coastal fortifications and air bases. Not however, until the Czechoslovakian crisis in September, 1938, was attention focused on the eastern coast as well. In this national defense program, by far the greater emphasis has been placed on the Royal Canadian Air Force, which received in 1939 nearly one-half of the total defense appropriations. A strong air force is to be Canada's first line of defense.

When President Roosevelt on August 18, 1938, in an address at Kingston, Ontario, declared that "the United States will not stand idly by if the domination of Canadian soil is threatened," he could not have anticipated the course of events since. Such an attempted domination has moved much nearer since the formal declaration of war, September 10, 1939, by the dominion on the German Reich. The president's pronouncement was not a declaration of a new policy but the recognition of a well-known elemental fact that a part or all of Canada in the hands of a power-hungry nation would be a very serious threat to American security and would bring Old World insecurity to the New. The United States cannot "stand idly by" if such a threat becomes imminent.

Toward the south Mexico's undeveloped and loosely held territory was the first to feel the full impact of North American expansion. It was inevitable that Texas, with its rich, well-watered lands contiguous to productive areas of the United States, should declare its independence from Mexico. The future of the people of Texas lay to the east and not to the south, across desert expanses; and the Lone Star state could not possibly have reached its present greatness as a part of Mexico or even as an independent state. Tariff hurdles would have been too high. Its annexation seemingly made inevitable the further acquisition of New Mexico and California. Unquestionably, these areas would soon have declared their independence also, had they not come into the American union. None of them involved any considerable alien population, nor did their loss retard the material development of present Mexico.

Economically, they were never a part of that Mexico which makes up the Central Plateau.

The many provocative incidents in Mexico during recent years have been a marked strain on all external relations. Its national conduct would probably not have been condoned by foreign powers had they felt free to act, or by the United States had it been waiting for an opportunity to acquire more territory. Perhaps physiographic and climatic factors, more than American patience, have preserved the present boundary line between the two countries. The aridity and general uselessness of the northern portion of Mexico, with its very sparse population, has offered little temptation to the aggressive American. The real Mexico is far to the south, centering in Mexico City and facing to the east through Vera Cruz, not to the north across the border deserts. Culturally and economically, Mexico is much farther away than its contiguity would seem to indicate. The comparison of Mexico to a cornucopia pouring out its rich resources across the north boundary is more fanciful than real. Little effort has been made by Mexico to meet the tenets of the "good-neighbor" policy which the United States now affects. The expropriation of farm and grazing lands and the confiscation of mineral and oil rights, together with certain industrial activities, indicate an opposing point of view. The overprint along the northern border shown on maps used in Mexican schools—"Territory temporarily in the hands of the United States"—does not help to build up neighborly relations.

Expansion in the direction of Canada, Mexico, or Central America is at present unthinkable. For the island republics the situation is much the same. Cuba, Haiti, and Santo Domingo are and should remain independent countries. Jamaica, as a British possession, has never caused this country any anxious moments. There has been, likewise, no reason for interfering in the affairs of the Lesser Antilles under the control of the British, French, and Dutch. Had all the islands of the Caribbean been in the hands of these nations, the history of the region would have been very different. Since the World War there has been some agitation for the transfer of the British and French islands to the United States in return for the cancellation of war and post-war debts. However much this might titillate national pride and afford greater security to the Americas as a whole, the United States economically would be the loser, even if it received the islands as an outright gift.

In the light of present economic conditions it seems strange that the Lesser Antilles at one time were prized so highly and were the scene of so many major naval operations and of so much bloodshed. In no other waters have European nations fought so doggedly for supremacy. With much truth has the Caribbean been called "the Cradle of British Sea Power." All of this seems the more strange in view of the large undeveloped continental land masses near by. The islands, however, are tropical, lending themselves to products that make the East Indies famous. Perhaps it was thought that the term "wealth of the Indies" was henceforth to apply to them alone. The individual islands are insignificantly small; they are the tops of extinct volcanoes resting upon a submerged mountain chain, with bare and rocky interiors. In the hands of a hostile power, however, any one of them would be potentially a very serious menace. But without some critical change in present conditions American political domination over them through aggression is as unthinkable as elsewhere.

The United States has taken a definite stand in the Caribbean, and there appears to be no reason for a withdrawal from it as a "sphere of influence." Local, as well as international, relations have too many possibilities of danger to take away the guiding hand. Under present Old World manifestations of land hunger the United States must be prepared, in co-operation with Latin-American nations, to uphold the spirit of the much discussed Monroe Doctrine; and it can in no case permit the transfer of any of the islands to another Old World power. This by no means involves any change in policy, nor does it presume aggressive tactics. The past policy may appear generous, perhaps even ridiculous, to some of the power-mad nations of the Old World. For the good of the Western world, geographical position and historical development have destined that the future of the Caribbean area should be indissolubly joined with that of the United States in an all-American effort to maintain peaceful relations. In a measure it may be to the interest of this combination to have one or more of the present Old World powers represented in the Caribbean.

As examples of American policy the relations with Haiti and Santo Domingo are fairly characteristic. The course of events in these countries more than once during the nineteenth century presaged their ultimate acquisition by the United States. During the present century both of them have experienced our military and fiscal supervision. Twice, at least, have American administrations entertained serious proposals to annex the Dominican Republic. Internal strife, impending bankruptcy, and threat of European intervention frequently have given full justification for supervision in both tumultuous republics. As late as 1914 both France and Germany threatened to intervene in Haiti and to take control of the customs in order to collect on defaulted loans. To save itself, Haiti appealed to the United States for help. At first our request for supervision of finances was refused; but after a particularly atrocious massacre, a treaty granted this power in 1915. This guardianship, continued by subsequent treaties and executive agreements, was not ended until the present decade, when our marines were finally withdrawn. The object had been accomplished, however; and Haiti again stood on its own feet financially.

The story of the Dominican Republic differs little from that of its colored neighbor. When, at the close of the last century, there were normal repercussions over defaulted loans, the United States in 1905, through executive agreement, established a financial protectorate over the country. In 1907, when further threats of European intervention arose, this relationship was continued under a definite treaty. Fiscal improvement followed but not political stability. Continual revolution and repeated threat of intervention from abroad led the United States in 1916 to assume full control of the island. The severe criticism which followed led to a withdrawal of the marines in 1924, leaving the Dominican Republic to pursue its own course. In spite of all this, both that country and Haiti still have an independent status with no direct political ties to the United States.

As characteristic as any of our island relationships and as revealing in tendency are those with Cuba. By all the principles of politico-economic gravity, Cuba ought by now to have come under the political control of the United States. It has long been recognized that islands which lie near the borders of continents tend to become subordinate to the nearest, most powerful mainland neighbor. Although conditions have brought about the economic dependence of Cuba, the wide variation in background, language, and social institutions has kept the fiscal tendency from becoming a political fact. Cuba's proximity to the United States, however, has been and will continue to be the most important economic factor in its evolution. Without a recognition of this fact its history becomes meaningless. No two areas are more complementary to each other, and no two should profit more from such vicinal location. As it is, contiguity has brought profit to both countries but without exhausting all possible advantages of the situation.

Cuba's nearness to the United States has given many favorable opportunities to American capital. Under the same flag, at least under the same tariff union, both countries could profit still more. At present the advantages lie with Cuba, which sells about 80 per cent of its products to the United States and takes less than 70 per cent in return. The extraordinary progress made by Cuba in the last three decades would have been impossible without American capital and technical skill. So important has the American market become to Cuba that a complete economic separation would mean a thorough collapse of the island's economic structure. Merely placing Cuba's sugar on a par with that of other nations of the world would necessitate a wholesale reorganization of its national economy. For the United States an increase in the tariff on Cuban sugar would mean higher prices and a great expansion of the sugar-beet industry of the United States. On the other hand, an elimination of the tariff on Cuban sugar would wipe out the American beet- and cane-sugar industries. At present the aim, theoretically at least, is to produce enough domestic sugar to guarantee an adequate supply in time of war and yet assure a reasonable price to the American consumer. Since the depression the tariff also has been adjusted in response to Cuban distress signals.

Cuba's proximity has kept it in the focal line of those who believed in "Manifest Destiny." Almost from the birth of the American republic the feeling arose that Cuba must inevitably be a part of the United States. The national area was sure to be increased; and the Appalachians were, it then seemed, enough of a barrier to prevent much expansion to the west. This was a period of water transportation, and blocks of land far from navigable waters had relatively little value. However, it was not until after the purchase of Louisiana in 1803 that the efforts of the expansionists became coherent in asking for the annexation or purchase of Cuba as being in line with needed expansion. It was at this time that President Jefferson made the pronouncement that the ultimate control of Cuba by the United States was absolutely necessary but that he would raise a monument at its southern tip with the inscription, "*Ne plus ultra*," as a limit to expansion in that direction. With the purchase of the Floridas in 1819 and the general crumbling of the Spanish empire during the following decade, renewed agitation again tried to get results. The chief arguments of the day seemed to be that unless the United States acquired the island, some other European power surely would. Even a conservative London paper commented on the certainty that, as the Floridas must belong to the United States, so likewise there was an "invincible necessity for the acquisition of Cuba by the British Crown."

All these efforts came to naught. Nevertheless, as the years advanced, annexation remained an open topic. It seemed very evident that inefficient Spain could not maintain indefinitely her traditional policy on the island. But Spain would not or could not change; and, as more repressive measures were added to the burdens of an already unhappy people, popular unrest grew in strength. This confirmed the belief in "Manifest Destiny," since political separation from the mother-country was a necessary preliminary step in any move toward annexation. Although there seems to have been little open encouragement in revolutionary activities, nevertheless Cuban *insurrectos* as early as 1849 were permitted to use bases on the mainland in furthering filibustering expeditions. During the following years, largely as a result of American initiative, commerce between the two countries made enormous strides and greatly furthered their interdependence. This was increased in 1893 by a reciprocity treaty that put sugar, cacao, coffee, and other Cuban products on the free list and reduced the duty on American flour by 50 per cent. For the first time economic forces between the two countries were given moderately free play. The result was an increased trade account as well as a tremendous increase in American capital investment in Cuba. It was a case of a people with surplus funds and technical skill finding increased opportunities for productive effort. The transformation resulting from this influx was so evident to the Cubans that handicaps to greater progress were laid at Spain's door. As a result, a prolonged revolution broke out in earnest in 1895; and, unfortunately for the mother-country, Cuba by this time had grown too powerful and was too aroused to accept any promises of reform.

The revolution brought forth a situation long hoped for by

those who expected to make Cuba a part of the United States. As stories of atrocity became widespread, American feeling against Spain was raised to a feverish pitch and led to a demand for the elimination of that country. The final step came with the sinking of the "Maine" in February, 1898, an event which doomed the last vestige of Spanish power in the New World. Annexation now seemed assured; but to satisfy critics and also cane- and beet-sugar growers a resolution was adopted "that the people of Cuba are, and of right ought to be, free and independent," with the significant addition "that the United States hereby disclaims any disposition or intention of exercising sovereignty, jurisdiction, or control of said island, except for the pacification thereof." Thus, when Cuba was virtually an American possession, events took a sudden turn, and Cuba was set free. However, the phrase "pacification thereof" made possible the much hated Platt Amendment, which restricted Cuba's freedom along certain lines. Its complete political independence, with the recent abandonment of the Platt Amendment, is most assuredly one of the strongest commentaries on the fundamental concept of justice and fair dealing which animates the American people. In Old World politics such a record is unthinkable.

Thus for good or evil has the United States spread its control across the North American continent and into the eastern, western, and southern seas. All in all, the benefits of this expansion quite surely far outweigh the evils. Each acquisition was regarded by those in authority as just and inevitable. None involved the ruthless uprooting of cultures except in the case of the Indian, who was tied loosely to the land. In no case was there a suppression or enslavement of peoples to further imperialistic aims. All acquisitions have been accompanied by such vigorous domestic criticism as a healthy democracy might engender and by unlimited and frequently unwarranted censure abroad, especially from Latin America. At times such criticism has seemed unduly severe, but much of it has had a salutary effect. In the long run, it has rendered the results of American activities overwhelmingly good for all concerned.

Many strictures from Latin America represent a dread that is honestly inspired by the unparalleled growth of the United States and by the resultant fear that the power thus acquired might be used to bully the Western world. Such apprehensions must have arisen from a mistaken interpretation of American character or from a failure to analyze thoroughly all factors—political, social, economic—involved in each successive phase of expansion. When its course is analyzed fairly and fully, judgment of the "Colossus of the North" in respect to its policy is likely to be more charitable. Certainly the Western Hemisphere as a whole is much better off than if the United States had repressed the natural expansive spirit of its people or, on the other hand, had followed the plans of conquest ordinarily pursued. Moreover, recent manifestations of its policy, such as those exemplified at Buenos Aires, Lima, and Havana, foreshadow a new American solidarity. The size and wealth of the United States make it the acknowledged head of the Western Hemisphere, but its position must be that of leader in a co-operative effort that includes the weakest nation and embraces the interest of all.

The spirit of "Manifest Destiny" may have run its course, but there can be no essential change in the native endowment that inspired it. Technical skill, progressiveness, and daring have carried and will continue to carry American influence far beyond the confines of its own borders. The experiences gained at home in the exploitation of rich resources on a large scale have opened the whole world to economic penetration. American enterprise is prone to undertake stupendous primary investments in which corporations of lesser capital might well hesitate to invest. American firms abroad are well known for their daring and are equally respected for their shrewd guessing. This economic penetration has had no small part in advancing our prestige abroad and in raising the standard of living at home.

This economic policy, however, has often provoked hostile criticism under the general topic of "economic imperialism." Various interpretations have been given to this term. Some regard it as benevolent political humanitarianism—an unselfish and, in a measure, a thankless civilizing process. Our most recent territorial acquisitions may be cited as examples. To others it is the ruthless placing of money above all human values, summed up fairly well in the phrase "dollar diplomacy." Those holding a more moderate view think of imperialism as having certain stages in its evolution: the accumulation of wealth and its investment abroad with the tacit assurance of protection under international law. In times of local disturbances protection may be asked for and received, if necessary through military intervention. Whatever the view held, it has been abundantly proved that, without such influx of capital, in relatively few cases would the nations involved have been able to realize a profitable development of their resources.

A great nation with hopes of permanency must, however, embody much more than wealth, territorial extent, or technical skill. The highest type of nation implies the existence of high moral standards and a policy determined by mutual benefit and the common good. This is the essence of democracy. Measured by such a standard, the United States is probably weaker with, than without, some of its overseas territory. This is the case, at least, in regions far away which play the role of a stepchild, possibly coddled but rarely regarded as one's own. To most Americans outlying territory is thought of in the light of possessions and not as integral parts of the country. Any legislation affecting it is almost invariably considered in the light of how it will affect home industries. Under the circumstances, the people of such areas, having no voice in national issues, can hardly be expected to feel themselves an essential part of the nation, nor are they surcharged with its ideals and aims.

The place of the United States in world economics, trade, and politics is, for the time being, assured. The advantages gained through good fortune, indomitable courage, and persistent faith in the future have given the nation leadership in both hemispheres. No longer may it isolate itself, for many of its problems are universal, affecting all continents and rendering untenable the separation of the New World from the Old. Although the Monroe Doctrine has been merged into one of multilateral enforcement, nevertheless aggression from abroad still threatens the Americas. The development of colonial Africa brings its European possessors much nearer to South America and exposes the politics of Hispanic America to infinite possibilities of intrigue. No one nation, however powerful, can ward off this peril. The Monroe Doctrine must perforce become a Pan-American pact supported by all the nations of the New World.

Primacy in this policy belongs to our country. Its commanding continental position, gained through a century of expansion, renders it a complementary, rather than a rival, force to Western nations facing on either ocean front. Its insular outposts secure not only its own approaches but also those of its neighbors. Lying athwart the long-sought passage from Europe to Asia, the United States constitutes a bulwark to encroachments from either continent, yet a link to bridge the interests of both with those of all the Americas. It is a trusted leader in the search for world-peace. May its protective and pacifying influence coincide with its remarkable growth and its present opportunities.

INDEX

INDEX